HIERARCHY AMIDST ANARCHY

Transaction Costs and Institutional Choice

KATJA WEBER

State University
of New York
Press

Published by
State University of New York Press, Albany

Production by Susan Geraghty
Marketing by Patrick Durocher

Printed in the United States of America

For information, address State University of New York
Press, State University Plaza, Albany, N.Y., 12246

Library of Congress Cataloging-in-Publication Data

Weber, Katja.
    Hierarchy amidst anarchy : transaction costs and institutional choice / Katja Weber.
        p. cm. — (SUNY series in global politics)
    Includes bibliographical references and index.
    ISBN 0-7914-4719-7 (alk. paper) — ISBN 0-7914-4720-0 (pbk. : alk. paper)
        1. International cooperation—Decision making. 2. International cooperation—Costs. 3.
International relations—Decision making. 4. International relations—Costs. I. Title. II.
Series.

JZ1318 .W43 2000
327.1'01—dc21
                                                                          99-059807

10 9 8 7 6 5 4 3 2 1

HIERARCHY
AMIDST
ANARCHY

SUNY series in Global Politics
James N. Rosenau, editor

For Elisabeth and Gunter Weber

CONTENTS

TABLES AND FIGURES

PREFACE

Even in a self-help system, self-interested actors voluntarily curtail aspects of their sovereignty to obtain needed assurances. These actors have a choice between cooperative institutional arrangements that entail different degrees of structural commitment. But what determines states' institutional choices, that is, whether states choose an entente over a confederation, a nonaggression pact over a more formal alliance, or a free trade area over a customs union? In short, what determines the varying degrees of hierarchy found amidst anarchy?

While in graduate school, I was struck by the inability of the main schools of thought in the field to account for the emergence of different types of hierarchical structures. This book now attempts to solve this puzzle. The book does not concern itself with the decision whether to cooperate or not. Rather, it assumes that states have decided in favor of cooperation (they have ruled out self-help or neutrality) and seeks to account for the degree of institutionalization elected at the founding moment. This theoretical framework can then be used as a building block to examine the evolutionary consequences of cooperation.

Scrutinizing states' security provisions, I show that realists and proponents of economies of scale arguments focus on size to explain cooperative behavior in the international environment, but that there is more to cooperation than the desire to be "bigger" or "stronger." Much like Keohane, Sandler and Cauley, or Martin, to name but a few scholars, I argue that economic theories of organization need to be looked at to account for institutional choices. What distinguishes my study from previous economic approaches is the way in which I operationalize transaction costs and then shed light on the relative causal weight of the various indicators of such costs.

Portions of this book originally appeared as "Hierarchy Amidst Anarchy: A Transaction Costs Approach to International Security Cooperation" in *International Studies Quarterly* 41 (1997): 321–40, and, in a revised version, are reprinted here with the permission of Blackwell Publishers. I also would like to thank James Rosenau, editor of the Global Politics series at SUNY Press.

As is so often the case with scholarly work, this book took longer than I expected. My interest in sovereignty issues and institutions dates back to my law school years in Germany in the late 1970s. My ideas then became more focused during graduate school at UCLA in the 1980s as a result of numerous seminars, hallway conversations, and lunch discussions with fellow students and professors. The "big break-through" occurred when I stumbled across Murray Forsyth's *Unions of States,* in which he discusses political communities spanning from the intrastate to the interstate world. His work prompted me to conceptualize a continuum of security arrangements ranging from alliances to confederations and to theorize about the determinants of states' institutional choices.

I presented a first draft of this project in Frieden and Lake's International Political Economy workshop and I am thankful to its members for their willingness to serve as sounding boards and critics. I also obtained valuable feedback in Rosecrance and Stein's Political Economy of Grand Strategy workshop that enabled me to refine my work and to establish a solid basis for field research in Washington and Germany. Since my UCLA days this project has undergone substantial revision and I conducted additional field research to produce the final manuscript.

Over the years I spent writing this book, I benefited enormously from the criticisms and support of colleagues and friends. My greatest debt is to Arthur Stein. Throughout the long gestation of this work he gave me invaluable intellectual guidance. When I ran into snares, he helped me to see the light at the end of the tunnel and encouraged me to persevere. For his support and friendship I will always be grateful. I also want to thank Michael Barnett, Mark Brawley, William Roberts Clark, David D'Lugo, Jeff Frieden, Lori Gronich, Mark Hallerberg, Jack Hirshleifer, Audie Klotz, Paul Kowert, John MacDougall, Ronald Rogowski, Richard Rosecrance, Cherie Steele, and my colleagues at Georgia Tech for their critical suggestions and comments.

In addition to the participants of the Strategy and IPE workshops at UCLA, special thanks are due the participants of the Political Economy Brown Bag seminar at Georgia Tech for their valuable feedback. Over the years, I also benefited greatly from various presentations at the annual meetings of the American Political Science Association, the International Studies Association, and the European Community Studies Association. I appreciate the insightful comments I received there. I also wish to thank the staffs at the National Archives in Washington, D.C., and the library of the Bundesministerium für Verteidigung in Bonn for their valuable research assistance.

I am also grateful for the generous financial support I received from UCLA's Center for Social Theory and Comparative History, the Social Science Research Council's Berlin Program for Advanced German and European Studies, and the University of California's Institute on Global

Conflict and Cooperation. Additional funding came from Lehigh University's Class of 1968 Junior Faculty Fellowship, and the Georgia Tech Foundation. I am deeply indebted to all of them.

Finally, special thanks go to my family. I am grateful to my parents, Gunter and Elisabeth Weber, for their love, moral support, and intellectual stimulation throughout the years and to my sisters, Barbara Busch and Eva Weber, for keeping the "Carpe Diem" motto alive. I hope they know how much I treasure the many hours spent with them in the "Nibelungenstadt" exchanging ideas. I dedicate this book to my parents, to whom I owe so much.

CHAPTER 1

Introduction

The field of international relations is built on a conception of autonomous and self-interested states interacting in an anarchic environment. And yet the history of international politics is replete with cooperative arrangements that are hierarchical, that is, that require the curtailment of some freedom of action, and that display different degrees of institutionalization.[1] In fact, the last couple of centuries provide numerous examples of international cooperative structures like the Concert of Europe, the League of Nations, various wartime and postwar alliances, or the vast array of regional trading blocs (EFTA, NAFTA, ASEAN, MERCOSUR, etc.). Whether one looks at Europe, North and South America, Africa, or the Pacific region, there is evidence of institution-building around the globe. And, as the latest debates concerning NATO and the European Union make clear, such cooperative international structures continue to be of great importance today.

Hierarchy clearly exists in the international arena, and our challenge as scholars is not only to explain why states cooperate, but, just as important, what form their cooperation takes. Because different degrees of institutionalization are possible at the founding moment of cooperative security and economic structures, it does not suffice to point to the existence of hierarchy amidst anarchy. One also needs to explain why international actors choose the specific type of arrangements they do. Why did NATO, at its outset, resemble a traditional guarantee pact and not take the form of a confederation? Why were the Swiss and the Germans, following the Napoleonic Wars, much more willing to curtail their sovereignty than Russia, Prussia, Austria, or Britain? Or why did several West European countries in the 1950s give rise to a free trade area rather than to seek a common currency as recently adopted by eleven European Union members?

The main schools of thought in the field cannot explain the emergence of such hierarchical arrangements, they cannot explain why states choose to confederate or even why they develop very institutionalized and binding alliances.

On the one hand, there are realists who argue that, since the international system is anarchic—that is, lacks a central authority capable of imposing order on the individual states—countries have to rely on self-help, and thus cooperation is rare and at best temporary.[2] In fact, for many scholars within the realist tradition, world politics, despite the end of the Cold War (the disintegration of the Soviet empire, the restructuring of East European governments, German reunification, etc.), has not fundamentally changed. John Mearsheimer, for instance, predicts that, due to the demise of bipolarity, the end of a rough military equality between the two superpowers, and the danger of mismanaged nuclear proliferation, we should see a return to greater instability and expect a decline in the number of international institutions.[3] Similarly, Kenneth Waltz continues to view the world in terms of power politics. He argues that, as a result of the collapse of the Soviet Union, the power of the United States is no longer held in check and he predicts that—as we have witnessed repeatedly in the past—other countries will assume Great Power status (Germany, Japan, China, Russia) to restore a balance. Or, put differently, Waltz suggests that we will see a return to multipolarity, since there are several countries whose interests dictate that they take on system-wide tasks and, in particular, balance against the preponderant power of the United States.[4]

On the other hand, there are functionalists, integrationists, and institutionalists who fault realists for being too pessimistic about the prospects of cooperation and who do see change.[5] Scholars like Robert Keohane and Charles Lipson, for instance, argued even before the end of the Cold War that institutions provide opportunities for further cooperation and predicted that, as long as interdependence is increasing, we should see greater institutionalization.[6] Although scholars within the institutionalist camp[7] have developed numerous theories to account for the emergence of cooperation, they have no clear conceptual basis for understanding different degrees of institutionalization. These scholars can explain how shared interests,[8] increasing interdependence,[9] informational problems, and transaction costs[10] lead to the creation of international organizations or international regimes,[11] yet they cannot account for why international actors choose the type of institutional arrangements they do.

To understand world politics one must recognize the importance of emerging hierarchies—with nation-states as their constituent elements and institutional structures that take substantial autonomy from the state.[12] Some such hierarchical arrangements are economic (free trade areas, customs unions, etc.), others are military (ententes, formal alliances, confederations).

This book studies countries' international institutional choices and seeks answers to questions such as these: Why do states create the type of cooperative international structures they do? What causes states to choose an entente over a confederation, a nonaggression pact over a more formal alliance, or a free trade area over a customs union? In short, what determines the varying degrees of hierarchy found amidst anarchy?

More specifically, the book highlights the importance of the founding moment of institutional structures. Assuming that states have decided to cooperate (rather than to engage in self-help), it seeks to explain the initial choice that leads to particular degrees of institutionalization.

Clearly, once cooperative arrangements have been formed, some dissolve quickly, others last for decades, and still others evolve into much more binding structures. However, since the causal connections between the initial choice to cooperate and the institutions that evolve over time are largely speculative, and considerations other than those that give rise to particular cooperative structures most likely would have to be factored into the equation to account for evolutionary developments (frequency of interactions, institutional inertia, organizational costs), it does not appear theoretically tractable to examine the founding moment and evolutionary consequences simultaneously.

The main purpose of this book thus is to account for the creation of different degrees of hierarchy in the international system. Having developed a theoretical framework that can shed light on the institutionalization "puzzle," in the conclusion, I then take up the issue of evolution. Specifically, I discuss how the variables scrutinized in this study can be expected to change over time, and thus how the argument developed can serve as a building block for examining the evolution of cooperative arrangements.

Although the framework put forth below has broad applicability to any voluntary curtailment of a state's freedom of action, regardless of whether cooperation is sought in the security, economic, environmental, or human rights domain, in the following, I will focus on security issues since they constitute the "hard case" for the theoretical approach employed in this study. However, in the conclusion, I will examine recent integrative moves within the European Union to test how my argument fares in the economic realm.

The remainder of this chapter takes a closer look at a continuum of cooperative security arrangements with different degrees of bindingness. It argues that realism barely recognizes such hierarchical arrangements and that, although it points us in the right direction, ultimately, is inadequate to explain them. The classical argument for the emergence of larger entities, that of economies of scale, explains size rather than "bindingness." But, recognizing that economists account for the creation of hierarchical arrangements like firms by focusing on transaction costs, the next chapter uses this insight to develop an autonomous inter-est-based explanation for cooperative governance structures in international politics. The chapter then discusses the operationalization of the main variables and explains the case selection. Subsequent chapters test the argument.

CONTINUUM OF INTERNATIONAL SECURITY ARRANGEMENTS

The history of international politics is replete with different security arrangements. These arrangements should be viewed as occupying various positions on a continuum that ranges from relationships characterized by high maneuverability or autonomy to highly structured relationships with significantly restricted maneuverability or autonomy (see Figure 1.1). The further a country moves away from arrangements that allow for a high degree of maneuverability toward the more restrictive arrangements, the more limited its freedom of action, the greater its delegation of authority to a centralized political structure, and the higher the costs of exiting the arrangement become. Thus, the closer countries move on the continuum toward the arrangements that curtail their freedom of action, the more "binding" their commitment will be, since the

FIGURE 1.1
Continuum of Cooperative Security Arrangements

Informal Alliances/ Informal Security Communities	Formal Alliances	Confederations/ Formal Security Communities
(entente; nonaggression pact; consultation pact)	(often w/ int'l organizations such as NATO)	(plans for an EDC)

→ freedom of action, sovereignty, autonomy, maneuverability decrease

→ costs of exiting the arrangement increase

→ likelihood of defection decreases

⇒ arrangements become more binding

costs of defecting from a highly structured arrangement are higher, and since the likelihood of defection is reduced. Or, put differently, binding-ness—which entails the voluntary curtailment of sovereignty in exchange for greater institutionalization—is likely to decrease opportunistic behavior, since it would be difficult, as well as costly, in terms of reputation and security for cheaters or defectors to find a replacement for a structurally sophisticated security apparatus.

Given this conceptualization, *alliances* constitute security arrangements on the less binding side of the continuum and *confederations* (or security arrangements like institutionally sophisticated security communities) represent arrangements on the more binding side. An alliance is a formal or informal relationship between two or more sovereign states that involves some measure of commitment to act jointly to bring about greater security and that assumes that a violation of any agreement would cost something.[13] A confederation, in contrast, entails a deliberate banding together of states to create a central, permanent, and state-like political structure that is capable of acting like a state, yet is not a single state but a union of states.[14] Hence, it is important to stress that in both alliances and more binding organizational structures like confederations states retain their sovereignty, in a nominal sense, but that in the latter arrangements states are bound much more significantly, due to an elaborate structural makeup that often includes a diet, a confederate army, and arbitration mechanisms.[15]

Moreover, it is imperative to distinguish between a confederation and a federation. Members of a confederation act as if they were a single state and curtail their freedom of action, but they never surrender their autonomy completely. In a federation sovereignty is surrendered to a higher authority so that the coordination found in a confederation gives way to subordination in a federation.[16] In other words, restricting the range of the continuum to confederations permits a focus on political units equal in status that continue to exist as independent (sovereign) political entities even after they have joined an alliance or a confederation. An extension of the continuum to federations would force one also to examine political units in which power is divided unevenly between "central" and "regional" authorities.[17] Put differently still, extending the continuum to include federations would require one to abandon the exclusive focus on *interstate* relations and to move into the *intrastate* world.[18]

Alliances and structurally binding security arrangements like confederations or formal security communities,[19] then, are the outer boundaries of the continuum under consideration here. But countries that have decided to cooperate do not only choose whether to ally or to confederate (face a dichotomous choice); they choose among a variety of security arrangements such as informal alliances (ententes, nonaggression pacts), more formal alliances, security communities with varying degrees of centralization,[20] or confederations. Stated differently, on this continuum ranging from security arrangements with great maneuverability and freedom of action to relatively binding security structures *intermediate* types of security arrangements exist as, for instance, alliances in which the members agree to found international organizations such as NATO.

Again, what needs to be stressed is that bindingness, as used in this essay, measures the degree of *structural commitment* allies agree to make. In that regard, this study differs significantly from the work of scholars like Sandler and Forbes, who examine states' financial commitments (military spending) as an indicator of bindingness,[21] or Sandler and Cauley, who rely on a combination of "tightness" measures such as "bindingness of decisions," "number of participants," "decision rule," and "scale of communication network."[22]

An understanding of bindingness requires scrutiny of the specific *institutional makeup* of security arrangements to ascertain how committed allies are to curtailing their discretionary powers. States that, for example, have agreed to forgo independent armies and instead have created a confederate army make a much stronger commitment than states that merely verbally commit to come to each others' aid or to provide financial support in the event of an attack by a third party. Likewise, cooperative arrangements with elaborate arbitration mechanisms, decision-making structures, and integrated military apparati are much more likely to be binding than arrangements lacking these components.

The literature has commonly treated alliances and confederations separately. Those who write of alliances do not address confederations and vice versa. Indeed, despite numerous studies in the field of international security, only a few scholars have treated security arrangements as matters of *choice*. Russett, Morgenthau, and Holsti, Hopmann, and Sullivan, for instance, all claim that states, when confronted with a threat, often align; thus they presume that states have a choice between a strategy of "going it alone" and allying.[23] Barnett and Levy focus on domestic sources of international alliances to account for a state's decision to ally or not to ally.[24] Similarly, Altfeld and Morrow develop a model of alliance choices by examining the trade-offs between autonomy and security;[25] Snyder compares the costs and risks of abandonment and entrapment to account for alliance strategies;[26] and Morrow focuses on the tightness of alliances as a signal of intentions.[27] Yet these scholars do not tell us why states choose one type of alliance over another, that is, they do not link the different types of alliances with their varying degrees of institutionalization to the issue of choice.

Some functionalists, integrationists, and institutionalists do allow for the fact that states can choose from a wide spectrum of institutional forms, but these scholars fail to offer a general argument for understanding different organizational outcomes. For example, Martin views institutions as solutions to dilemmas of strategic interaction, yet stresses that a functional approach leaves one ill-equipped to account for specific organizational outcomes.[28] As she puts it herself, her type of analysis, at best, "provid[es] rational-choice baseline expectations about behavior."[29] Similarly, Garrett warns that, although transaction costs economics holds that cooperative security arrangements represent uniquely efficient solutions to problems, often it is impossible to discriminate between different potential outcomes in terms of their efficiency.[30]

Finally, there are scholars who are interested in accounting for one particular type of political structure. For instance, classical political theorists like Rousseau, Abbé de Saint Pierre, Kant, and List[31] try to distinguish confederations from other types of political unions. Sandler and Cauley engage in a cost-benefit analysis to design an optimal supranational structure.[32] Breton and Scott focus on organizational costs to explain the origin of federal states.[33] Sandler and Forbes examine the relationship between defense burden-sharing and NATO's structure.[34] And Weber analyzes political ideas of U.S. decision-makers to shed light on the specific institutional form NATO took in the postwar period.[35]

The argument developed here departs from the studies just mentioned. Beginning with realist premises, that is, accepting that the international system is anarchic,[36] it arrives at an explanation of international hierarchy that is rooted in the choices of sovereign states. More specifically, it begins with the standard realist assumption of self-interested states in an anarchic environment, acting to assure their survival. It claims that states (as rational, unitary actors)[37] choose whether to ally or not, with whom to ally, and, very important, what degree of commitment and what kind of relationship they desire.

Of course there are many scholars who reject the economistic view of realists. Constructivists, in particular, argue that to understand international relations one must adopt a sociological or social/psychological approach and recognize that "the fundamental structures of international politics are *social* rather than strictly material."[38] As Wendt explains, "these structures shape [states'] identities and interests, rather than just their behavior," and thus realists are wrong in claiming that identities and interests are "exogenously given."[39] Similarly, Dessler finds fault with the realist conceptualization of structure and proposes that, rather than to view structure as "an environment or 'container' in which behavior takes place," structure should be seen as a "medium, a means to social action."[40] In sum, what matters most in obtaining a better understanding of international politics, constructivists tell us, is a focus on ideational forces to ascertain how ideas, norms, rules, learning, and so on, affect states' behavior and their interests.[41]

However, as Waltz correctly points out, assumptions are neither true nor false, but merely more or less "sensible."[42] One relies on assumptions for the purpose of theory development and then asks how useful specific assumptions are in explaining a particular puzzle under investigation. Thus, despite the objections raised by members of the English school, constructivists, and others,[43] this study builds onto realist propositions and, as will be developed below, argues that the basic assumptions of realism provide an excellent basis for examining the determinants of states' institutional choices.

REALISTS AND HIERARCHY

Realists like Hans Morgenthau and Kenneth Waltz tell us that, in a self-help world, self-interested states either act to assure their survival or perish.[44] The need to rely on themselves "leads states to value autonomy and independence."[45] It is clear that, if all states pursued their self-interest, the creation of alliances—which indicate the existence of convergent interests—would be unlikely. At best, alliances would be temporary and would function as signaling devices with which states would inform each other of their individual interests.[46]

Yet situations do arise in which unilateral action cannot assure the survival of states, that is, in which a strategy of "going it alone" would be inferior to cooperation.[47] Common interests often do exist, particularly in cases of high (external) threat.[48] As Stephen Walt convincingly shows, states ally against threats rather than to balance against power alone.[49] And states are much more likely to balance than to bandwagon, since the latter (joining the stronger side) would leave an ally "vulnerable to the whims of its partners."[50]

The problem, however, is that even states that ally against a threatening power have to fear opportunistic behavior on the part of others; that is, their allies could defect or cheat. States thus seek to devise institutions that facilitate cooperation by safeguarding against opportunism.[51] Or, put differently, states seek hierarchical arrangements to decrease chances that their allies will defect when cooperation is needed to offset relative weaknesses vis-à-vis enemies. Hence, even in an anarchic environment that stresses survival and autonomy, self-interested actors voluntarily reduce their freedom of action to obtain necessary assurances.

In the military realm, the level of threat is instrumental in determining the nature and degree of states' commitment. That is, if the level of external threat countries face is low, there is no need for a strong commitment, and therefore if countries choose to cooperate, an alliance might be chosen over a more binding security arrangement. On the other hand, if the level of external threat is high, countries are likely to prefer an arrangement that gives them greater assurance (that is, one that is more binding, thereby reducing the risk of defection), and thus to opt for a formal security community or a confederation.[52]

In sum, what extant international relations theory by itself can tell us is that threat leads to alliances, since alliances are viewed as political structures that are militarily capable of dealing with a security problem. Moreover, realists like Walt can explain who is likely to ally with whom and, by pointing to the centrality of threat, realists make an important contribution to finding an explanation for states' institutional choices.

However, realism cannot definitively tell us how binding a relationship countries will enter into. That is, even if we try to use the degree of threat to explain various gradations of bindingness, such an explanation is incomplete since it cannot account for a case like NATO where external threat was high yet the countries did not confederate. And, in fact, it is likely that reactions to threat may include hierarchical structures not at all envisaged by realism. Put differently, given that alliances offer a presumptive organizational solution to security issues, what we need is a theory of alliances that links institutional structures to the issue of providing security. More specifically, what needs to be articulated is the exact relationship between increased security and different organizational arrangements. Absent such knowledge, all international relations theory currently can explain is that a high level of threat might be a *necessary* condition for a confederation to come about but that it is not sufficient.[53]

The following section turns to the classical argument made for the emergence of larger entities, for hierarchy, and for integration, namely, that of economies of scale.

ECONOMIES OF SCALE AND INTERNATIONAL INTEGRATION

Security arrangements between states are mechanisms for aggregating the capabilities of states in situations in which individually the states have inadequate capability to deal with threats that confront them. In fact, the scale required to generate the capability to assure survival often exceeds any one state, so that cooperation becomes necessary.

Focusing on European military history, Richard Bean, for instance, argues that changes in the art of warfare (military technology) can alter the efficient size of political units.[54] More specifically, he claims that, just as gains from specialization in different activities can give rise to economies of scale for firms, there are advantages of large size among political organizations. Defense costs, for example, should decrease for individual members as organizations increase in size, since "doubling the area of a state usually less than doubles the border needing defense and so more resources are available per linear mile." But, as Bean puts it, "economies of scale are checked at some point by decreasing returns"; that is, the larger political units become, the greater their problems of command and control, so that there is an "optimal range of size."[55] States that exceed this optimal range are likely to break apart, whereas those that are smaller are likely to be integrated into other political units.

A good example of how technological innovation can bring about change in the relative size of states is provided by the development of gunpowder weapons in the fifteenth century. As William McNeill explains, prior to the manufacture of the cannon, numerous castles were spread throughout Western Europe that were almost immune from attack. Then, in the middle of the fifteenth century, the introduction of heavy artillery pieces not only rendered existing fortifications useless, but also greatly diminished the power of smaller states (like the Italian city-states) that could not afford these costly new weapons. The new gunpowder arms began to favor larger, centralized states that possessed the means to extract resources from their populations.[56] Or, more general, as increasingly powerful and mobile weapons were being developed that made it possible for countries to express their military power over greater distances, the necessity to defend larger territories led to the need for larger armies, and hence bigger states.

In short, what Bean, McNeill, and many of their colleagues suggest is that institutions are created to allow individual members to reap the benefits inherent in economies of scale. If we can pinpoint the factors that force political or economic actors to merge or collaborate to attain a sufficient size to assure their survival, we then can account for institutional change.[57]

It is important to stress that the economies-of-scale approach (much like the traditional realist model) focuses on *size* rather than bindingness. Thus, all economies-of-scale proponents can tell us is that size considerations may lead to institutional change, but they cannot specify the exact nature (structural makeup) of the new institutional arrangements.[58]

The next chapter extends the realist argument by adding transaction costs as a further explanatory variable and, in doing so, provides an alternative to economies-of-scale approaches. As will become clear, the application of a transaction costs argument to international relations is not new. Building onto the work of others, I develop several indicators of transaction costs and then test them in what constitutes the "hard case"—the security realm.

CHAPTER 2

Developing the
Transaction Costs Model

For some time, international relations scholars have borrowed essential ideas from economics to enhance our understanding of how the international system operates. Waltz, for instance, draws an analogy between the anarchic international system populated by competing states and the economic market populated by competing firms.[1] States, like firms, he posits, are self-interested actors who worry about their survival. Moreover, just as economists seek to explain the behavior of firms on the basis of the competitiveness of markets, Waltz seeks to explain the behavior of states on the basis of the struggle for survival in a self-help world.[2] Similarly, Kenneth Boulding compares "states of the international system" with "states of the market"; that is, he likens a balance of power system with few actors to monopolistic competition, a loose bipolar system to oligopoly, a tight bipolar system to duopoly, and so forth.[3]

Yet the competitive market model has proved inadequate in economics, and is thus flawed as an analogy for international politics. That is, although the competitive market analogy is consistent with a world in which small unit-level actors (producers) engage in cooperative exchange, the market analogy cannot account for the creation of larger economic structures such as firms and regional arrangements. To explain the emergence of these larger aggregates, economists like Ronald Coase and Oliver Williamson tell us to focus on transaction costs.[4]

ECONOMISTS AND HIERARCHY

Neoclassical economists view the economic system as coordinated by price mechanisms (supply is adjusted to demand), hence basically "working itself."[5] The market, these scholars argue, is superior to more centralized organizations, since the market is the "natural and efficient" way to mediate transactions.[6]

Yet, as Coase in his seminal 1937 article "The Nature of the Firm" explains, the use of the price mechanism to organize production costs something, since economic agents have to establish what the relevant prices are at a given time and then incur costs in preparing, negotiating, and concluding agreements.[7] Firms thus arise because they are a more efficient way of organizing production. Or, put differently, as Coase argues, firms are a response to market failures, that is, transaction costs.[8]

Coase then qualifies his argument in two important ways. First, he claims that, as a firm gets larger, the costs of organizing additional transactions within the firm may increase, so that a firm can be expected to expand only "until the costs of organising an extra transaction within the firm become equal to the costs of carrying out the same transaction . . . on the open market."[9] This suggests that the coordination of transactions between a large number of economic actors tends to be more efficient if left to the market than conducted by a firm.[10]

Second, without uncertainty a firm probably would not emerge. Frank Knight in *Risk, Uncertainty and Profit* illustrates this point.

> With uncertainty entirely absent, every individual being in possession of perfect knowledge of the situation, there would be no occasion for anything of the nature of responsible management or control of productive activity. . . . With the introduction of uncertainty—the fact of ignorance and the necessity of acting upon opinion rather than knowledge— . . . the primary problem . . . is deciding what to do and how to do it.[11]

Since it is costly to make decisions concerning transactions in an uncertain environment (due to a lack of information, communication problems, etc.), economic actors can benefit by delegating decision-making to hierarchical organizations. That is, as a result of their specialized governance structure (centralized decision making), firms can reduce the costs of deriving decisions, can consider many more options than an individual actor, and thus reduce the risk of suboptimal or disadvantageous decisions.[12]

Although Coase—by arguing that hierarchical institutions can be more efficient than the market, and hence are alternative ways of coordinating production—significantly contributed to the economic theory of organization, a coherent theory did not come about until the 1970s, when Williamson began to operationalize the concept of transaction costs and to assign different transactions to different governance structures.

Williamson's analysis relies on two assumptions about human nature. Borrowing from Chester Barnard and Herbert Simon,[13] Williamson stresses, first of all, that people possess only "bounded rationality," that is, they are limited in their ability to formulate or solve complex problems and to process information.[14] Second, people act opportunistically. This means they occasionally engage in undesirable behavior such as "lying, stealing, and cheating" that also includes "calculated efforts to mislead, distort, disguise."[15] Due to these two behavioral characteristics (bounded rationality and opportunism), Williamson argues, not only do people differ substantially from the ideal-type described in neoclassical economics—a "trustworthy maximizer"[16]—but also they make it impossible for economic activity to be organized effectively by contract.

Williamson then claims that, when the behavioral attributes of bounded rationality and opportunism join with two environmental factors—namely, uncertainty and small-numbers bargaining—transaction costs difficulties arise that often lead to organizational failures.[17] As mentioned above, a high degree of uncertainty is likely to raise transaction costs. Yet transactions are further complicated by the fact that, although a large number of bidders might exist at the initial bargaining stage, this does not have to be the case at a later stage. That is, "a condition of large numbers bidding at the outset" can be transformed into a bilateral exchange relationship thereafter—and thereby become more vulnerable to opportunism—if, as Williamson argues, transactions involve specific assets.[18] Since the concept of asset specificity will be discussed in more detail below, here it suffices to stress that the transformation from large-numbers bargaining to small-numbers bargaining is likely to increase transactional risks, and thus transaction costs.

Refining an earlier definition of transaction costs by Kenneth Arrow,[19] Williamson then differentiates between *ex ante* and *ex post* transaction costs. *Ex ante* transaction costs include the costs of "drafting, negotiating and safeguarding an agreement," whereas *ex post* transaction costs consist of "haggling . . . setup and running costs of governance structures . . . and bonding costs of effecting secure commitments."[20] Yet, occasionally, Williamson also refers to transaction costs as "the economic equivalent of friction in physical systems."[21]

As did Coase and Arrow before him, Williamson claims that, if transaction costs are high, the market is no longer the most efficient governance structure. The objective thus is to identify the most effective institutional or organizational framework for each transaction, that is, to assign transactions to appropriate governance structures. To accomplish this task Williamson seeks to ascertain how transactions differ and focuses on three attributes of transactions.

First, he studies the frequency of transactions. He differentiates among transactions that occur only once, those that occur occasionally, and transactions that are recurrent. He claims that the creation of a specialized institutional framework is easier to justify for transactions that are recurrent rather than occasional, since the setup costs of a highly specific structural apparatus often cannot be recovered for occasional transactions.[22]

A second dimension of transactions Williamson looks at is asset specificity, that is, the degree to which transaction-specific investments are incurred.[23] Williamson argues that an asset is specific if it is "less transferable to other uses or users."[24] To determine the degree of asset specificity one thus needs to ask how specialized investments are, that is, whether their assets are redeployable.[25]

If the supplier of an asset can easily find other buyers, or if other suppliers are available to the buyer, both parties are protected by the availability of alternative partners so that they incur few transactional risks.[26] If, however, an asset is designed for a particular use by a particular person, and the value of the asset would be significantly reduced if the asset were used otherwise or by another person, a breakdown of this relationship would cause serious damage. In situations like this, Williamson claims, all parties have an incentive to bring about a "fundamental transformation," that is, to move their relationship out of the market and into a hierarchical governance structure to obtain additional safeguards.[27]

Third, Williamson examines the uncertainty under which transactions take place. He argues that, if transactions are nonspecific, an increase in the degree of uncertainty has little effect, since new trading partners can easily be found.[28] However, if transactions entail specific assets, an increase in the degree of uncertainty makes it necessary to move transactions out of the market into firms, since "the costs of harmonizing a relation among parties vary directly with the need to adjust to changing circumstances."[29]

A TRANSACTION COSTS MODEL
OF INTERNATIONAL HIERARCHY

Given that defense is plagued by the public good problems of nonrivalness and nonexcludability,[30] states often free ride on the efforts of others or seek efficiency through integration, rather than rely on market forces. At a first glance, this suggests that the market analogy might not apply to security issues. However, as Sandler and Forbes rightly point out, "it is doubtful whether [even] deterrence as provided by strategic nuclear weapons is fully nonexcludable,"[31] so that defense is best viewed as an *impure* public good. This implies that the existence of rivalry and the possibility of exclusion will diminish the likelihood of free riding so that states can be expected to decide security issues via market transactions. In fact, as the degree of impurity (nation-specific benefits) increases, states should be more likely to opt for greater autonomy by resorting to the market—unless the existence of transaction costs makes such behavior undesirable.[32]

If defense is indeed best viewed as an *impure* public good, then—just as economists claim that hierarchical governance structures are more efficient than the market in the presence of high transaction costs—there are situations in international relations where it is beneficial to replace anarchy with hierarchy. As discussed above, in cases of high external threat states seek to create institutions that facilitate cooperation by raising the costs of opportunistic behavior. Thus, even in a self-help system that stresses autonomy, self-interested actors voluntarily curtail their sovereignty to obtain needed assurances.

Or, in other words, international relations resembles the world of firms in that the provision of security can require replacing anarchy (market) with hierarchical governance structures (firms), at least among a subset of states. Whereas in the economic realm a transaction consists of the trade of goods or services between parties to organize production, in the military realm, states trade goods or services to enhance their security and assure their survival. A transaction, for instance, might entail the provision of certain types of raw materials, specialized equipment, skilled labor, or the dispatch of specially trained troops to aid allies in organizing their defense.

However, it is important to stress that the substitution of hierarchy for anarchy is costly,[33] so that hierarchical governance structures come about not only because they promise greater security, but also because they can reduce transaction costs. That is, just as economic agents—to minimize transaction costs—tend to arrange themselves hierarchically, threatened states weakened by the enormous costs involved in gathering and evaluating information, in preparing for, negotiating, and concluding agreements, and so on, seek allies. Given that coordinated efforts are often more efficient than individual efforts, threatened countries facing high transaction costs could benefit from joining political entities with well-developed, cooperative organizational structures.

Clearly, the level of transaction costs is important in determining which security arrangement countries choose. If transaction costs are negligible, the organization of military activities for efficiency reasons seems to be irrelevant. If transaction costs are low, countries should strive for greater freedom of action, and hence prefer a less binding security arrangement. Yet, as the level of transaction costs increases, the likelihood of a country preferring a confederation over an alliance will also increase.

It once more needs to be stressed that the use of a transaction costs approach to examine international institutional structures is not unprecedented. Keohane in his path-breaking work on regimes, for instance, builds a strong case for importing theories of market failure into the realm of international relations. Institutions are formed, he tells us, to reduce informational costs and to lower the likelihood of opportunistic behavior "to facilitate negotiations leading to mutually beneficial agreements among governments."[34] Similarly, Yarbrough and Yarbrough, Caporaso, Frieden, Moravcsik, and Trachtman,[35] to name but a few, all focus on transaction costs as a factor to be looked at in explaining states' choices. However, much like Martin and Garrett's work discussed earlier,[36] this type of scholarship does not provide us with a clear conceptual basis for understanding different degrees of institutional bindingness.

Most closely related to the argument advanced here are the previously cited studies by Lake and by Sandler and Cauley.[37] In *Entangling Relations* Lake employs theories of relational contracting to make sense of U.S. foreign policy. He argues that "[t]he choice between unilateralism and cooperation, and among alternative forms of security cooperation . . . is determined by . . . joint production economies, the expected costs of opportunism, and governance costs."[38]

What sets my study apart from his is the way in which I operationalize transaction costs. Although we both rely on Williamson's work and scrutinize asset specificity to ascertain the magnitude of transaction costs, I pay much greater attention to the role of uncertainty in giving rise to opportunistic behavior and, as will be seen shortly, expand on Williamson's framework by introducing two additional factors—technological development and heterogeneity.

Sandler and Cauley analyze the role of transaction costs in creating an optimal supranational political body. The two scholars first propose to conduct a cost-benefit analysis to determine whether the creation of a cooperative structure is beneficial. They then argue that, since transaction costs and benefits depend upon the "tightness" of a political body, the structure of such a body should be loosened "when tightening adds more to costs than benefits at the margin."[39]

Whereas Sandler and Cauley break down transaction costs into decision-making costs, interdependency costs, and enforcement costs,[40] following Williamson, my study lays out several factors crucial in determining the degree of transaction costs. And, whereas Sandler and Cauley shed light on the various components of transaction costs, I develop proxy measures for them.

My study thus combines one of the main variables used by international relations scholars—level of (external) threat—and one of the main variables used by economists—transaction costs—to explain the type of hierarchical security structures countries choose.[41] (See Table 2.1.) That

TABLE 2.1
Summary of the Determinants of States' Choices in the Security Realm

| | | Level of Threat | | |
		Low	High	Extreme
Transaction Costs	Low	No cooperation	Binding alliance	Wartime alliance
	High	No cooperation or informal alliance	Confederation or formal security community	Wartime alliance (no time for more binding security arrangement)

———→ High threat and high transaction costs are both necessary conditions for a confederation to come about, but neither is sufficient.

is, first, the greater the external threat, the greater the need for assurance and the greater the willingness to forgo some freedom of action; and hence the greater the likelihood a country will enter a binding arrangement, provided time constraints (as in situations of extreme threat) do not forclose this option. Thus, a high level of threat is assumed necessary for a confederation to come about. Second, the higher the level of transaction costs, the greater the likelihood a country will prefer a more binding arrangement. Hence, in situations characterized by high external threat and high transaction costs, a confederation would be most likely. If the level of threat is low, countries can be expected to choose less binding arrangements, even if transaction costs are high. Conversely, if the external threat is high but transaction costs are low, countries should seek binding alliances, yet not confederate, since chances for opportunistic behavior are reduced so that the creation of a confederation is not essential. Therefore, both high external threat and high transaction costs are necessary to bring about a confederation (they are separately necessary), but neither is sufficient (only jointly are they sufficient).

Moreover, my study presumes *symmetrically high* perceptions of threat and vulnerability to transaction costs if prospective partners are to create a very binding security apparatus. Where symmetry can be found, the tie between states' preferences and institutional outcomes is expected to be quite close. But even in situations characterized by asymmetry, knowledge of the actors' preferences should go a long way to shed light on the degree of commitment sought by the various parties. Or, since asymmetry does not prevent cooperation per se, but merely a serious curtailment of autonomy on the part of the country that feels less threatened or less vulnerable to transactional risks, a careful assessment of threat and transaction costs should still tell us a great deal about structural compromises obtained. In fact, given the model developed above one can hypothesize that truly binding arrangements should be more likely to occur among weaker states and less likely with a Great Power, if for no other reason than that the concern about threat and opportunistic behavior is unlikely to be both high and symmetrical for a Great Power and its weaker allies.

ASSESSING THREATS AND TRANSACTION COSTS IN INTERNATIONAL POLITICS

Two indicators help to determine the amount of external threat countries confront. First, the *military capability* and the *military potential* of countries—measured in terms of the number of men in the armed forces and the resources availability to create military forces during crises—are important. The greater a country's military capability/military potential, the greater a threat it can pose to others, and therefore the greater the likelihood the threatened countries will seek a more binding security arrangement.

Second, the *geographic proximity* between countries matters. Since a nation's strength and ability to project power decline over distance,[42] states can be expected to pose a greater threat when they are near than when they are far away. Proximity, clearly, played a greater role in the past when countries threatened each other with spears, cannons, and rifles. Even in today's world, however, where many countries can threaten each other with bombs and nuclear weapons, the geographic distance to one's enemy remains important—despite the fact that the "loss-of-strength gradient" for air power is less than that for land power.[43]

In sum it can be said that geographic proximity, like military capability/military potential, increases the potential threat, and thus the demand for binding security arrangements.[44]

The remainder of this section delineates the security analogues for the factors that generate transaction costs. Four factors in particular are critical in determining the magnitude of transaction costs.

First, as Williamson shows for contractual relations in the economic realm, the degree of *uncertainty* under which transactions are executed appears to be crucial. He differentiates between two types of uncertainty, namely behavioral uncertainty—which is attributable to the fact that humans must be expected to behave opportunistically—and a nonstrategic kind that arises due to a lack of communication.[45] The greater the uncertainty of transactions, the higher the transaction costs, and thus the greater the need for institutional structures that facilitate communication and cooperation between the parties involved. For instance, a businessman who lacks certainty regarding his partner's behavior needs to acquire additional costly information or engage in negotiations with other businessmen to reduce his transactional risks, unless he can convince his partner to institutionalize their transactions.

Williamson, however, argues that an increase in the degree of uncertainty only seriously impacts transactions that entail specific assets. That is, for nonspecific transactions an increase in uncertainty has virtually no effect, since alternative trading partners can easily be found. Yet, if transactions are specific, the greater the degree of uncertainty, the more likely the creation of an institutional framework capable of dealing with contractual gaps, that is, one that can mediate between the parties and thus help to "work things out."[46]

An analogous argument can be made for cooperative security arrangements. If transactions are executed under a low degree of uncertainty, countries are expected to prefer greater freedom of action over more binding institutional arrangements. However, as the degree of uncertainty increases, so does the likelihood that countries will create more binding security arrangements, since countries now have to fear opportunistic behavior on the part of their allies that could endanger their security. A good example provides the Swiss' reaction to Napoleon's escape from Elba. When the French general once more threatened the Swiss cantons and it was not clear whether all cantons, when called upon, would contribute to the common defense, or whether some would attempt to free ride or defect, the Swiss decided to create a confederation to obtain greater assurances.

To measure the degree of uncertainty in the international system this study examines two factors. First, it focuses on the number of Great Powers to deduce hypotheses concerning cooperative behavior; that is, the larger the number, the greater the likelihood states will defect from security arrangements, since other countries might be available that could make more attractive offers.[47] Conversely, in a system of only two Great Powers, that is, a bipolar system, states should be less likely to act opportunistically, since only one other potential ally is available.

Aside from Great Power considerations, the signals (signing of treaties, arms negotiations, adherence to previous agreements, etc.) states send and receive also reveal uncertainty.[48] Specifically, the clearer and more consistent the signals sent, the less likely states should be to seek reassurance in structurally binding security arrangements provided benevolent intentions were signaled. On the other hand, the less clear and consistent the signals, the more likely states are to be concerned about the intentions of others, and thus the greater the need for binding security structures to safeguard against opportunistic behavior.

A second indicator of transaction costs that, according to Williamson, influences states' behavior significantly is *asset specificity*. He argues that transactions that do not entail specific investments, that is, that are easily transferable to other uses or users, pose few hazards, since both buyers and suppliers can redirect their investments to alternative sources.[49] However, as assets become more specific (impossible or very costly to redeploy) economic agents have to fear opportunism by others (cheating or defecting), and thus are likely to design specific governance structures with "good continuity properties."[50] Or, in other words, if—due to a high degree of asset specificity—transactional risks are high, economic agents are likely to move their relationship out of the market and into a hierarchical governance structure to obtain additional safeguards.

The same rationale can be applied to security relations. As assets become more specific, states have to fear opportunistic behavior on the part of their allies—that is, that allies seek to cheat on their defense contributions or defect from the security arrangement—and thus are more likely to create more binding security arrangements with highly developed institutional structures.[51] Conversely, if assets can be used in various ways, an elaborate institutional structure seems unnecessary, since states face fewer transactional risks. It can therefore be hypothesized that the more specific the assets involved in a transaction, the greater the likelihood countries will confederate rather than ally, since the chances of opportunistic behavior would be significantly reduced in a more binding security arrangement, due to the high reputation or security costs defectors or cheaters are likely to incur. The desire for binding security arrangements, in fact, should persist even if investments in specific assets are reciprocated, since, in an uncertain environment, structural sophistication would improve the chances of detecting undesirable behavior. Or, in other words, reciprocity, although likely to reduce opportunism, would not eliminate it, hence perpetuating the need for safeguards.

Like Williamson, this study differentiates among three types of asset specificity, namely site, physical, and human asset specificity, to demonstrate how the above propositions might be operationalized. Williamson argues that *site specificity* arises when economic agents are located in "cheek-by-jowl relation to each other so as to economize on inventory and transportation expenses."[52] If the parties to a site-specific transaction complete their contract as specified, they can reduce their cooperation costs due to their unique location. Yet, if a contract between such parties should be interrupted, the parties are likely to suffer high exit costs since a site-specific investment cannot be moved—except at prohibitive cost.[53]

An analogous argument can be made for security arrangements. Allies that are in a geographically strategic position or are located very close to each other can be expected to be able to reduce their transportation and coordination expenses as a result of their special location. However, since it could be detrimental to the allies' security if a member of their defense system were to act opportunistically—cheating or defecting could leave a big gap in the security system or raise cooperation costs significantly—site specificity helps to account for why states at times choose to confederate rather than to ally. Or, since site specificity increases the potential for opportunism, allies subject to this condition can be expected to prefer a more binding defense structure.[54]

Physical asset specificity arises in situations where special ingredients or specialized equipment are required to produce a particular component.[55] It is assumed that the value of these ingredients or of the equipment in its "next-best alternative use" is substantially lower, and hence that both parties to the transaction have a strong interest in the continuity of their exchange relation.[56] Economic agents planning to make investments entailing special ingredients, yet fearing opportunistic behavior by their partners, can therefore be expected to safeguard their transactions by moving them out of the market and into hierarchical governance structures.

Physical asset specificity can also arise in the security realm and can force states to structure their transactions carefully. If a country, for instance, is asked to join a military arrangement that calls for a sizeable investment in sophisticated military hardware, the country has to fear that its allies (or at least one of its allies) might eventually try to cheat, make extortionary threats, or even defect—that is, act opportunistically—and thus the country can be expected to become a member of the arrangement only if it receives greater assurance in the form of a more binding arrangement.[57] If, on the other hand, countries are members of security arrangements involving assets that can be used in various ways (troops, guns, etc.), the chances of opportunistic behavior are much smaller. Not only is it less likely that countries possessing generic assets would find better deals elsewhere that would tempt them to defect, but there is also less possibility for extortion. Hence, countries engaging in transactions entailing nonspecific physical assets can be expected to prefer greater freedom of action over a more binding arrangement, that is, to ally rather than to confederate.

Human asset specificity arises in a "learning-by-doing fashion."[58] If, for instance, workers are trained to run complicated machinery they—due to their expertise—cannot easily be replaced.[59] Thus, if economic agents conduct transactions that involve investments in human capital, these agents are likely to protect their investments against opportunism by embedding them in hierarchical governance structures.

An analogous claim can be made for security relations. Soldiers who receive special training to operate sophisticated military equipment or to fight certain types of war (guerilla warfare, sea warfare, etc.) cannot easily be substituted. Hence, if states enter security arrangements that depend upon highly specific human assets, one would expect these countries to seek binding commitments to safeguard themselves against opportunistic behavior.

Williamson argues that economic actors are said to act opportunistically if they cheat, steal, lie, distort information, mislead, and so on.[60] Yet what do we mean when we refer to "opportunism" or "transactional risks" and "defection" or "exit costs" in the security realm? Here, opportunistic behavior can take several forms such as cheating, using extortionary threats, or defecting (free riding, exiting) and each form of opportunism brings with it specific reputational and security costs the magnitude of which varies with the degree to which transactions entail specific assets.

For instance, if a country promises to aid its allies by sending troops rather than specialized military equipment, yet cheats (only partially fulfills its promise) or defects (reneges on its promise, as did Prussia under Frederick II in 1742 when it abandoned the French and signed the Peace Treaty of Breslau), the country, in addition to hurting its allies, damages its reputation as a dependable partner and thus incurs reputation costs. But, provided the defector's reputation has not been damaged to the point where no one else would want to ally with it, the defector could redeploy its troops and therefore avoid security costs. On the other hand, if a country commits itself to contribute to an integrated military force by providing highly specialized military equipment (as, for instance, the Royal Navy in NATO), yet cheats or defects, in addition to leaving its allies in a very vulnerable position, the country not only seriously damages its reputation, it also jeopardizes its own security, unless it can reequip itself and then join some other security arrangement.

In short, the asset-specificity component of my transaction costs argument implies that alliances are most likely in cases in which states do not feel the need to invest in specific assets. On the other hand, where security arrangements require investing in highly trained men, specialized equipment, or specific sites that states otherwise would not invest in or could not readily shift to, then there is a desire for greater bindingness to reduce transactional risks.[61]

Third, in international relations—and particularly security studies—the level of *technological development* (transportation and communications) at the time of transactions appears to be important. If the state of technology is not very advanced, that is, if it takes days to relay messages, to arrive at certain destinations via horseback, and so forth, countries will be exposed to higher coordination costs and will be more vulnerable to opportunistic behavior (an ally might be able to defect and go undetected for some time) than in a technologically more sophisticated environment. These costs, moreover, are likely to be exacerbated by an increase in the number of allies. In fact, a "backward" state of technology coupled with a large number of allies would be a costly position to be in. Hence, it can be hypothesized that the less sophisticated the state of technology and the larger the number of allies, the higher the costs of coordinating operations, the greater the risk of opportunism, and thus the greater the likelihood that countries will prefer more binding security arrangements.[62]

Fourth, the degree of *heterogeneity* of states seeking to cooperate is crucial. That is, the greater the degree of heterogeneity between countries, the greater the likelihood of language problems, misunderstandings, and disagreements,[63] and therefore the greater the need for translation, arbitration, and costly coordination, which increases transaction costs significantly. Or, put differently, the more varied the religious, language, cultural, and political backgrounds of countries seeking to cooperate,[64] the higher their transaction costs, and thus the greater their need for political structures that can reduce these costs. Hence, all else being equal, if France, Germany, and Italy, for example, were to cooperate, one would expect them to favor a more binding security apparatus than if the United States and Britain sought to cooperate. It is important, however, to understand that a high degree of heterogeneity is neither a necessary nor a sufficient condition for the creation of a confederation. A study of the cost-benefit implications of heterogeneity merely explains why a high degree of heterogeneity raises the transaction costs countries incur, and thereby contributes to our understanding of why states choose the security arrangements they do.

The argument developed here thus differs substantially from the standard view put forth by scholars such as Guetzkow and Deutsch who view confederations as rooted in culture rather than in terms of costs and benefits.[65] Whereas the explanation put forth here is consistent with international relations arguments about power and interests, their cultural explanation disconnects them from such arguments and makes it impossible for them to account for other interstate arrangements. More specifically, these scholars claim that states sharing the same religion, language, cultural, and political traits are more likely to ally than states that differ on those counts.[66] Factors like "mutual identity," "loyalty," and "a sense of we-ness," we are told, aid in the creation of a security community,[67] yet there are historical cases that do not fit such sociological (cultural) arguments. That is, even if a high degree of homogeneity would be a helpful condition for a confederation (security community) to come about, the degree of homogeneity is not sufficient to explain the creation of such a security arrangement and, in fact, countries could be homogeneous, yet prefer to ally rather than to confederate. Good examples are Austria and Germany before World War I as well as the Australian colonies before 1901. Moreover, since one can think of heterogeneous countries confederating, the Swiss cantons did so in 1815, a high degree of homogeneity should not be viewed as an essential condition for the creation of a confederation. Finally, if trust already exists between homogeneous countries,[68] one could argue that there may be no need to build a more binding security structure so that homogeneous countries—from a purely cultural perspective—might be expected to ally rather than to confederate. Heterogeneous countries, lacking a similar degree of trust, and therefore much more fearful of opportunism, on the other hand, should favor structurally binding security arrangements.

Having discussed the measurement and consequences of threat and transaction costs, the argument can now be further refined. Given high threat, the more numerous and severe the transaction costs (uncertainty, asset specificity, technological development, and heterogeneity) a state faces, the greater the likelihood it will seek structurally sophisticated security apparati to reduce these costs. Thus, seriously threatened countries whose transactions are plagued by great uncertainty and the presence of asset specificity can be expected to seek more binding security arrangements than seriously threatened countries whose transactions are plagued by uncertainty alone. Or, facing high threat, heterogeneous states engaged in transactions involving specific assets should be more likely to opt for binding security structures than homogeneous states conducting the same transactions.

To summarize, this study begins with realist premises and points to the centrality of threat in security concerns. Since realism, by itself, cannot explain gradations of bindingness—states may respond to threat by creating hierachical security structures not envisaged by realism—I then extend the realist framework by adding transaction costs. As discussed above, this is not the first time a transaction costs argument is being made in the context of international relations; but, by applying the argument to security issues rather than the economic realm, I choose to investigate the "hard case." Nevertheless, the argument presented here has broad applicability to any states voluntarily curtailing aspects of their sovereignty to bring about binding international institutional arrangements. In fact, a transaction costs argument should be able to account for any hierarchical structure in international relations. Finally, by stressing the importance of transaction costs and providing proxy measures for them, a transaction costs approach can be seen as an alternative to economies-of-scale explanations that, like realism, can only account for size (aggregation), not bindingness.

CASE SELECTION

To test the above propositions I conduct a cross-sectional study of historical periods in which a reevaluation of the level of threat, and the creation of new security arrangements can be expected. The final years of major wars and postwar periods are ideal testing grounds in that they represent periods of flux. That is, states that have been at war for some time and are still engaged in battles, or that have experienced war recently, are likely to reassess their security provisions. In these situations states typically reexamine the degree of threat they face and readjust their defense systems according to their security needs.[69]

First, I examine security arrangements during the last years of the Napoleonic Wars and the period of the Congress of Vienna (1812–15). During this three-year time-span several different types of security structures existed. When Napoleon was defeated in Russia in the winter of 1812, the potential power of France nonetheless remained great; Russia and Prussia, for instance, formed an alliance against France (Treaty of Kalisch) that Austria joined in June 1813 (Treaty of Reichenbach) and Great Britain in March 1814 (Treaty of Chaumont, which set up the Quadruple Alliance). Although the allies sent Napoleon into exile in April 1814, he managed to escape and forced them to renew their union and once more build a common defense. When Napoleon was finally defeated in June 1815, that is, when the common danger was removed, the wartime coalitions began to disintegrate (the Quadruple Alliance became less and less important), and Great Britain, more and more, withdrew from continental politics to pursue an insular policy. Those countries that still felt threatened, however, gave rise to new security arrangements. The Swiss and the Germans created confederations, and Russia, Prussia, and Austria united in the Holy Alliance.

As a careful study of this historical period will show, the degree of threat the European countries were exposed to varies with changes in Napoleon's behavior. Furthermore, the level of transaction costs—which one would expect to be significant, due to the high degree of uncertainty in the international system (multipolar) as well as the backward state of technology at that time—varies with the specificity of the countries' assets and their degree of heterogeneity.

Second, I turn to the post-1945 period,[70] again a period in which threats were reevaluated, in which changes in technological developments and the creation of new security arrangements were likely, yet, in which the degree of uncertainty can be expected to be lower, due to the bipolar nature of the international system. Here I contrast two security arrangements in particular. On the one hand, I analyze the founding of NATO—an alliance that, at its outset, resembled a traditional guarantee pact, but, shortly thereafter, became much more formalized. I argue that, absent symmetric assessments of threat and transaction costs, the West Europeans had to settle for fewer guarantees than they would have liked.

Thereafter, I examine plans proposed by the French in the 1950s for the creation of a European Defense Community (EDC). When the Korean War broke out in June 1950, the United States and Europe discussed an all-out rearmament program as well as changes in their existing security provisions. It was clear to both the United States and the Europeans that German rearmament was necessary to deal with an increase in Soviet threat, yet there was no agreement as to how the German army should be integrated into the Western defense system. The United States merely sought to increase the number of troops within NATO—that is, place a German army under NATO command—to decrease the American defense burden. France, fearful that German rearmament could lead to opportunistic behavior (Germany could defect and bandwagon, or once more seek to become a military power), favored the creation of a European Defense Community that would prevent the revival of an independent German army.

Although the United States—upon realizing that France would not allow German rearmament outside an EDC—declared its willingness to support such a security structure, an EDC did not come about since the French, following Stalin's death, began to see a reduction in Soviet threat, and thus were no longer willing to curtail their freedom of action significantly. Had the French continued to perceive a high Soviet threat, one might speculate, chances for a ratification of the EDC should have been good, since France faced the highest transaction costs of all the Western powers, and since obstacles to a ratification on the part of France's allies had been removed.

In short, the cases are chosen to maximize variation on *both* independent and dependent variables. This mixed-selection procedure, King, Keohane, and Verba tell us, is "wise" in situations in which the dependent variable has a "rare value" (confederation) to assure that "a number of observations having the rare value . . . [will] be included."[71] The case selection rule adopted in this study is also referred to as the "most different" selection design in which "the overall influence of systemic factors is assessed step-by-step with the addition of each new variable."[72] More specifically, first the magnitude of threat is ascertained to determine what the threat variable by itself can tell us about states' institutional choices. Then the various indicators of transaction costs are examined one by one to determine their role in solving the puzzle.

Since there is no common metric (like price) with which to measure transaction costs, as discussed above, the latter are operationalized by focusing on four separate indicators—uncertainty, asset specificity, technological development, and heterogeneity. Once the magnitude (value) of each indicator has been established, transaction costs are then classified as "high" or "low" compared to other cases. Hence, comparisons across cases both within and between centuries will be conducted and it is hoped that such comparisons will not only serve as a test of the theory, but will also yield information concerning the relative causal weight of different kinds of transaction costs, and thereby pave the way for future research.

The next four chapters contain in-depth case studies. Each begins with a discussion of the theoretical expectations, then operationalizes threat, and explains how realism, by itself, cannot account for the institutional choices made. I then turn to an analysis of transaction costs and, building on the insights of Williamson, Keohane, and other institutionalists, show how this additional factor can shed light on the degree of structural commitment chosen.[73] For each case I study the main actors seeking cooperation and try to make sense of their various calculations.[74]

Chapter 3 examines wartime alliances during the final years of the Napoleonic Wars. Chapter 4 scrutinizes security arrangements following Napoleon's abdication. Chapters 5 and 6 focus on the post-1945 period and analyze the founding of NATO and the failure of the European Defense Community, respectively.

Having developed and assessed an argument about the determinants of different forms of cooperative security arrangements, chapter 7 summarizes the empirical findings. It then ascertains the applicability of the transaction costs model for the present period of flux in the international system. After an examination of the new world (dis)order, the chapter analyzes developments within the European Union to test the explanatory power of the transaction costs approach outside the security realm. The chapter concludes by drawing out the implications of a transaction costs argument for international relations theory.

CHAPTER 3

Wartime Alliances during the Final Years of the Napoleonic Wars

The Napoleonic period can be characterized as an era of almost continuous warfare and great upheaval.[1] Ever since Napoleon seized power in 1799 he pursued an expansionist policy and extended French control over the European continent considerably. Since the numerous battles of the Napoleonic Wars are well documented,[2] it here suffices to stress that, prior to the French invasion of Russia, "Napoleon's dominion extended from the Atlantic to the Vistula and from the Baltic to the Mediterranean," and that the French army was the "most imposing" on the whole continent.[3] Clearly, French expansionist policies posed a serious threat to the European powers and, in fact, they had to fear that further consolidation of French control would eventually jeopardize their existence as independent nation-states.[4] Given this dangerous situation, the continental powers (Austria, Russia, and Prussia) and Britain were forced to reevaluate their security provisions.

NAPOLEON'S RUSSIAN CAMPAIGN AND THE WARTIME ALLIANCE OF PRUSSIA AND RUSSIA

The following discussion shows how Prussia—which prior to the French invasion of Russia saw itself unable to join ranks with its eastern neighbor—reexamined its position and elected to ally with Russia, once it became convinced of the seriousness of the French threat. Or, faced with the choice of risking to be run over by Russian troops in pursuit of the French, or to be annihilated by Napoleon, who, in the near future, was bound to turn against Prussia, the latter came to conclude that it should cooperate with Russia.

Due to the serious time-constraints the allies confronted, their security arrangement had to take the form of a wartime alliance. Russia was already at war with France, thus precluding other types of security relationships with more binding structural commitments that would have taken additional time to bring about. And yet, given that absent extreme threat a number of security arrangements with differing degrees of bind-

31

ingness would have been plausible, in addition to studying threat I will examine transaction costs to be able to speculate about likely outcomes. As will be shown, although the case study confirms realist predictions regarding the choice of alliance partners, realist propositions by themselves face problems accounting for the structural makeup of states' institutional choices.

Letters by European statesmen in 1811 make clear that the continental powers were not surprised by the French invasion of Russia. On the contrary, they were quite aware of the threat they were about to face. Metternich, for instance, wrote to Emperor Francis in 1811 "that the year 1812 will lead to greater disturbances than any of the former ones must be apparent to the most superficial observer."[5] And, in the same year, Metternich informed the British Foreign Office of his conviction that Napoleon is determined to destroy Austria as well as every other government on the continent.[6] The Russians held similar suspicions. Alexander knew that Napoleon felt threatened by Russia's growing independence[7] and, fearing that he would shortly be at war, the Russian emperor employed his espionage service to learn more about French preparations for war.[8]

By the end of 1811, there were no longer any doubts as to French intentions. In an interview with Napoleon on December 17, 1811, Schwarzenberg found out that war was to commence in April of 1812.[9] Alexander, lacking the finances for an offensive policy, thus began to prepare for a defensive war and immediately sought help from Prussia and Austria. As will be seen, however, he did not succeed in his efforts to recruit allies.

Given that the continental powers felt threatened by Napoleon, why did they not combine their efforts at this point against their common enemy? Austria, situated between two Great Powers (France and Russia) in the center of Europe without natural frontiers, clearly was in a vulnerable position and should have had an interest in reducing the power of France.[10] Metternich, however, saw two main obstacles to an Austrian-Russian alliance. On the one hand, as long as friendly relations were to exist with France, it would be impossible actively to cooperate with Russia.[11] On the other hand, and probably more important, Metternich was "still afraid to fight even a shattered Grand Armée,"[12] and saw the need to buy time to strengthen his army. More specifically, in a letter to the British Foreign Office in 1811 he explained:

> My principal and sole Object therefore is to gain sufficient time to enable the military Department to organize the most effective Force which the reduced state of our Finances will permit; but in order to accomplish this end, It is necessary that not only the French Government, but that the greater Part of Europe should be deceived as to my

Principles, and Intentions. I declare, however, in the most solemn manner that so long as I am Minister, I never will listen to any Proposal of active Cooperation between this Country and France.[13]

Hence, the best Austria could do for Russia at the time was to promise it neutrality.

Prussia, after the harsh settlement at the Peace of Tilsit (where it had to agree to phenomenal territorial losses) was a third-class power.[14] It faced serious financial problems and needed time to become important again militarily. Thus, unless Prussia's existence as a sovereign power were to be threatened, Prussia could not be expected to contribute in a meaningful way to any type of security arrangement with Russia. Like Austria, Prussia had to submit to Napoleon's demands and contribute troops to the French army.[15]

And Britain did not have direct influence on Austrian, Prussian, or Russian decisions, yet. In fact, as Gulick points out, at that time, she is best viewed as having potential rather than actual power.[16] Moreover, as a maritime power, Britain's interests on the continent were secondary at best, explaining why, for the most part, she still pursued an insular policy.

During the spring of 1812 several factors contributed to an increase in Russia's threat perception. First, Napoleon assembled an immense army made up of French, German, Italian, and Polish troops.[17] Second, the French emperor managed to draw Prussia and Austria into an alliance with him, since both countries feared that France would crush them before moving into Russia.[18] Third, it had become clear that, aside from being a charismatic and militant leader, Napoleon possessed "intimate knowledge of his own trade as soldier."[19] Fourth, the French army's aggressive tactics, speed of march, and strategic concentration became known[20] so that Alexander had to hasten his preparations for war.

In June 1812 Napoleon moved into Russia. With an army of about 680,000 men he hoped to end the war with one crushing blow, particularly since his enemies—with only about 400,000 men—appeared to be quite vulnerable.[21] Yet, even though Napoleon, on September 7, 1812, won a costly victory in an artillery duel at Borodino and forced the Russians to retreat, he did not manage to talk them into surrendering and had to march into Moscow.[22] Even there Alexander rejected a truce and a combination of severe weather, hunger, and constant enemy attacks eventually forced Napoleon's troops to retreat. The Russian campaign ended with phenomenal losses on both sides. The French army was reduced from about 680,000 to 108,000 men, and Russian troops shrank from about 400,000 to 200,000 men.[23]

Even after the Russian campaign, however, Napoleon's situation was not unfavorable. Given that he had Italy, Illyria, the Netherlands, and all of Germany (with the exception of Prussia) on his side, his potential power continued to be enormous.[24] In fact, it was estimated that he remained capable of raising an army of up to 650,000 men. And, despite his losses in Russia, he "retained the prestige of the greatest military genius of all time."[25] This explains why the continental powers continued to view Napoleon as a major threat and were forced to reevaluate their security provisions.

It became increasingly clear that to overthrow Napoleon united action would be needed. Yet neither Austria nor Britain were ready to join Russia. And Prussia did so only as a last resort. In the winter of 1812 Metternich decided that Austria should begin to play the role of a "mediatory armed power," but stressed that it would need time to prepare adequately.[26] Since 1809 the Austrian army had been reduced to 150,000 men and, due to budgetary constraints, in early 1813 had no more than 60,000 men ready to fight in a new campaign.[27]

British statesmen acknowledged that their country should become more active in European politics since the continent, if unified under a single rule, would pose a great threat to British interests.[28] In fact, Castlereagh proposed Britain assume the role of balancer and "unite in one unbreakable block all the enemies of France."[29] But in reality, Britain, in early 1813 did not have any direct influence on the continent yet.

Prussia, initially, was no more prepared to enter an alliance with Russia than Austria or Britain, but soon had to reevaluate its position. When the Russian army advanced toward Prussian territory in December 1812, Prussia concluded that it should seek more amicable relations with Russia to prevent being run over by Russian troops. Hence, as a first step toward greater cooperation, Prussia signed an armistice with Russia at the Convention of Tauroggen (December 30, 1812). And, since Alexander left no doubt that he would continue his war against Napoleon, Prussia—situated between France and Russia, and thus particularly vulnerable—decided to aid the defender (Russia) in the hope of destroying Prussia's greatest enemy once and for all. Or, in other words, given the choice of siding with the aggressor or the defender, Prussia opted for a wartime alliance with Russia, since Prussia feared that Napoleon soon would also turn against it.

The details of the alliance were worked out in the Treaty of Kalisch on February 28, 1813. It specified the number of troops Prussia was to provide, discussed the exchange of information and the regulation of Russian soldiers on Prussian soil, and stipulated that no separate peace should be negotiated.[30] Thus, a first step toward a general reversal of European diplomatic alignments was taken.[31]

The above discussion lends support to realist propositions concerning state behavior. One sees clearly that the individual nation-states were preoccupied with security concerns and recognized that they would be penalized by the international system, should they fail to protect their interests. Metternich, for example, contemplating the "relative strength of states" in 1811,[32] knew that Austria would have to increase its military capabilities before it could influence the European balance of power. Similarly, Prussia—hit hard at Tilsit—had to rebuild its army and, afraid of being crushed by French troops en route to Russia, together with Austria elected to bandwagon, that is, join the stronger (French) side. And, as a maritime power, Britain opted to pursue an isolationist policy, thus causing Russia to stand alone when Napoleon attacked in the summer of 1812.

Following the invasion of Russia, Austria, Prussia, and Britain once more behaved consistent with realist predictions. Aware that France still possessed great potential power, and that greater cooperation among the continental powers and Britain would soon become necessary, Austria and Britain—as "defensive positionalists"—[33] sought to enhance their own capabilities before playing a more active role in restoring the European balance of power. Prussia, which not only feared being run over by Russian troops in pursuit of Napoleon's forces but also an outright attack by France, opted, as expected, to ally with Russia. Or, deeply concerned about its security, Prussia chose to join the weaker side, that is, to balance with Russia in the hope of defeating France for good.

Since Russia was already at war with France when Prussia decided to ally with its eastern neighbor, the allies had no time to create a sophisticated structural apparatus that would have given their commitment greater bindingness. What mattered most at the time was the immediate fulfillment of mutual obligations to enhance the allies' chances of survival.

And yet, had it not been for serious time-constraints, would Russia and Prussia have sought to bring about a security arrangement of a more binding nature? In the following, I analyze the level of transaction costs the allies experienced at the time they discussed the creation of a joint security apparatus. I show that, although several factors were present that contributed to such costs, the risks associated with the allies' transactions remained moderate.

First, the degree of behavioral uncertainty at the time was substantial and it was not always clear who would ally with whom. Metternich, for instance, who had promised neutrality to Russia in 1811, had reneged on his promise and, as already discussed above, joined Napoleon in the spring of 1812. Hence, in the winter of the same year, it was impossible to know how Austria would behave as a "mediatory armed power." Similarly, Prussia—which repeatedly sent mixed signals by frequently changing sides[34]—had joined Napoleon's Russian campaign prior to allying with Russia, thus making it difficult to predict its future behavior. It was clear, in the winter of 1812, that France remained a serious threat and that the tsar would pursue French troops into Prussian territory. Moreover, one could be reasonably certain that British influence on the continent, for the near future, would remain indirect.

Second, the state of technology (communications, transportation) during the Napoleonic Wars was not very advanced. The system of communication, for instance, particularly when compared to the post-1945 period, was still fairly primitive. Although Napoleon experimented with a semaphore telegraph for passing on news and, occasionally, information could be sent as far as 400 kilometers a day,[35] the usual way of communicating was via courier who would deliver letters by horse. Thus, especially where great distances between the people seeking communication existed, for example, when a letter had to be sent from the continent to Britain, the letter could take several weeks to reach its destination. It is estimated that "[m]ost politico-military information probably traveled at from 60 to 90 kilometers a day."[36]

One, however, has to be careful not to overstate communication problems. What needs to be kept in mind is that representatives of the continental powers and France were frequently assembled at the same conference places, and thus could reduce the number of written accounts of their meetings.[37] Communication via courier then was only needed when representatives had to keep informed about military developments or relay messages to their home countries.

Turning to an examination of the transportation system one finds that Napoleon had initiated several changes. He, for instance, improved roads leading to the borders of his empire, created new roads over mountain passes for armies with cannons, constructed tunnels, and improved the canal system.[38] And yet, since one of the most crucial modes of transportation, the railways, did not become important until the 1830s,[39] the changes Napoleon undertook were of relatively minor significance.

Clearly, an underdeveloped state of technology raised coordination costs, but, even more important, it increased the risk of opportunism. In one instance, as will be seen below, slow communications led to a defection that went undetected for some time.

Third, the heterogeneous cultural background of the allies made transactions more costly. To coordinate military activities of soldiers from different countries, speaking different languages, required higher cooperation costs than coordination among culturally homogeneous countries. But since, in this case, the number of allies seeking cooperation was small and there was no evidence of strong feelings of distrust between Russia and Prussia, the impact of heterogeneity is likely to have been minor.

Fourth, an analysis of the military equipment used during the Napoleonic period shows that weapons entailed generic rather than specific assets. As a result, the transactional risks the allies faced were relatively low. In fact, the industrial revolution clearly came too late to affect the Napoleonic Wars[40] and weapons underwent little modification between 1799 and 1815. Armies, to a large extent, depended on the infantry and their principal weapon was the musket.[41] The cavalry only played a secondary role. Since there was no significant change in weaponry, tactics did not change much either and there was no need for special training.

What did change, however, was the magnitude of war. Instead of conflict involving tens of thousands of men, now it took place between hundreds of thousands.[42] This increase in the size of armies explains the need for conscription,[43] but, since draftees did not receive improved and more specialized training, human asset specificity did not exist.[44]

It also deserves mention that the degree of threat and transaction costs the allies were subjected to was roughly equal. Russia, which most recently had been attacked by France, still felt seriously threatened. Likewise Prussia, aware of the enormous potential power of France and particularly vulnerable due to its geographic closeness to the enemy, perceived a significant danger. Moreover, high behavioral uncertainty, underdeveloped technology, and cultural heterogeneity impacted the allies similarly. Even though these factors increased the allies' costs of cooperating, absent asset specificity and feelings of distrust, the risk of opportunism was significantly reduced.

In sum it can be said that not only the wartime nature of the alliance between Russia and Prussia precluded the creation of a very binding security arrangement like a confederation, but that, with a reduced likelihood of opportunistic behavior, the allies saw no need to curtail their autonomy significantly. Or, although a high degree of uncertainty plagued the allies' coordination efforts, generic assets, a lack of distrust, and the relatively small number of countries seeking cooperation kept transaction costs down. Put differently still, the symmetric assessment of threat and transaction costs leads one to predict that—even absent serious time pressures—ceteris paribus, the allies would have refrained from building a highly sophisticated security structure.

THE WARTIME ALLIANCE OF
RUSSIA, PRUSSIA, AND AUSTRIA

This case demonstrates that Austria joined the wartime alliance since it increasingly felt threatened by Napoleon's offensive behavior. Although Metternich managed to make use of his diplomatic skills to postpone Austria's entry into the war on the side of the allies, he could not hold out on making a firm commitment to the continental powers for long without seriously jeopardizing the security of his country. Thus, when he became convinced that the French would soon be fighting on Austrian territory, he took immediate action.

As in the Russo-Prussian alliance, the allies faced serious time-constraints that precluded the creation of a time-consuming, structurally sophisticated security apparatus. The tsar and Prussia were already at war with France, and Austria saw itself on the brink of war. But, as will be developed below, the magnitude of the allies' transaction costs also did not warrant greater institutional bindingness.

Taking a closer look at threat first one finds that, despite France's recent defeats, the allies continued to perceive the country as "powerful and dangerous."[45] Whereas, in April 1813, they had 80,000 men, Napoleon had about 145,000 men (including 10,000 cavalry), and both sides were mobilizing rapidly.[46] Hence, to improve their chances of withstanding renewed French attacks and reach their ultimate goal—the defeat of Napoleon and the reduction of France to her natural frontiers[47]—Russia and Prussia targeted Austria for further assistance.

Efforts to improve the allies' security were complicated by the difficulty of predicting Austrian behavior in early 1813. On the one hand, Metternich was hesitant to join the allies since he feared Russia and wished to maintain a strong France for balancing purposes.[48] On the other hand, he was convinced that Napoleon would commence a new campaign in Germany very soon,[49] and thus had no choice but to make military preparations to enter the war against France.[50]

In a first attempt to remove the uncertainty surrounding his country's future actions the Austrian statesman met with Alexander to explain Austria's continued need, in the short run, to play the role of mediator. More specifically, Metternich informed the tsar, Austria would offer to mediate between France and the allies and, should Napoleon decline, friendly relations between France and Austria would end. In the event of French acceptance, Metternich assured Alexander, demands would be put to Napoleon that the French general would have to reject.[51] Hence, the only importance of mediation attempts, Metternich stressed, was to buy Austria time to position its armies.[52]

During the following weeks the Austrian statesman used his diplomatic talents wisely. In frequent consultations with the continental powers he devised a plan to persuade Napoleon to participate in a conference that the French emperor hoped would allow him to win back Austria, but that was really designed to give the latter additional time. Lured by the prospect of improved French-Austrian relations, Napoleon not only agreed to such a meeting but also signed an armistice at Pleswitz (June 4, 1813) that was to last until July 20, 1813.[53]

Meanwhile, Prussia, Russia, and Austria worked feverishly to consolidate their position. They met repeatedly to work out the terms to be put to Napoleon and, on June 12, agreed on a final version of their demands that would require territorial losses on the part of France, and thus was sure to be rejected. Moreover, the continental powers convened at Reichenbach and on June 27, Austria secretly allied with Russia and Prussia.

To avoid arousing French suspicions Metternich also met with Napoleon and continued Austrian efforts to win time. Although the Conference of Prague began in mid-July, the allies did not give their demands to the French delegation until August 7, and then in the form of an ultimatum. The French had to make a decision by August 10, and in case of noncompliance Austria would enter the war against Napoleon. Not surprisingly, the deadline passed without France being able to reply.[53]

On August 12, 1813, Austria finally officially joined the allies by declaring war on France, but it took the continental powers a couple of months to defeat Napoleon seriously. Although, for the first time, Russia, Prussia, and Austria were aligned against Napoleon and, consequently, outnumbered his troops (Napoleon had about 700,000 men compared to the allies' 865,000 men),[54] the allies' war efforts were weakened by jealousies and dissensions between their military leaders,[55] as well as the greater military experience of their French counterparts.[56] Thus, in the Battle of Dresden (August 26–27) Napoleon defeated the allies, but by October they had learned to cooperate more effectively and in the Battle of Leipzig rendered a decisive blow to the French that forced them to retreat.

Aside from Austria's membership in the wartime alliance, British subsidies played an inceasingly important role in the defeat of Napoleon. Although Britain's voice in Central European affairs was still largely ignored during the fall of 1813,[57] British subsidies and weapons became more readily available to remedy shortages in the continental armies' equipment so that, when "the material means and the will to overthrow Napoleon came together," the French could be defeated.[58]

In sum, it can be said that, at a time when Britain exercised little political influence on the continent, and Russia and Prussia felt increasingly threatened by France's superior military capabilities, the allies sought Austrian assistance to prevent French hegemony.[59] As realism predicts, Metternich was primarily interested in restoring an equilibrium.[60] He recognized the danger stemming from French expansionism, but also knew that France had to remain strong to check the power of Russia, since gains by the latter could also lead to Austria's decline. Hence, as a "defensive positionalist" the Austrian statesman sought to mediate between Napoleon and the allies to buy time—until French noncompliance with the ultimatum obliged Austria to balance, that is, to join the weaker side and aid in Napoleon's defeat.

While the outcome—a wartime alliance between Russia, Prussia, and Austria—confirms realist expectations regarding alliance partners, I once more examine transaction costs to ascertain whether, in the absence of extreme threat, the allies might have chosen a higher degree of institutionalization.

First, as expected, one can see the greater uncertainty associated with a multipolar world in British and Austrian behavior and others' assessment thereof. As discussed above, in 1813 it was particularly difficult to predict how Austria would act. Since Metternich in the past had promised neutrality but then reneged and sided with France, the tsar had to feel uneasy about Austria's delaying tactics. Even though the continental powers met several times to discuss the terms to be presented to Napoleon, Prussia and Russia had no way of knowing what really took place during repeated meetings between Napoleon and Metternich. Moreover, it was unclear whether Britain would play a more active role on the continent. After all, Castlereagh still resided in Britain and there was no guarantee that subsidies and weapons shipments would continue.

In short, the signals sent by Austria and Britain were not always easy to interpret and therefore raised transaction costs. Until Austria declared war on France it was not always clear who would ally with whom. The only thing the continental powers knew for sure was that France posed the most serious threat to their security and that it would take their combined efforts to defeat Napoleon.

Moreover, as explained previously, communications and transportation were underdeveloped and made diplomatic efforts difficult. Castlereagh, for instance, was well aware that delays in receiving information seriously reduced his effectiveness as negotiator. In fact, "the difficulty of communication caused [his] dispatches always to lag at least ten days behind events."[61]

Most importantly, however, slow communications increased the risk of opportunism. Metternich's doublecross of France in 1813 provides a good example.[62] The incident shows how the Austrian statesman, aided by a "backward" state of technology, managed to deceive Napoleon for some time by secretly negotiating with the continental powers—a development almost unthinkable today where most parts of the world are equipped with satellites, phones, and computers.

Lacking the necessary data to ascertain the magnitude of transaction costs stemming from the allies' heterogeneous backgrounds, it nevertheless stands to reason that cooperation costs were slightly higher than during the wartime alliance of Russia and Prussia. Three countries with different language, cultural, and religious backgrounds in this case sought to cooperate, thereby increasing both the need for translation and the cost of military coordination. And, given their lack of cultural affinity, the allies must have been concerned about opportunistic behavior; but, since there is no mention in the literature of deep-seated distrust, heterogeneity is unlikely to have led to significant transactional risks.

Similarly, since weapons remained unchanged, that is, still largely consisted of generic rather than specific components, the allies' vulnerability to opportunism continued to be relatively low. Occasionally, some men attended military schools—Napoleon for example trained to become an artillery specialist[63]—but the average soldier lacked any kind of specialized education so that there was no human asset specificity to speak of either that might have raised transactional risks.

Finally, as in the previous case, the magnitude of threat and transaction costs Russia, Prussia, and Austria confronted was nearly symmetric. All three countries perceived France as a serious threat and their cooperation efforts were plagued by high uncertainty, an underdeveloped state of technology, and cultural heterogeneity. This suggests that the allies once again should have been in agreement on the degree of institutionalization needed to enhance their security.

In sum, not only the wartime nature of the alliance between Prussia, Russia, and Austria stood in the way of a very binding security arrangement, but the magnitude of transaction costs also did not call for a substantial curtailment of sovereignty. As in the alliance between Russia and Prussia, the absence of asset specificity and feelings of distrust moderated transactional risks, and thus kept transaction costs manageable.

THE QUADRUPLE ALLIANCE

A final security arrangement prior to Napoleon's abdication that deserves closer attention is the Quadruple Alliance. It demonstrates how Britain—aware of France's immense military capabilities, Napoleon's unwillingness to surrender, and the allies' leadership struggles—decided to take action to prevent disaster. Given that the allies faced a serious threat (the year 1814 saw continuous fighting), and that they had to coordinate their military efforts under great time-pressure to offset the power of Napoleon, the Continental states and Britain formed a wartime alliance—known as the Quadruple Alliance.

Realism, as in the previous cases, sheds light on the choice of alliance partners and here provides an excellent account of British behavior. To be able to speculate, however, whether, absent extreme threat, the allies might have sought greater structural commitments, traditional realist accounts once again need to be augmented with an analysis of transaction costs.

By the end of 1813, the alliance between the continental powers faced serious problems. Napoleon rejected a peace offer, jealousies and suspicions among the allies threatened to impair their military effectiveness, in fact, it was no longer clear whether the coalition would survive. Whereas Russia and Prussia sought the total defeat of France, Austria merely aimed for a reduction in power, since Metternich was convinced that an independent French state was needed to keep Russia and Prussia in line.[64] To complicate matters further, the present coalition consisted of nine separate treaties of alliance,[65] and, as Castlereagh feared, if not "welded together by some firm and unequivocal Act of General Alliance,"[66] the coalition might collapse.

In the spring of 1814, the British foreign minister therefore arrived at the continent, determined to take charge. At the Congress of Chatillon (February 5 to March 19) the allies made one last attempt to arrive at a peaceful solution by offering Napoleon the French frontiers of 1792. Yet, encouraged by recent military successes at Champeaubert, Montmirail, and Chateau-Thierry,[67] the French emperor refused the offer, thereby signaling to the allies that they would have to make a greater commitment or risk defeat.

Convinced of their helplessness vis-à-vis the overwhelming military capabilities of the French, except in combination,[68] the continental powers finally reaffirmed their commitment to fight against their common enemy. In the Treaty of Chaumont (signed on March 9, 1814) Austria, Russia, Prussia and now also Britain pledged to continue their struggle against France and, in seventeen regular and several secret articles,[69] specified the nature of their security relationship. Each ally, for instance, was to put 150,000 men in the field to fight Napoleon, Britain was to pay five million pounds in subsidies, and no one should conclude a separate peace.[70] Moreover, in the secret articles the allies vowed to restore sovereignty to those states that had lost their independence as a result of Napoleon's expansionist campaigns. Or, in other words, the allies secretly pledged to reestablish the independence of the German states, Italy, the Swiss cantons, Holland, and Spain, thus expressing their desire to restore the state system as it existed prior to French expansionism.[71] And, to mention but one further safety measure, the allies vowed to keep their forces in existence one year beyond France's defeat.

Yet probably of greatest importance was the stipulation that the alliance should last for at least two decades. As article XVI makes clear

> The present Treaty of Defensive Alliance having for its object to maintain the equilibrium of Europe, to secure the repose and independence of its States, and to prevent the invasions which during so many years have desolated the World, the High Contracting Parties have agreed to extend the duration of it to 20 years, to take date from the day of its Signature; and they reserve to themselves, to concert upon its ulterior prolongation, 3 years before its expiration, should circumstances require it.[72]

This twenty-year duration reflects two crucial concerns of the treaty drafters. First, the long time-span indicates the allies' assumption that France would continue to pose a threat to their security, even after Napoleon's defeat.[73] Second, the twenty-year stipulation demonstrates the allies' willingness, automatically, to enter into a peacetime security arrangement to preserve the European balance of power.[74]

In sum, since they felt seriously threatened by constant French military attacks and were unable to attain a peaceful solution, the allies had to put their differences behind them and consolidate their war efforts. To assure the continuity of their common security endeavors, the signatories to the Treaty of Chaumont furthermore pledged that their defense efforts should last for a minimum of twenty years.

As alluded to earlier, realism does a good job accounting for the events leading to the Quadruple Alliance. In fact, two different realist schools can be invoked to explain the behavior of the European powers.

On the one hand, balance of power theorists argue that, given the severity of the French threat, the European powers had to combine their efforts to balance against this threat, and thereby increase their chances of survival. Since the continental powers lacked the military capabilities to defend themselves against French attacks, Britain had to join the allies to offset the power of France. Or, in other words, Britain elected to join the weaker side to balance against an increasing threat.[75]

On the other hand, hegemonic stability theorists focus on the power and interests of Britain to explain the creation of the Quadruple Alliance. Countries that possess preponderant power (naval power), we are told, "organize global order, since, as holders of monopolies," they obtain large benefits by doing so.[76] Thus, as hegemon, Britain had a major incentive to restore stability on the European continent to defend its position as world leader.

Although both strands of realism (balance of power and hegemonic stability theory) can explain why there was a need for the Quadruple Alliance and why Britain decided to play a more active role on the European continent, neither, by itself, can shed light on the institutional form the allies might have selected, had there not been serious time-constraints. Historical accounts of the Napoleonic wars make clear that the wartime nature of the Quadruple Alliance precluded the creation of a very binding security structure. But, less pressed for time, would the allies have sought greater commitments, that is, chosen to confederate? Clearly, a structurally more sophisticated security arrangement with a central decision-making apparatus and arbitration mechanisms would have been better equipped to settle the allies' differences. To find an answer, again, traditional realist explanations have to be complemented with a transaction costs analysis.

Focusing on the degree of uncertainty the allies had to contend with one quickly discovers that one set of doubts was replaced by another. The big question no longer was who would side with whom, but whether the coalition would survive. As discussed above, while Russia and Prussia hoped to defeat Napoleon once and for all, Austria sought to assure France's continued existence as a Great Power, and there was no guarantee that Castlereagh's diplomatic skills would suffice to keep the coalition intact. In fact, this uncertainty concerning the longevity of cooperation efforts was not diminished until the allies pledged a long-term commitment at Chaumont.

Moreover, transaction costs resulting from an underdeveloped state of technology remained high—particularly when compared to the post–World War II period. Castlereagh's move to the continent, without a doubt, diminished the costs of negotiating agreements since now all the allies were assembled at the same conference places. But the slow speed of communication and transportation assured that the stakes would remain great. The likelihood of opportunistic behavior going undetected for some time continued to be substantially greater than in a technologically more sophisticated age.

Given that the degree of cultural heterogeneity increased further with Britain's entry into the alliance, it stands to reason that the transaction costs brought about by the varied language, religious, and political backgrounds also rose. However, as explained earlier, absent serious distrust, heterogeneity is likely to have led to greater coordination costs, not transactional risks.

Finally, the nature of the allies' weapons employed in their fight against Napoleon assured low vulnerability to opportunism. Since the musket continued to be the principal weapon and, in 1814, Russia, Prussia, and Austria fought French troops on land rather than at sea, the fact that Britain possessed the largest navy with highly specialized physical and human assets, from a transaction costs perspective, was of little importance. Or, even though the British Navy in the past had played a crucial role in the struggle against France (one only needs to recall Napoleon's defeat at Trafalgar in 1805), in this instance, the continental powers had little reason to fear British opportunism since they sought assistance in the form of soldiers, not naval vessels. Stated differently still, since the members of the anti-Napoleonic coalition vowed to provide 150,000 men each and there was no mention of additional British naval support, any assets the allies possessed outside of the ones pledged should not have entered risk assessments or cost-benefit analyses, and thus should not have influenced the institutional outcome.

What sets the Quadruple Alliance apart from the two security arrangements discussed previously is asymmetric threat perception. Britain, as a maritime power and holding naval supremacy, felt less threatened than the continental powers on whose soil the war was being fought. This suggests that, under less pressure to act, Russia, Prussia, and Austria should have sought a more binding security arrangement than Britain.

To summarize, confronted with an extreme threat that was expected to last for some time, the allies chose to give long-term assurances to each other. Even without serious time-pressure, however, they should not have formed a very binding security structure. Although they had to cope with great uncertainty, a backward state of technology, and cultural heterogeneity, as in the previous cases, the absence of deep-seated distrust and specific assets moderated the risk of opportunism. Moreover, one finds that Britain, feeling less threatened, had no incentive to curtail its freedom of action significantly. Thus, under such circumstances the allies might have created an alliance with the structural means to coordinate military operations (maybe a security arrangement resembling NATO), but should not have surrendered a substantial amount of their sovereignty to a central decision-making body.

As with the two prior alliances, realism—stressing the centrality of threat—can explain both the need for a Quadruple Alliance and the choice of alliance partners. If one wants to know what type of security arrangement the allies would have chosen, had they not been at war with Napoleon already, one needs to expand traditional realist explanations and, additionally, examine the magnitude of transaction costs.

NAPOLEON'S ABDICATION
AND THE ALLIES' PEACE EFFORTS

In the days following the Treaty of Chaumont the allies fought numerous battles and began to advance upon Paris. On March 10, 1814, the allied armies defeated Napoleon in the Battle of Laon. On March 12, the British captured Bordeaux. Eight days later Napoleon suffered serious losses in the Battle of Arcis-sur-Aube, and on March 25 was defeated in the Battle of La Fere-Champenoise. Finally, on March 30, the allies stormed the Montmartre and forced the French to capitulate.[77]

Shortly after their victorious march into Paris, the allies forced Napoleon to abdicate and exiled him to the island of Elba. Louis XVIII was restored as king of France and efforts were made to reestablish order through a series of peace settlements. In the First Treaty of Paris (May 30) the allies put moderate terms to France to strengthen Louis XVIII and to preserve France "as an effective member of the European balance of power."[78] Among other points the treaty specified that France would retain the boundaries of 1792, and that it would have to recognize the independence of the German states, the Netherlands, and Switzerland. Due to the complexity of some of the problems before them, the allies further agreed to hold a congress at Vienna that should settle unresolved territorial issues.[79]

From September 1814 to June 1815 most European rulers attended the Congress of Vienna, but negotiations did not always work as smoothly as hoped. Repeatedly, the allies reached a deadlock over territorial questions and by January 1815 were on the verge of war over disagreements concerning Poland and Saxony.[80] In fact, Russia and Prussia decided to ally against Austria and Britain, causing the latter two to seek the support of France and to create a Triple Alliance (Austria, Britain, and France).

Before the disagreements among the former allies could become more serious, the congress was interrupted by Napoleon's escape from Elba (March 1815) and his return to Paris (Hundred Days). This obvious common danger had a unifying effect, causing the four big powers to put their differences aside and to renew their coalition against Napoleon.

Remarkable are the speed and efficiency with which the coalition was relaunched. Given that the representatives of the Great Powers were assembled in Vienna, that they had a "common and recent experience with coalitions," and that their armies could be employed quickly, the allies managed to restore their security arrangement by March 25, 1815.[81] By June, Napoleon's armed forces numbered over 500,000 men and the coalition agreed to put 600,000 soldiers in the field.[82]

The allies had to fight a series of battles before they could force Napoleon to abdicate a second time. On June 14, the French general marched into Belgium. On June 16, his troops were engaged in the Battles of Ligny and Quatre Bras. Finally, on June 18, the allies managed to defeat Napoleon for good in the Battle of Waterloo.[83] Four days later he had to relinquish power and was imprisoned on the island of St. Helena. Paris once more was captured by the allies and Louis XVIII returned to the throne.

CHAPTER 4

Security Arrangements Following Napoleon's Abdication

Following the above described period of intense fighting the allies had to restore order. In addition to dealing with territorial issues that were likely to cause new problems, the allies had to reevaluate their security provisions and, where necessary, modify them. As expected, one finds that countries that still felt seriously threatened and believed their security arrangements to be insufficient to counter such threats created new security structures (examples are the German states and the Swiss cantons). On the other hand, countries that felt less threatened merely sought to renew existing arrangements (renewal of the Quadruple Alliance during the Second Peace of Paris), or to withdraw altogether (Britain which more and more began to pursue an insular policy).

THE GERMAN CONFEDERATION

This case examines the drawn-out negotiations between the European powers and the German states concerning German security provisions. It shows that realism focusing on power considerations does a good job explaining the need for a binding German security apparatus as well as individual preferences regarding alliance partners. Since realism, by itself, cannot shed light on the structural makeup of the security arrangement chosen by the German states, I then scrutinize transaction costs and find that the Germans were exposed to much greater transactional risks than the members of the previously discussed wartime alliances.

The German states, as a brief historical overview of their plight shows, faced security problems for some time prior to the creation of the German Confederation in 1815. A first step toward the disintegration of the Holy Roman Empire was taken in 1801, when, as a result of the Treaty of Luneville, the left bank of the Rhine fell into French hands.[1] During the following years, secularization and mediatization further curtailed the power of the German emperor,[2] making it impossible for him to maintain peace. Before the German states—left virtually defenseless by this internal turmoil—could consolidate their power and improve their security, Napoleon imposed a political system on them known as the Rheinbund. The German emperor was forced to abdicate and, with his removal from power in 1806, the Holy Roman Empire collapsed.

From 1806 to 1813 the German states were "trapped" in a confederal body under French protection (Rheinbund) that reduced their freedom of action severely.[3] Unlike Prussia, which could decide for itself whether it would fight on the side of Napoleon or on the side of the Great Powers, the German states were forced to fight with the French. Moreover, the German states had to adjust to significant structural changes. By suppressing a number of smaller states, destroying ecclesiastical principalities,[4] and allowing medium-sized states like Bavaria, Württemberg, and Baden to increase their territory,[5] the French General greatly reduced the number of "sovereign" German units, and thus decreased the fragmentation of power that plagued the old German Reich.

However, since the Rheinbund was imposed on the German states, resistance against the French grew quickly. Physically exhausted and economically depleted by almost continuous warfare, the Germans desperately were waiting for an opportunity to free themselves from French control. When the great European powers formed a coalition against Napoleon and began to advance toward French territory, the members of the Rheinbund deserted Napoleon, thus causing the disintegration of the artificially created German government.[6]

Following Napoleon's overthrow in 1814, German sovereignty had to be restored, but it was not at all clear what form the new German political system should take. Representatives of the Great Powers and German statesmen put forth various proposals that they debated at the Congress of Vienna. Early on, they managed to rule out three possible solutions.

First, since the German states, to a large extent, tacitly accepted Napoleon's political restructuring of the Rheinbund years, too many changes (particularly a reduction of the number of sovereign units from over 300 to 38) had occurred to reinstate the old Reich.[7] Or, in other words, since several German states—due to the secularization of ecclesiastical principalities and the suppression of numerous small states during the Rheinbund—had experienced significant territorial gains, they were unwilling to return to the old, fragmented German Empire and surrender their new possessions.[8]

Second, plans for the unification of Germany were "not in the realm of practical politics in 1815."[9] The rivalry between the two big German powers clearly prevented the creation of a unified state—in fact, Prussia and Austria abhorred this notion.[10] And in the south of Germany several medium-sized states had been created (Bavaria, Württemberg, and Baden) that were determined to defend their sovereignty along with the smaller states.[11]

Third, the representatives at Vienna rejected the complete independence of the various German states. On the one hand, as Metternich pointed out, it was feared that too much autonomy might encourage some states "to gravitate toward France and would leave Germany as a whole too disorganized to resist Russian encroachments."[12] On the other hand, the representatives at Vienna doubted that all German states would be able to fend for themselves, and thus sought to create an arrangement that would give the small or geographically more vulnerable states greater assurances, while setting some boundaries to their political maneuverability.[13]

Aside from agreement on the proposals for a German solution that could be rejected immediately (a reinstatement of the old German Empire, German unification, and the complete independence of the individual German states), there was consensus that, even after Napoleon's overthrow, Germany's external security remained seriously threatened. Although the level of threat posed by France diminished with Napoleon's defeat, it did not disappear. That is, whereas prior to the French general's overthrow the continental powers were *extremely* threatened and engaged in continuous warfare with France, following his defeat threat continued to be *high*, due to the potential power of France. One only needs to recall that the signatories of the Treaty of Chaumont expected France to pose a significant threat for some time, and thus vowed to keep their alliance in existence for twenty years.

Additional cause for concern stemmed from the fact that Napoleon's overthrow left the immense power of Russia, at least temporarily, without an "effective counterpoise" on the continent.[14] What the German states sought at Vienna, thus was a security system that would protect them from French pressures and that would offset the newly created Russian danger.[15]

"Sprawled across Central Europe, with arbitrary and indefensible frontiers, afraid of French designs on the Rhineland and Russian ambitions on Poland,"[16] it was clear that Germany was in need of a binding security arrangement. The form this arrangement should take, however, was seriously disputed. As the following study of the negotiations of 1814/1815 shows, the European powers and the German states were unable to reach agreement on the German question until Napoleon's escape from Elba increased the urgency to find a compromise. Or, stated differently, one sees how an increase in threat caused the negotiating powers to put their differences aside and to cast their votes in favor of a binding security arrangement.

To obtain a better understanding of the intricate debates concerning Germany's future it is essential to differentiate between the goals of the European powers and those of the German states. As realists would predict, after Napoleon's defeat, the European powers were mainly interested in restoring the balance of power and in maintaining peace and order. To achieve this goal the representatives of the Great Powers concluded several important steps had to be taken. For instance, the French borders of 1792 needed to be restored to assure that France would remain a Great Power. Russia could not be allowed to obtain all of Poland to prevent a Russian dominance on the continent. Prussia would have to receive parts of both Saxony and Poland to restore Prussia's Great Power status; and Austria would have to regain its territorial possessions of the pre-revolutionary era.[17] Moreover, since the German states—located in the middle of Europe and surrounded by powerful countries—could be expected to pose a continuous threat to European peace unless their security problem was to be alleviated,[18] the Great Powers at Vienna decided to treat the German question as a European question.[19]

German statesmen had a much more narrow goal. Rather than to concern themselves with balance of power considerations in all of Europe, they were mainly interested in restoring the sovereignty of their former territories and in protecting Germany's regained autonomy.

The German question was further complicated by the fact that neither the European powers nor the German statesmen could agree on Germany's new political structure. Focusing on the European powers first one finds that France and Russia, for instance, favored the creation of an independent third Germany, that is, a German union without Prussia and Austria.[20] This can be explained in that both France and Russia would have felt threatened by a too powerful Germany and that they sought to avoid a strong and united Central Europe.[21]

The British were of exactly the opposite opinion. Castlereagh argued that amicable relations between Austria and Prussia would be "essential to the stability of the Continent,"[22] and thus suggested that the two big German powers should function as the "main pillars" of a newly created German political body.[23] Any solution other than dual leadership, the British statesman feared, would merely reignite the rivalry between Prussia and Austria, and therefore pose a new danger to European peace.

Prussia and Austria agreed that they needed to increase their security vis-à-vis France and Russia. To achieve this goal the two great German powers sought to subordinate the smaller and medium-sized German states to Prussian and Austrian control.[24] That is, Prussia and Austria envisioned a political structure in which they would hold dual leadership, yet for some time could not reach agreement on its final form.

Numerous German statesmen, simultaneously, debated various proposals. In August 1813 the Prussian reformer Stein, for instance, envisioned an arrangement of the small and medium-sized states that should enter a union with Austria and sign a guarantee pact with Prussia.[25] In the spring of 1814, another Prussian, Hardenberg, suggested to divide Germany into nine districts.[26] In October of the same year, Austria, Prussia, and Hanover reached agreement on a plan that resembled Hardenberg's, yet favored the division of Germany into only seven districts and sought to institutionalize the dual hegemony of Austria and Prussia.[27] That is, whereas all of the German states should be allowed to cast a maximum of one vote each, the two big German states should be allowed two votes each.

A German committee (Austria, Prussia, Hanover, Bavaria, and Württemberg), specifically created to discuss the German question, debated the seven district/dual hegemony plan in October 1814. Yet both Bavaria and Württemberg found the institutionalized hegemony of Prussia and Austria unacceptable and rejected the plan.[28] Before new proposals could be discussed Württemberg, dissatisfied with the work of the German committee, resigned. And, due to increased tensions over territorial questions concerning Saxony and Poland, cooperation between Austria and Prussia became virtually impossible.[29]

From mid-November 1814 until May 1815 official negotiations on Germany's future were interrupted. During this stalemate, however, new proposals were made and the German states upheld their diverse positions. Fearing that they could be drawn into future wars of the two big German powers, the medium-sized German states, for instance, wanted to keep Austria and Prussia outside a new German structure. The small German states, on the other hand, expressly sought Austrian and Prussian membership, hoping that the two big powers would protect them against potential infringements by the medium-sized states.[30]

In short, the security debates show that both the European powers and the German states assumed the role of rational, calculating actors, weighing the costs and benefits of the various options before them. Time and again, representatives of the negotiating parties voiced concerns about relative gains and, consistent with realist predictions, sought to make sure that no single country would become so powerful as to pose a threat to others.

The stalemate on the German question could only be overcome when Napoleon escaped from Elba and, on March 1, 1815, landed in France. The French general's return demonstrates how an increase in threat forced the great European powers and the German states to compromise and strengthen their security provisions.

Since, as discussed above, aside from threat, the magnitude of trans-action costs is instrumental in determining states' structural commit-ment, the next section examines these costs and then takes a closer look at the compromise solution obtained. Having established high threat, if transaction costs are low, one would expect to see a binding alliance, but there should be no need for a confederation. Conversely, if transac-tion costs are high, ceteris paribus, one would expect a structurally sophisticated security arrangement like a confederation to reduce trans-action costs and to guard against opportunistic behavior.

An analysis of the period of the Congress of Vienna indeed shows that transaction costs were substantial and this can be attributed to a number of factors.

First, the allies sought to cooperate in an environment characterized by multiple uncertainties. Although the great European powers in the Treaty of Chaumont had pledged to maintain their alliance, it was not always clear how Austria and Prussia would act. Would they cooperate or compete against each other? Would they pursue their own agendas or share interests with the other German states?

Similarly, it was impossible to know which of the numerous Ger-man states would side with whom, whether some states might gravitate toward the enemy or even engage in outright aggression. After years of inconsistent signals, frequently changing alliances, and countless wars between the territories of the old German Empire,[31] the possibility of internal upheaval could not be ruled out. That is, given little semblance of domestic order and a whole gamut of conceivable opportunistic behavior, the Germans—unlike the members of the previously discussed wartime alliances—additionally feared that some of their allies might turn against them. This suggests that the uncertainty about the future behavior of the various German states became intertwined with a new kind of threat—one *internal* (from the German states themselves) to the security arrangement and thus excluded from the argument advanced here. But this threat was merely derivative of the larger French threat discussed above.[32]

Second, the relatively underdeveloped state of technology raised the allies' transaction costs. As mentioned previously, communications and transportation were not very sophisticated. It still took several days (sometimes even weeks) to relay messages from one place to another, travel continued to take place mainly on horseback, and it remained cumbersome and costly to send troops for combined military maneu-vers. Even though it is conceivable that the geographic proximity of the allies may have moderated transaction costs and risks somewhat, there can be no doubt that the very large number of states seeking to cooper-ate (thirty-nine German states in 1815)[33] had the opposite effect (raised transaction costs). Any effort to gather information, exchange ideas or conclude agreements among that many states had to be costly, unless a central, state-like political structure were to be created to help offset these costs. For instance, if representatives of the various states were to reside in the same city year-round and their respective governments were to delegate decision-making powers to them, negotiation, monitoring, coordination costs, and the risk of opportunism would be significantly reduced, since it would be more difficult for undesirable behavior to go unnoticed for any length of time.

Third, the varied cultural background of the German states increased transaction costs. Some states could be classified as hereditary monarchies or princedoms, others as city republics,[34] and there was a significant difference of interests between northern and southern German states.[35] For transactions to be handled smoothly in this diverse environment conflict-solving mechanisms were needed to mediate between the various parties. Differences in military training and military customs, moreover, raised the Germans' cooperation costs. In fact, at times, there was so little standardization that one state's signal to attack was identical with another's signal to withdraw.[36]

In addition to raising coordination costs cultural heterogeneity increased transactional risks. "Deep-cutting differences of confession" and the divergent political interests of the German states repeatedly led to belligerence, and over time brought about the "decay of any sense of common German nationality."[37] Long-lasting struggles such as the Wars of Religion or the Thirty Years War were especially damaging and seriously undermined feelings of trust. Hence, although the degree of heterogeneity was lower in the German case than the Quadruple Alliance since the German states shared a common language, the Germans, nevertheless, lived in constant fear that some of their allies (other German states) might behave opportunistically—if not engage in outright aggression—and thus, were in need of a structurally sophisticated security apparatus that would diminish transaction costs and risks.

Focusing on the allies' military equipment one finds that, much like in the above described alliances, the absence of asset specificity had a moderating effect. In this case, too, the lack of highly specialized armament ingredients and of human asset specificity (in the form of sophisticated weapons training) helped to reduce transactional risks. Yet, due to the high degree of uncertainty, the backward state of technology, the varied cultural backgrounds, the significant level of distrust, and the unusually large number of states seeking to cooperate, any joint efforts to enhance German security would be subject to high risks and costs.

Furthermore, unlike the Quadruple Alliance where the British perceived a lesser threat than their allies, the Germans agreed on the magnitude of threat. That is, even though it stands to reason that the smaller German states should have felt more threatened than the medium-sized and larger ones, the above described security debates make clear that all Germans perceived a high French threat and therefore sought a binding security arrangement that would enhance their chances of survival. Similarly, all Germans were subjected to high transaction costs. Each state had to come to terms with great uncertainty, make the best of an under-developed state of technology, and cope with the costs associated with cultural heterogeneity.

To summarize, given high threat, the German states—unless they were willing to jeopardize their survival as independent entities in the international system—had no choice but to aggregate their capabilities against their common enemy. And, since in 1815 the Germans confronted significantly higher transaction costs than Russia, Prussia, and Austria when they formed their wartime alliance, the German states were in need of a structurally sophisticated security apparatus that would reduce these costs.

In the following, I return to the negotiations between the great European powers and the German states to explain how the German problem was solved. As will be seen shortly, the final outcome (a confederation) lends support to the argument developed in this book and points to the importance of opportunism in giving rise to a structurally binding security arrangement.

Clearly, the news of Napoleon's escape from Elba was the deciding factor in overcoming the stalemate that had been reached on the German question. Having received word of Napoleon's return to France (on March 1, 1815), the Great Powers and the German states again saw peace in Europe significantly threatened[38] and decided to act immediately to find a solution to the German problem that would increase everyone's security.

Driven by a new urgency to reach a compromise, the great European powers quickly came up with a list of reasons why they favored a centralized and cohesive German political structure. First, such a structure might keep France in line and, should renewed French aggressions occur, provide an adequate defense.[39] Second, a binding arrangement between the numerous German states would create a neutral mass in Central Europe, and thus reduce the risk of war among the Great Powers.[40] Third, a centralized German political body would be best equipped to control the rivalry between the two big German states—Austria and Prussia.[41]

Yet, at this time, the Great Powers did not think it wise to prolong finding a compromise by attempting to dictate to the Germans what their security system should look like. Any structure the German states were willing to bring about was seen as a major improvement of the disorganized state of affairs, and therefore believed to strengthen the security of all of Europe.

In short, after Napoleon's return to the continent the Great Powers indicated what type of German arrangement they would prefer, but, as realists would predict, decided not to intrude in the domestic affairs of the German states and allow them to draft their own constitution.[42]

Signaling their acquiescence for the Germans to find their own solution without outside interference, the Great Powers facilitated negotiations tremendously. In May 1815 the German committee continued its work and particularly striking was the greater willingness to make concessions. In fact, the May negotiations make clear how an increase in threat had a unifying effect and caused the Germans to exercise greater flexibility to reach a compromise. On May 23, 1815, Austria and Prussia, for example, announced that they would no longer insist on their institutionalized hegemony within a newly created German executive.[43] This decision, of course, was greatly welcomed by the medium-sized states that had fought for equality all along. Further concessions were made to the small German states by allowing them to participate in the negotiations. Thus, in June of the same year the committee finally decided to curtail the autonomy of the individual German states in exchange for greater security, that is, it voted in favor of a confederation.

To recapitulate, realists can explain the need for and timing of a binding security arrangement as well as the choice of alliance partners. An additional study of transaction costs yields that, in the German case, these costs differed markedly in degree from those found in the security arrangements examined previously. Given much greater uncertainty and substantial transactional risks the Germans had no choice but to make firm structural commitments to enhance their security.

Convinced that they would have to do substantially more to assure their survival than to pledge troops in the event of an attack by France (or Russia), the Germans decided to create a sophisticated structural apparatus that would be able to address their problems. On June 8, 1815, the German states signed the Federal Act that specified common external defense and internal arbitration as the basic goals of the newly founded confederation.[44] As article 11 explains:

> The States of the Confederation engage to defend not only the whole of Germany, but each individual state of the Union, in case it should be attacked, and they mutually guarantee to each other such of their possessions as are comprised within this union. . . . The Confederated States engage, in the same manner, not to make war against each other, on any pretext, nor to pursue their differences by force of arms, but to submit them to the Diet, which will attempt a mediation by means of a Commission.[45]

A study of the individual members' rights yields that, although each state was allowed to enter into alliances,[46] it had to delegate a significant amount of its authority to the "confederal" body (Bund), and thus curtail its freedom of action. Several articles of the Final Act of Vienna (Wiener Schlußakte) deal expressly with the powers of the Bund. Article 35, for instance, assigns the Bund the right to decide upon war, peace, and treaties. Article 40 provides for a two-thirds majority in the plenary assembly to declare war. Article 50 grants the Bund the right to send and receive ambassadors.[47] To name but one further power of the Bund regarding external relations, article 51 gives the Diet the right to create the necessary military institutions.

Although negotiations to develop a military constitution took place in 1817 and 1818, it could not be ratified until 1821/22, since the German states disagreed on the composition of the federal army corps.[48] The compromise that was eventually reached called for an army that was to consist of one percent of each member's population. This amounted to 300,943 men who were to be divided into ten army corps and financed by a quota system.[49] More specifically, "Austria and Prussia each [were to provide] three corps, Bavaria one, and the remaining three corps were [to be] mixed units made up of troops from the remaining states."[50] The constitution did not name a permanent supreme commander, but specified that the Inner Council of the Diet would select one, should the need to mobilize the troops arise.[51]

The powers of the German Confederation regarding internal relations were also impressive. As already mentioned, article 11 instructed the individual states not to resort to self-help in settling their disagreements, but to refer disputes to the Bund, which then would appoint a commission to arbitrate.[52] Moreover, the Bund engaged in legislation. That is, it could make up rules that did not have to be ratified by the individual states but merely had to be made public to become immediately binding.[53] This type of legislation therefore not only speeded up the process of making rules, but also eliminated the costs normally associated with lengthy ratification processes.

A few words remain to be said about the special relationship between the two big German states (Prussia and Austria) and the Bund. For instance, only those Prussian and Austrian territories that formerly were part of the German Empire joined the German Bund.[54] When it came to their other territories, Prussia and Austria pursued their own policies. The two big German states thus were European powers as well as members of the Bund.[55] If Austria or Prussia were to fight a war in their capacity as European powers, the German Bund would not automatically be pulled into this war, but would only find itself at war if hostilities were to be "dragged" into its territory.[56] Finally, the fact that

Prussia and Austria were members of the Bund gives important structural information about a confederation, namely that it is not a security arrangement solely for small states.

To summarize, given that the German states following Napoleon's overthrow still felt threatened (both by France and Russia) and that with his escape from Elba this threat increased even further, the Germans sought to combine their efforts to enhance their security. In need of a binding commitment, the German states—once they had received the acquiescence of the European powers to create their own security arrangement—essentially had a choice between an alliance and a very binding security structure like a confederation. Since they sought to cooperate in an environment characterized by great uncertainty and high transactional risks, they opted for a confederation to reduce these risks and to make their transaction costs more manageable. That is, they chose voluntarily to cede some aspects of their sovereignty and to delegate a part of their authority to a centralized political structure in exchange for greater security and lower transaction costs. A confederate army and arbitration mechanisms were counted on to diminish uncertainty. And allies that could not be trusted were to be imbedded in a political structure that would raise the costs of opportunism noticeably (a defection from a confederation presumably would lead to security costs in addition to reputation costs, and thus render the costs of such behavior prohibitively high).

In a final analysis, substantial transactional risks (further exacerbated by the large number of allies) set the German case apart from the previously discussed alliances and tipped the scale toward a confederation.

THE SWISS CONFEDERATION

Particularly striking are the many similarities between the German and the Swiss case. After Napoleon's defeat the Swiss, much like the Germans, continued to feel threatened by France. Since Napoleon also had imposed a political system on the Swiss, once freed of French control, the cantons had to restore an independent political structure that would protect their sovereignty. Here too, only the news of Napoleon's escape from Elba could convince the deeply divided cantons to reach a compromise on the specifics of such a structure. Thus, as in the previous case, high threat had a unifying effect and called for a substantial commitment.

As one would expect, realists once more do a good job explaining the need for a binding security arrangement, its timing and membership. Yet, as in the cases discussed above, realism by itself cannot account for

the specific structural outcome chosen by the cantons and again a transaction costs analysis is needed to shed light on the degree of institutionalization elected. High uncertainty, severe cultural cleavages, and the
presence of site specificity, as will be seen, played a crucial role in Swiss
calculations.

To make sense of the security debates following Napoleon's defeat
some knowledge of past Swiss struggles is essential. For at least five centuries prior to the occupation of their country by French troops, Swiss
people repeatedly had to defend their independence against foreign foes.
In 1291 the three forest communities of Uri, Schwyz, and Unterwalden
swore to assist each other to prevent being dominated by the Habsburgs.
Throughout the fourteenth century neighboring communities joined the
original three to build a common defense and what started out as a mere
alliance, by the end of the fourteenth century, had been transformed into
a confederation.[57] In the sixteenth century the Swiss fought in northern
Italy, sometimes with the French and sometimes against them.

The outbreak of the Reformation weakened the Swiss Confederation considerably. To already existing internal difficulties—stemming
from the division between town and country[58] and the division between
cantons in the west and east[59]—a new factor was added, namely the division between Catholics and Protestants. As a result, the confederation
sought to pursue a policy of international neutrality to free up time to
tend to its internal problems. And even though the Swiss designed various peace settlements to restore internal order, the French Revolution of
1789 caused further political unrest that once more spread throughout
the cantons.[60]

The French, interested in Switzerland for strategic military purposes, decided to exploit this vulnerability. Rather than to attack outright, they chose to distribute revolutionary materials throughout the
region to create further unrest.[61] When internal disorder had reached crisis proportions in April of 1798, and the Swiss were no longer able to
assure their external or internal security, Napoleon occupied Swiss territory and replaced the confederation with the Helvetic Republic—a
unitary state.[62]

A closer look at cantonal developments in the years immediately following the French Revolution yields interesting parallels to the German
case. First, the Helvetic Republic was imposed on the Swiss just as the
Rheinbund was imposed on the Germans. Second, the political structure
of the Helvetic Republic, similar to that of the Rheinbund, was specifically created to lessen the fragmentation of power, and thus allow the
French to exercise greater control. Yet, whereas in the German case
Napoleon settled for a reduction in the number of German states
(through mediatization and secularization), in the Swiss case, he forced

the cantons—despite their significant differences—to unite in a single, centralized state.[63]

The Helvetic Republic, however, did not last long. Napoleon soon came to conclude that the unitary structure he imposed on the Swiss, in the long run, might do more harm than good, and hence replaced it with a Mediation Constitution. Or, fearing that it would not be in France's interest to allow a strong, central power to consolidate itself on Swiss territory (such a power might later strive for independence), Napoleon in 1803 reverted the Republic to a union of states.[64]

The second imposed political system—the Mediation Constitution—was in place from 1803 until 1813. During this ten year time-span nineteen Swiss cantons coexisted in a "loose" association of states that lacked a strong central government (the diet was dependent on instructions from the various cantons)[65] and central arbitration mechanisms. Napoleon himself assumed the role of the mediator,[66] and made clear that the Swiss, like the Germans, had to fight on the side of France.[67]

When Napoleon was defeated the Swiss were finally freed of French rule and had to reconstruct a political body that would assure their sovereignty. This, however, proved to be a difficult undertaking. Since the divisions that existed prior to French interference in Swiss politics had never been overcome (Napoleon more or less had forced the cantons to cooperate),[68] these divisions came to the forefront again and had to be dealt with. To discuss their internal differences and to write a new constitution, in April 1814, the nineteen cantons agreed to open a Tagsatzung (diet).

Yet, although the representatives of the various cantons, in what became known as the "Lange Tagsatzung" (a Diet that was in session from April 1814 to August 1815),[69] undertook substantial efforts to iron out their problems, these men failed to reach agreement. In fact, by spring 1815 the degree of internal disorder had reached crisis proportions. The canton Schwyz threatened to resort to war, should the territory of Uznach not be returned to it.[70] Berne, Waadt, Aargau, Fribourg, and Soleure argued over both territorial and religious matters and were making preparations to fight each other. At the same time, Uri, Schwyz, and Nidwalden debated whether they should resign their membership in the Tagsatzung and create a union of their own.[71]

Had it not been for an external danger, namely Napoleon's escape from Elba, the Swiss in spring 1815 most likely would have gone to war with each other. In many ways similar to what happened in Germany, however, the news of the French general's return to the continent convinced the Swiss to unite and to rethink their security provisions. After brief deliberations the cantons concluded that it would be best not to be drawn into a renewed war with Napoleon and to strive for neutrality.

That is, if they could stay out of future wars between the Great Powers, the cantons calculated, they could strengthen their external security and thus focus on their internal problems. In order to defend their borders, and thereby give credibility to their quest for neutrality, the Swiss in an emergency meeting of the Tagsatzung, agreed to mobilize fifteen thousand men.[72]

However, when Austria, Russia, and Prussia—determined to defeat Napoleon once and for all—asked for Swiss support the cantons agreed to strike a deal with them. Convinced that Napoleon still posed a great threat to their security, the Swiss concluded that they should aid the allies in exchange for additional guarantees. In a convention, on May 20, 1815, the Swiss pledged to join the Great Powers in their fight against Napoleon in return for recognition of Swiss neutrality, which was to be spelled out in the peace settlement following the war.[73]

From June until Napoleon was defeated in August of 1815 the Swiss once more fought on the side of the allies. Although the threat the Swiss faced clearly diminished after Napoleon's overthrow in 1815, it did not disappear. On the contrary, despite a reduction in the severity of the threat, the Swiss still had plenty of reasons to be concerned about their security. First, although protected by mountains that render attacks more difficult, the Swiss continued to feel vulnerable due to their geographic proximity to the enemy (Swiss territory borders on French territory). Second, French aggressive intentions repeatedly had come to the forefront and there was no guarantee that the French would behave differently in the future. Third, since French military capabilities were much greater than Swiss, and it had to be assumed that France's potential power remained enormous, the Swiss still felt seriously threatened.

Much like in the German case, the above analysis supports realist predictions regarding states' behavior in the international system. One sees how, as a result of high threat, security concerns became of utmost importance and forced the cantons to function as one coherent unit—despite domestic differences. Moreover, balance of power considerations, as expected, made it necessary for the cantons to join the allies in their fight against French hegemony before plans of Swiss neutrality could be entertained seriously. As rational actors the Swiss understood that they needed allies to assure their survival and that it would be in their best interest to make short-term sacrifices for long-term gains.

To summarize, the Swiss cantons, like the German states, knew that they had to create a political structure that would improve their security vis-à-vis the enemy. Since the Swiss, like the Germans, felt seriously threatened, they too were in need of a binding security apparatus. To account for the structural makeup of the arrangement the Swiss ultimately settled on, however, one once again needs to examine transaction costs.

One quickly learns that similarities with the German case are not confined to threat perception, but largely persist as one compares indicators of transaction costs. What sets the Swiss apart from the Germans, for the most part, is the presence of site specificity, which, as will be seen shortly, raised transaction costs even further.

Focusing on uncertainty first, there can be no doubt that the Swiss felt deeply troubled. It never appeared to be clear whether all cantons, when called upon, would contribute their share to the common defense or whether some might attempt to free ride or defect. For instance, when at the end of the eighteenth century the French directorium ordered military preparations to attack Berne, the other Swiss communities did not come to its aid, causing Berne to be defeated.[74] Moreover, in an environment where it was difficult to ascertain who would side with whom at any given moment, bandwagoning could not be ruled out. And since Switzerland in the early nineteenth century had become a multilingual political body,[75] there was no guarantee that the newly added cantons would not return their loyalty to their former rulers. In fact, as history readily shows, for centuries the Swiss had been sending mixed signals (sometimes indicating cooperation and at other times noncompliance) to each other and not seldom had engaged in outright aggression. One only needs to recall the war between Zurich and Schwyz in the middle of the fifteenth century, or the religious war Berne and Zurich waged against five Catholic states (Uri, Schwyz, Unterwalden, Lucerne, and Zug) in 1656.[76] The Swiss, like the Germans, therefore feared the possibility of internal upheaval as much as desertion by one (or several) of their allies who might be needed to prevail against an external threat.[77]

It stands to reason that the large number of allies seeking cooperation exacerbated transaction costs further. In this case twenty-two cantons sought to coordinate their security efforts—a substantially bigger group than in the previously discussed security arrangements, except the German one. Given this large number of actors, both cooperation costs and transactional risks should have increased noticeably.

The state of technology remained unchanged—that is, particularly when compared to the post-1945 period, rather backward. And again, the fact that a sizeable number of cantons sought to cooperate under such conditions rendered transactions more costly. Moreover, as experts on Swiss history explain,

> [b]ecause of the awkward natural obstacles common in the lower reaches of Alpine valleys, circulation tended to cross from one valley to the next over some convenient pass rather than to descend towards the lowlands.[78]

This suggests that alpine passes played an important role in communications and transportation, but the mountainous terrain also assured that the transaction costs the allies encountered in passing on information, or sending troops and materiel were high.

An examination of Swiss cultural backgrounds yields that, of all the cases examined, the cantons by far score the highest when it comes to heterogeneity. First, as in the German case, there were differences of interest stemming from the numerous types of government.

> Uri, Schwyz, the two Unterwalden, Zug, Glarus, and the two Appenzells were democratic cantons governed by *Landsgemeinde* or rural communes. Grisons and Valais were rather federations of autonomous communes. Zurich, Basel, Schaffhausen, St. Gallen and, to a lesser degree, Biel, Mulhouse and Geneva were more oligarchies based on corporations. In Bern, Luzern, Fribourg, Solothurn, all aristocratic States, sovereignty was in the hands of an exclusive patriciate. And there were even monarchical forms, for instance in the Principality of Neuchatel, the Bishopric of Basel and the Abbacies of St. Gallen and Engelberg.[79]

Furthermore, "divisions between town and country" repeatedly led to struggles,[80] but, as mentioned above, religious differences were especially problematic since the outbreak of the Reformation had resulted in a clear denominational division. Whereas Uri, Schwyz, Unterwalden, Zug, Lucerne, Fribourg, and Solothurn remained Catholic, many of the densely populated cities (Zurich, Berne, Basle, Schaffhausen) were Protestant,[81] and members of the two different faiths entangled each other in fierce battles to reach an equilibrium.[82] Even when there was no open warfare, religious hatreds were so strong and there was so little trust that the potential for renewed fighting remained high.

To make matters worse, the different languages (German, French, and Italian) spoken in the Swiss cantons further raised the allies' cooperation costs that were already substantial, due to the high transactional risks described. Sometimes "representatives of the people understood one language only, so that interpreters had to be employed for voting in the chambers."[83] Moreover, it stands to reason that language problems complicated military coordination considerably and, most likely, not only increased the need for translation and language training, but—given frequent misunderstandings—also the need for costly arbitration.

Finally, although the Swiss did not have to be concerned about physical and human asset specificity (due to the underdeveloped state of military technology), the presence of site specificity was absolutely crucial and had to be dealt with to make the costs and risks of transacting more manageable. Given the centrality of geography in Swiss life and the fact that the mountain passes, and to a lesser extent the waterways, are believed to "have shaped Swiss policy,"[84] a transgression into alpine geopolitics is needed to comprehend why site specificity was of such importance to Swiss security decisions.

The construction of the St. Gotthard pass provides a good starting point for this alpine excursion. The completion of the pass in the thirteenth century unearthed the shortest route through the Alps, and, as a result of the St. Gotthard's strategic position (a passage way to Italy), the pass became extremely important to trade, communications, and military endeavors.[85] Moreover, the pass put the valley of Uri on the map, that is, it changed Uri from "a remote cul-de-sac [to an] indispensable link in an international traffic artery to Italy."[86]

Given the strategic value of the St. Gotthard, it was only a matter of time until foreign rulers would seek to gain control of the pass, and thus force the Swiss to respond. When the Habsburgs made threatening gestures, Uri and the neighboring communities of Schwyz and Unterwalden who also feared for their security decided to cooperate and in 1291 gave rise to the Swiss Confederation. But it was not long before other areas started to feel threatened and asked to join the three forest communities. As will be seen, in each case, the new ally brought territory of strategic importance to the confederation in exchange for greater security.

Lucerne, for instance, "an important strategic link both on the north-south trade routes and in the Habsburg military drive against the forest communities,"[87] approached the confederates since its economy suffered greatly from the oppressive rule of the Habsburgs and their ongoing struggle with the Swiss. More specifically, the people of Lucerne asked to join the confederation and vowed to provide the rural cantons with much needed goods. In return Lucerne hoped to secure the openness of its main trade routes as well as its allies' support in the event of an attack by Austria. The confederates, on the other hand, were interested in admitting Lucerne into their circle to increase the difficulty of a Habsburg attack from the direction of the city, that is, to close the "ring of allies around Lake Lucerne."[88]

Similarly, when Zurich and Berne were challenged by Habsburg vassals, they applied to become members of the confederation and again offered to supply the forest communities with much sought-after goods.[89] Even more important from the confederates' perspective, however, was the strategic territory they would gain (and then jointly control) as a result of this increase in membership. The admission of Zurich would bring "mutual assistance within a large area which includ[es] important passes in the Gotthard region," and the addition of Berne would provide "an important outpost in the west."[90] To give but one further example of the salience of geographic factors in security decisions one can focus on the Glarus Valley. When the people of Glarus asked for help to rid themselves of Habsburg oppression the confederates were eager to oblige because, "[s]o long as the Ha[b]sburgs ruled Glarus, Schwyz was exposed to attack from the east."[91] Hence, Glarus mainly was allowed to join the allies to remove an enemy by expanding the eastern border of the confederation.

This account of Swiss security provisions demonstrates that "the process [of admission to the confederation] was not simply fortuitous; a conscious effort of expansion was sometimes dictated by the necessities of 'pass policy'."[92] And since attacks through the mountain passes occurred frequently, in addition to possessing the pass itself it was imperative to gain control of the approaches to it, thereby necessitating further expansion.[93] As the Swiss brought more and more territory of strategic value under joint control, a tight net of alpine passes was woven[94] and the confederation grew from the original three to twenty-two members.

As rational, calculating actors the Swiss understood that their unique geographic location (surrounded by mountains and situated very close to each other) would allow them to economize on transaction costs—provided they were to cooperate. For instance, if military equipment were to be distributed throughout the cantons, troops moved to a specific site, or information passed on to several locations, coordination expenses could be kept down as long as each ally were to play its specified role in any of these transactions. Conversely, if one or more cantons were to act opportunistically, that is, free ride on an obligation or defect, this would increase the remaining allies' transaction costs and risks significantly. In fact, in the above envisioned scenario of troop movements, for example, the defection of a single ally could prove detrimental to the security of the others.

Given that, throughout history, geostrategic considerations played an important role in Swiss political developments and significantly influenced the behavior of the individual cantons, the allies should have had a strong incentive to cast their vote in favor of a binding security arrangement that, by virtue of sophisticated structural mechanisms, would minimize the risks of transacting in a site-specific environment.

To summarize, much like in the German case, close scrutiny of the Swiss situation yields that the cantons' cooperation attempts promised to be plagued by substantial transaction costs. Again, behavioral uncertainty was high, technology remained underdeveloped, and a large number of actors sought to cooperate. Making matters worse, however, were an even greater degree of cultural heterogeneity and the presence of site specificity—both factors that could be counted on to heighten transactional risks further.

The above analysis also shows that the degree of threat and transaction costs the allies experienced was symmetric—another parallel to the German situation. Subjected to French control in the past, the Swiss feared that they could face a simliar fate again, and thus elected to cooperate to enhance their chances of survival. At the same time, great uncertainty, underdeveloped technology, and a high degree of heterogeneity assured that every canton would be exposed to high transaction costs and risks, even though not all communities shared the same geostrategic importance.[95]

As expected, symmetrically high assessments of threat and transaction costs in the end convinced the Swiss to give rise to a structurally sophisticated security apparatus. On March 20, 1815, a first step toward improved relations between the various cantons was taken when territorial differences were settled at the Congress of Vienna.[96] Upon further negotiation the Swiss cantons, on August 7, 1815, signed a new federal contract and signaled their willingness to curtail their autonomy in exchange for greater security. As the first article of the Federal Pact explains

> The XXII sovereign Cantons of Switzerland, . . . unite by the present federal Pact, for their common security, for the preservation of their liberty and their independence against all attack from foreign powers, and for the maintenance of order and peace within.[97]

Once their new constitution was in place the Swiss turned to their main foreign policy goal—the solidification of their neutrality. On November 20, 1815, the Great Powers realized their earlier promise and officially recognized Swiss neutrality;[98] yet the cantons knew that to enhance their security they would have to back their neutrality with a credible military. That is, whereas prior to the Federal Pact each community provided its own military (a confederate army and confederate money for military purposes did not exist),[99] it had become clear that such a system of self-defense was no longer viable and would have to be replaced by an organized and trained military.[100] On August 20, 1817, the Tagsatzung (Diet) passed a "Militärreglement" for the Swiss Confederation that called for the creation of an agency to oversee the training of the troops.[101] A year later a central military school and several training camps were established in Thun and, in 1820, various cantons began to combine their military exercises.[102] Thus, with the piecemeal creation of a confederate army the Swiss achieved a major breakthrough in the field of defense and security.[103]

A further accomplishment regarding Switzerland's external relations entailed granting the Tagsatzung the power to declare war, to make peace, and to enter alliances with foreign countries. This was a major improvement over the pre-1798 period during which the individual cantons conducted their own foreign policy.[104] In fact, by surrendering a substantial amount of their autonomy the cantons for the first time enabled the confederation to pursue a common foreign policy.

Aside from provisions to enhance external security, the Federal Pact specified the creation of common institutions to improve internal order. For instance, an elaborate system of arbitration was worked out to settle disputes between the various cantons and reduce their costs of interacting. Yet in other areas such as the economic sphere the sovereignty of the cantons remained virtually intact.[105] This last observation is crucial in that it shows clearly that the Swiss Confederation was not rooted in economic issues.

To sum up, following Napoleon's defeat in 1815, the Swiss—like the Germans—still felt seriously threatened by France, largely because of the enormous potential power the latter continued to possess. Given that Swiss cooperation efforts also were plagued by high transaction costs, the cantons decided to seek structurally binding commitments from each other and to vote for a confederation. Whereas in the German case great uncertainty and distrust, for the most part, caused the allies to be concerned about opportunism, the Swiss confronted an additional potential liability—site specificity. Hence, exposed to even greater transactional risks, the Swiss, as predicted, also had no choice but to give rise to elaborate institutional structures that would enhance their security.

THE RENEWAL OF THE QUADRUPLE ALLIANCE

In the aftermath of the Napoleonic Wars the European powers had to reassess their security provisions. As explained above the Swiss and the Germans, who still felt highly threatened, sought to counter future French aggressions by creating confederations. The Great Powers, perceiving a lesser threat, saw no need to surrender a substantial amount of their autonomy and, as realists would predict, settled for an informal alliance. But would the outcome have been different had Austria, Russia, Prussia, and Britain not been convinced of a reduction in threat? Transaction costs, as will be seen shortly, were moderate and did not call for a very binding security structure, but neither, in this case, would have the combination of high threat and high transaction costs.

Having been subjected to protracted warfare, the European powers took several precautionary measures to enhance their security. In the Final Act of Vienna, as previously mentioned, they, for instance, specified the restoration of Prussia's Great Power status and the augmentation of Austrian territory.[106] In the Second Peace of Paris the allies, moreover, agreed to build a defensive barrier along French borders to enhance the security of neighboring countries and to impose "heavy pecuniary indemnities" on the French.[107]

However, since these measures merely diminished the French threat and could not make it disappear entirely, additional safeguards had to be taken. On November 20, 1815, the allies renewed the Quadruple Alliance and vowed to prevent the return of Napoleon or any member of his family to the throne.[108] Moreover, they agreed to treat any attempt by Bonaparte once more to usurp power as an immediate renewal of French aggression that would require each of the contracting parties to furnish a specified contingent of troops.[109]

The renewed Quadruple Alliance, also the same in name, differed substantially from the original version. As a result of the downgrade from wartime to informal peacetime alliance,[110] the allies, for example, scaled back the number of troops to be provided in case of an enemy attack from the original 150,000 to 60,000 men. And, as article 6 of the treaty makes clear, the Great Powers agreed to convene conferences on a regular basis to exchange ideas.

> [I]n order to assure and facilitate the execution of the present Treaty, and to consolidate the intimate relations now uniting the Four Sovereigns for the welfare of the world, they have agreed to renew, at fixed epochs, either under the immediate auspices of the sovereigns, or through their respective ministers, meetings devoted to the grand interests they have in common and to the discussion of measures which, at these several epochs, shall be judged to be most salutary for the repose and prosperity of the nations, and for the maintenance of the Peace of Europe.[111]

Once again, the security provisions chosen thus confirm realist expectations regarding states' behavior in the anarchic international environment. As balance of power theory would predict, the allies first sought to restore the equilibrium that, as a result of the continuous warfare with France, had been upset. And when, after Napoleon's defeat and a series of negotiations (Vienna and Paris), the Great Powers perceived a reduction in threat, they no longer saw the need for a binding security arrangement and, as expected, elected to protect their freedom of action.

Yet would the allies have sought greater cooperation had they continued to feel seriously threatened? One would assume so, but, as an analysis of the magnitude of transaction costs makes clear, the Great Powers should not have created a highly institutionalized security arrangement since the cooperation costs they confronted were moderate at most.

First, the high degree of uncertainty that accompanied previous transactions diminished. The numerous treaties signed by the European statesmen put an end to territorial disputes and established a record of cooperation. The Congress of Vienna in particular helped to acquaint the allies and by addressing balance of power considerations clearly specified where state boundaries should be redrawn and who would side with whom in the event of renewed French aggression.

Although communications and transportation remained underdeveloped, and hence transaction costs stemming from this unsophisticated state of technology promised to be high, the allies, as discussed above, managed to defray these costs by periodically meeting at the same conference places. Moreover, one would expect the small number of countries seeking cooperation also to be beneficial.

The cultural background of the allies, obviously, remained the same as in the original Quadruple Alliance—it was varied. Repeated signals of benevolent intentions and frequent interaction at conferences, however, suggest that the allies might have developed some degree of trust, which in turn would have diminished their fear of opportunism.

And, once again, the absence of asset specificity had a moderating effect. Unlike the Swiss case where site specificity greatly increased the allies' transactional risks, the Great Powers merely pledged to supply each other with generic assets (troops) in the event of an attack, and therefore were less vulnerable to opportunistic behavior.

In sum, the above analysis demonstrates that in 1815 the great European states faced no more than moderate transaction costs. This can largely be attributed to relatively low uncertainty and the absence of specific assets. The small number of countries seeking cooperation and frequent conference meetings also worked in the allies' favor.

This then leaves one to speculate whether the Great Powers would have sought a structurally sophisticated security arrangement had they experienced both high threat and high transaction costs. One would think not since it has to be assumed that asymmetric threat assessments would have stood in the way of such binding commitments. More specifically, much like in the original Quadruple Alliance so too in the renewed version the allies faced differing degrees of threat due to their geographic locations. Britain as an insular country, for instance, never experienced the same degree of threat as any of the continental powers.[112] Similarly, Russia, once the fighting had ceased, felt less endangered than Prussia or Austria, whose geographic proximity to the enemy made them more vulnerable. This explains why Britain was able to maintain much greater freedom of action than any of the other European powers and why she could afford to return to an insular policy in the 1820s.[113] (See Table 4.1.)

TABLE 4.1
Summary of Security Choices in the Napoleonic Period

		Level of Threat		
		Low	*High*	*Extreme*
Transaction Costs	*Low*	Renewed Quadruple Alliance		Wartime Alliance R & P R, P, & AU Quadruple Alliance
	High		German & Swiss Confederations	

Abbreviations: R = Russia; P = Prussia; AU = Austria

In a final analysis, given a significant reduction in threat and transaction costs, the great European powers saw no reason to curtail their autonomy seriously and opted for an informal alliance. But, even if both threat and transaction costs had been higher, it seems unlikely that the allies would have given rise to a very binding security apparatus since their assessment of threat was asymmetric.

CONCLUSION

The late Napoleonic period and its aftermath (1812–15) show that the security arrangements chosen reflect the specific needs of the individual European countries. That is, those states that felt seriously threatened and experienced high transaction costs confederated. Those countries that felt less threatened sought to maintain greater maneuverability by avoiding binding commitments. Put differently, the above analysis confirms that states value their freedom of action. Only in situations where symmetric assessments of high threat and high transaction costs made allies equally vulnerable were they willing to surrender a substantial amount of their sovereignty to obtain additional assurances.

The Napoleonic cases also allow one to speculate about the relative causal weight of the individual indicators of transaction costs. Aside from threat, most important in determining the degree of institutional-ization appears to be the risk of opportunism states confront. As the above security debates have shown, high uncertainty and the presence of specific assets (in the Swiss case site specificity) seem to increase the risk of opportunistic behavior the most. Cultural cleavages, if they manifest themselves in deep-seated feelings of distrust, also raise the allies' trans-actional risks, whereas different language backgrounds, for the most part, exacerbate cooperation costs by requiring translation. Similarly, a backward state of technology can lead to opportunistic behavior (recall Metternich's doublecross), but, most of the time, merely appears to raise transportation and communications costs.

Thus, if in fact it is possible to rank the various measures of trans-action costs in terms of their causal importance, then, assuming high threat and symmetry, structurally binding security arrangements should be most likely in uncertain environments where countries distrustful of each other see the need to engage in transactions entailing specific assets—a proposition to be tested next in the post-1945 period.

CHAPTER 5

In Search of Security via NATO

The defeat of Germany and Japan at the end of World War II left a tremendous vacuum to the west and east of the Soviet Union[1] and the United Kingdom, France, and the United States were not at all sure how the USSR would react to this change. That is, would the Soviet Union cooperate with the United States, as indicated at Yalta where the Soviets promised free elections in Poland and the rest of Eastern Europe, or would it pursue an expansionist policy and thereby pose a threat to the security of independent countries?

Three developments almost immediately convinced the Western powers to rethink their security provisions and, over the course of the next few years, made them realize that they would have to cooperate to prevail against the Soviets. First, at the United Nations Conference in San Francisco on April 25, 1945, serious disagreements emerged between the United States and the USSR over the imposition of Soviet puppet governments in some of the East European countries.[2] Churchill as well as several U.S. advisers claimed that the Soviet government was pursuing an "obstructive and unfriendly course"[3] that required a response. If the United States were to allow a limited Soviet sphere of influence, there would be no guarantee that the Soviets might not try to extend their influence later.[4]

Second, there was the need to deal with the immense military imbalance between the Soviet Union and the Western world.

> On the day that Germany surrendered, the American armed strength in Europe amounted to 3,100,000 men: within a year it had melted to 391,000. On VE Day the British armed strength in Europe was 1,321,000: one year later there were only 488,000 left. . . . Meanwhile, the Soviet Union continued to maintain their forces on a war footing, and to keep their armament production going at full blast.[5]

Thus, after the war about "a dozen scattered, under-strength Western divisions" in Europe faced twenty-five fully armed Russian divisions in Central Europe, in addition to at least 140 Russian divisions at battle strength.[6]

Despite this enormous discrepancy in military capabilities and Stalin's increasing expansionism (he annexed sections of Finland, Estonia, Latvia, Lithuania, a part of East Prussia, and one-third of Polish territory),[7] however, the Soviet Union was not yet viewed as a serious military threat. To the extent that a Soviet problem existed at the end of 1945, it was political, not military.[8]

Third, in the immediate postwar period advances in military technology—particularly in the field of aircrafts, rockets, and nuclear weapons—called for collective defense. With increases in speed and range, for instance, the geographic space of countries had shrunk, thereby rendering an effective defense on a national basis impossible.[9] Moreover, due to the higher sophistication of weapons, individual states—except for the United States and the USSR—could no longer afford them,[10] and thus were in need of allies.

As the following dicussion will show, by 1946 the West Europeans already felt threatened by the Soviet Union and some (foremost among them France) additionally feared a resurgent Germany. To enhance their security, much like realism predicts, these countries solicited United States support. Drawn-out security debates ensued, yet it was not until the United States became convinced of a significant Soviet *military* threat in 1948 that progress toward the creation of a common security arrangement could be made. Since the Western powers merely agreed on the existence of a threat, and not its magnitude (the United States and the United Kingdom perceived a lesser threat than France, the Benelux countries, and Germany), they settled for a security apparatus that, at its outset, resembled a traditional guarantee pact.[11]

Realism, as in the previous cases, can explain the need for cooperation. Knowledge of asymmetric threat assessments, moreover, allows one to narrow the range of structural outcomes. One can, for instance, hypothesize that those parties feeling less threatened should be protective of their freedom of action and stand in the way of a highly binding security apparatus. Conversely, those feeling more threatened should seek strong commitments.

A sole focus on the allies' threat perceptions, however, once again does not suffice to shed light on the degree of commitment ultimately elected. Rather, threat assessments need to be exceeded by an examination of the allies' exposure to transaction costs. As with threat, scrutiny of the various indicators of transaction costs yields pronounced asymmetry—the United States (and to a lesser degree the British) experienced lower transaction costs than the French, Benelux, and Germans—and thus makes clear why the allies could not reach agreement on a structurally more sophisticated security arrangement.

SECURITY DEBATES LEADING TO THE DUNKIRK TREATY

Already in the spring of 1946 several events convinced the Western powers to adopt a tougher policy toward the Soviet Union. In a speech on February 9, for instance, Stalin stressed the incompatibility of communism and capitalism and hinted toward potential conflict between the Eastern and the Western world. On February 16, the world was stunned by the news of a Canadian spy case—apparently an attempt by the USSR to steal information concerning the atomic bomb.[12] And, although the Great Powers had pledged to withdraw their troops from Iran by March 2, 1946, the Soviets began to annex the Iranian province of Azerbaijan.[13] Moreover, Stalin sought to gain control of Bulgaria, Romania, Poland, and East Germany by imposing Moscow-oriented governments on them,[14] and he began to exert pressure on Turkey.[15]

The West's response to Stalin's behavior was not only immediate, but differed from country to country. Churchill, for example, in his famous "iron curtain" speech at Fulton, Missouri, on March 5, 1946, described how the Soviet Union was gradually bringing Central and Eastern Europe under its influence, and thus called for the revival of an Anglo-American alliance to enhance Western security.[16] Truman, unwilling to accept that Soviet influence necessarily would have to spread, ordered the Joint Chiefs of Staff (JCS) to undertake a detailed study of U.S./Soviet relations. It here suffices to report that by the middle of 1946 the West Europeans as well as numerous U.S. officials started to perceive the USSR as a threat to the European balance of power. Yet, whereas the French, Benelux, Germans, and, to a lesser extent, the British—due to their geographic closeness and military inferiority to the Soviet Union—felt seriously threatened, the United States believed the Soviet threat to be political and economic in nature, *not* military.[17]

If one compares Soviet and Western military capabilities one initially questions why the United States did not perceive the USSR as a *military* threat. After all, in 1946 the Soviet Union had an armed strength of 6 million men, compared to only 391,000 U.S. and 488,000 British men.[18] But at that time the United States possessed nuclear capabilities that the USSR lacked. As Special Counsel Clark Clifford pointed out to President Truman on September 24, 1946:

> The Soviet Union's vulnerability is limited due to the vast area over which its key industries and natural resources are widely dispersed, but it is vulnerable to atomic weapons, biological warfare, and long-range air power.[19]

To summarize, in 1946 the United States was aware of a political and economic threat emanating from the USSR, and thus talked about pursuing a tougher policy to contain Soviet influence. Although the West European countries, feeling less secure than the United States, would have liked a cooperative security arrangement, such an arrangement did not come about since the United States, merely perceiving the USSR as a *potential* enemy,[20] sought to maintain its freedom of action.

A careful analysis of the year 1947 similarly reveals that the Western powers' security demands varied according to their threat perceptions. Consistent with realist expectations those countries that felt more threatened sought greater commitments than countries that perceived a lesser threat.

A good place to begin is the Foreign Ministers Conference of March 1947 in Moscow. It signals a major turning point in postwar Soviet/U.S. relations since the failure to reach agreement on the German question led to a substantially changed international environment.[21] Not only did the United States have to become involved in European affairs to defend the balance of power, but it also had to give assurances to France, the Benelux countries, and, to a lesser degree, the British, who feared a resurgent Germany.[22] Put differently, since there was no European country capable of maintaining an equilibrium, or willing to integrate West Germany into the Western state system without prior U.S. guarantees,[23] the United States had to aid the West Europeans.

It is important to stress that, whereas the United States largely saw the Soviets posing a political threat to international peace, the West Europeans (although to varying degrees) focused on two sources of threat—a rearmed Germany and an expansionist USSR. This explains why the West Europeans had different security needs than the United States, and why the former acted first to improve their security.

British foreign minister Ernest Bevin, a shrewd diplomat, understood that the West Europeans would have to demonstrate their willingness to help themselves, before they could expect U.S. assistance.[24] Hence, in early 1947 he took the first step to coordinate a West European defense system by offering a treaty to France. In his mind such a treaty should accomplish two objectives. First, since he was convinced that better relations with France would be essential for further cooperation,[25] Bevin hoped to win French support by promising British assistance in the event of renewed German aggression. Second, he sought to reduce the influence of the French Communist Party and to put a "check to undesirable Soviet weight" in France.[26] This twofold objective required that the text of an Anglo-French alliance would be worded carefully so as not to antagonize the USSR any further or seriously offend Germany. That is, the language of the treaty should not give the Soviets the impression that it could be directed against them, nor should it alienate the Germans, since the latter eventually might have to be included in a Western security system.[27] Thus, the United Kingdom and France could only settle on an acceptable treaty text after long deliberations.

A Treaty of Alliance and Mutual Assistance was finally signed on March 4, 1947, at Dunkirk—in the form of an old-fashioned military alliance. With it the United Kingdom and France promised each other immediate assistance in the event of an attack upon either[28] and provided a starting point for later Western defense systems.[29] Although the United States in the spring of 1947 was aware that no single power existed in Europe capable of balancing the USSR, at that time the United States was not willing to play a more active role in Western Europe's defense.[30]

FROM DUNKIRK TO BRUSSELS

Only days after Dunkirk, the American position began to change. U.S. decision-makers started to attribute recent unrest in Greece and Turkey to Soviet infiltration attempts and therefore persuaded President Truman to take action to stop Soviet influence from spreading. On March 12, 1947, the American president (in what became known as the Truman Doctrine) asked Congress for the appropriation of direct financial aid "to support free peoples who are resisting attempted subjugation by armed minorities or by outside pressure."[31] And, as an additional safeguard against Soviet infiltration, U.S. Secretary of State George Marshall, on June 5, 1947, introduced a plan to aid European economic recovery.

This clearly shows how threat perception drove American behavior. As long as the United States felt no significant Soviet threat it saw no need for action. But when the United States became aware that Soviet interference in West European affairs could destabilize the international system, the United States chose to free up financial resources to avoid the further spread of Soviet influence.

Judging by the type of action taken (the appropriation of money) the United States still viewed the Soviet threat as political in nature[32] and felt it could afford to gamble by not making military commitments. In fact, on December 8, 1947, Secretary of Defense Forrestal explained

> As long as we [the U.S.] can outproduce the world, can control the sea and strike inland with the atomic bomb, we can assume certain risks otherwise unacceptable in an effort to restore world trade, to restore the balance of power—military power—and to eliminate some of the conditions which breed war.[33]

How firmly the United States wished to maintain its freedom of action became obvious when the United Kingdom asked for additional help. Following the Council of Foreign Ministers meeting in London (December 1947), which had shown that Germany's Four Power supervision (as specified in the Potsdam Agreement) would be impossible,[34] Bevin immediately proposed the formation of some form of union that should be backed by the United States and the Dominions. The United States, on the other hand, lost no time arguing that a military alliance was premature.[35] It feared that an Atlantic security arrangement might unduly provoke the Soviets,[36] and it was determined to "beware of entangling alliances."[37] The United States thus asked the West Europeans to demonstrate their willingness to engage in self-help before any further U.S. commitment would be discussed.[38]

Unwilling to watch Western Europe succumb to Soviet pressure, Bevin once more took the lead and, on January 22, 1948, officially called for the creation of a Western union in the House of Commons.[39] Next he sought to win French foreign minister Bidault as an ally, while continuing his attempts to bring the United States on his side. By the end of 1947, however, Bevin could get no greater commitment from the Americans than financial aid for Western European economic recovery.

In 1948 a series of hostile Soviet incidents forced the Western powers to reevaluate their security provisions. Again, in line with realist arguments, those countries that felt most threatened acted first and sought greater assurances. Conversely, those countries that perceived a lesser threat continued to defend their freedom of action.

Since the events of the year 1948 are well documented and most readers are familiar with them, I merely enumerate the main developments. First, on February 22, the Communist Party of Czechoslovakia seized control of the government in Prague.[40] Then, on March 5, General Clay sent a telegram from Berlin warning the United States that war "could come with dramatic suddenness."[41] Also in March there were rumors about a Soviet-Norwegian nonaggression pact,[42] as well as talk that Denmark feared an armed invasion by the USSR.[43] And, with elections impending in Italy, there was the danger of a Communist victory.[44]

Needless to say these developments were viewed with alarm and confirmed the Western powers' belief that Soviet political infiltration had to be stopped. France, convinced that Western Europe could not defend itself since it still had most of its financial resources tied up in aiding economic recovery, reacted first and asked the United States for help.[45] This request for immediate U.S. military assistance is not surprising given that the French government perceived a dual threat: a short-term threat stemming from the USSR, and a long-term threat emanating from Germany.[46]

Yet the United States remained unwilling to curtail its freedom of action[47] and reiterated that the West European powers should demonstrate their willingness to help themselves. Again, the United Kingdom assumed leadership and more firmly pursued its previous call for a Western union. Bevin, at once, suggested using the Dunkirk model for further treaties with the Benelux countries, but encountered strong opposition. For several days various versions of a treaty text were debated. The Benelux countries increasingly supported a text that would allow for a regenerated Germany to join the union; the French very much opposed any reference to a possible future collaboration with Germany; and the United Kingdom played the role of a mediator between the two camps.[48] Finally, on March 17, 1948, Belgium, France, Luxembourg, the Netherlands, and the United Kingdom signed a Treaty of Mutual Assistance and vowed to build a common defense system and to strengthen economic and cultural ties.[49] In its final version this treaty, also known as the Brussels Treaty, largely resembled the text of the Inter-American Treaty of Reciprocal Assistance, that is, the Rio Treaty.[50]

PREPARATIONS FOR A
NORTH ATLANTIC TREATY (NAT)

Since with the signing of the Brussels Treaty the West Europeans demonstrated that they were doing everything in their power to improve their security, the United States had to reevaluate what type of aid it should give. A review of military capabilities in 1948 revealed that Soviet troops still vastly outnumbered U.S. troops.[51] And yet the Americans continued to view war with the Soviets as unlikely in the near future.[52] In fact, the USSR had to be cautious, due to its continuing strategic weakness—its lack of nuclear weapons.[53]

Even though war with the Soviet Union was not imminent, the Czechoslovakian coup, the March crises, the Europeans' repeated pleas for help, and the fulfillment of their end of the bargain (self-help via the Brussels Treaty) convinced the United States in the spring of 1948 to take action. After drawn-out debates considering various U.S. moves,[54] President Truman, on March 22, gave permission to begin secret North Atlantic Treaty (NAT) talks with the United Kingdom and Canada.[55]

The most important topic of discussion was the form a North Atlantic defense system should take. Initially, several possibilities were scrutinized. One plausible solution was simply to extend the Brussels Treaty and to include the United States and Canada. Yet, although this might have been acceptable to the United Kingdom and Canada, the United States voiced strong objections. Since the obligations under the Brussels Pact are "automatic"—if one member is attacked the others are obliged to act immediately—the United States opposed a formal adherence to the Brussels Treaty to safeguard as much maneuverability as possible.[56]

Instead of a multilateral security system, the United States proposed a unilateral presidential guarantee. With it the United States would oblige itself to "regard any threat to the free countries of Europe as a threat to its own national security, . . . and it would act accordingly."[57] The other NAT talk participants, however, deemed this solution unacceptable. Most importantly, it lacked the guarantee that a future U.S. president would uphold his predecessor's commitment.[58] And the United Kingdom was convinced that the United States would have to be truly committed in Europe.[59]

A third possibility was the creation of a North Atlantic alliance. The United States envisioned a "two-pillar" concept—one pillar consisting of the United States and Canada, the other of the European countries. Canada, however, fearing that its influence would be dwarfed by the United States, voiced immediate opposition.[60] The "two-pillar" concept thus was discarded and replaced by the more general idea of a multilateral security arrangement based on mutual assistance.

Convinced that the combined power of several countries would provide both a more effective deterrence and defense,[61] the NAT talk participants did manage to settle on a multilateral (rather than bilateral) arrangement within a few weeks. Yet by far the greatest obstacle to a NAT—disagreement regarding the nature of the allies' pledge—remained. As will be seen shortly, the negotiating parties discussed several versions of a pledge with varying degrees of commitment, which indicates that they had a choice between different types of security arrangements.

FROM THE BERLIN BLOCKADE
TO THE SIGNING OF THE NAT

Meanwhile, since the failure of the Council of Foreign Ministers meeting had made clear that Soviet cooperation on the German question could not be obtained, the United States, the United Kingdom, and France engaged in trilateral discussions to normalize living conditions in the western zones. The Soviet Union viewed such western cooperation as a provocation and, on April 1, responded with a partial blockade of Berlin. Debates ensued how best to respond to the USSR. Churchill, outraged by Soviet behavior, suggested to threaten the USSR with nuclear war, unless it were to withdraw from Berlin and East Germany: "we cannot appease, conciliate or provoke the Soviets; . . . the only vocabulary they understand is force."[62] However, neither the British nor the U.S. government supported such a position and argued that a diplomatic solution should be tried first.

On June 24, hostilities escalated even further when the Soviets replaced their partial blockade with a full blockade. Due to American hesitancy,[63] the United Kingdom had to carry the lion's share of managing the Berlin crisis. When it had become clear that diplomatic attempts were deadlocked (the USSR was unwilling to end the blockade unless the entire German question was reopened, and the Western powers would not agree to Four Power talks until the blockade was lifted),[64] the United Kingdom initiated an airlift and thereby demonstrated its determination not to yield to Soviet pressure. The United States only joined in the airlift and sent B-29s (atomic bombers) to bases in Britain *after* the British had taken the initiative to stand up against the USSR.[65]

Despite this delayed U.S. response the West Europeans, however, were not the only ones who perceived a steady increase in Soviet threat. President Truman, the director of the Office of European Affairs, Hickerson, and his subordinate Achilles had supported a North Atlantic alliance for some time, and by now the chairman of the Senate Foreign Relations Committee, Vandenberg, and some of his colleagues were convinced that greater commitments would be necessary to enhance Western security.[66] Consequently on July 6, 1948, President Truman gave the official go-ahead for NAT talks between the United States, the United Kingdom, Canada, France, Belgium, and the Netherlands. Moreover, on September 27, the defense ministers of the Brussels Treaty powers decided to create a Western Union Defense Organization as a first step to a larger association that the United States should join.[67]

By winter, U.S. policymakers had reached consensus on the presence of a Soviet threat as well as its nature. Many experts who had studied Soviet military capabilities and political moves for some time finally concluded that the Soviet Union was *militarily* strong, increasingly hostile, potentially "war inducing," and hence a threat that needed to be balanced.[68] As a result the NAT talks progressed rapidly. On December 10, 1948, a third stage of intergovernmental meetings began (with Luxembourg added as discussant), and only fourteen days later a first draft of a NAT was written. A fourth and final stage of negotiations (January 10 to March 28, 1949) followed these meetings and culminated in an agreement by the Brussels Treaty countries, the United States, Canada, and (as of March) Norway on a final treaty text.[69] On March 15, the negotiating countries asked Denmark, Iceland, Italy, and Portugal to join the North Atlantic Treaty.

To recapitulate, already in 1946 the West Europeans, devastated by World War II, concerned about the possibility of German rearmament (an eventual threat), and frightened by recent Soviet expansionist moves (an actual threat), sought U.S. support. Given that it took the Americans until the winter of 1948 to view the Soviet Union as sufficiently belligerent to pose a military threat, the former, throughout the early post-1945 period, remained reluctant to curtail their autonomy. Or, exposed to a dual threat, the West Europeans—consistent with realist predictions—asked for U.S. assistance to balance against this threat and to restore a power equilibrium in the international system. Initially unconvinced of the seriousness of the Soviet threat, the United States, as expected, sought to protect its freedom of action and instructed the West Europeans to rely on self-help.

Although realist theory, by focusing on the centrality of threat, provides a strong case for why the Western powers had to cooperate, it cannot explain why they chose the security arrangement they did. Absent symmetrically high assessments of threat, realists can tell us, those countries preceiving a lesser threat should stay aloof of highly binding commitments, whereas those countries experiencing a high threat should seek great assurances. Hence, in the case of divergent threat perceptions realists, at best, can narrow the range of possible outcomes, that is, explain why structurally sophisticated security arrangements like confederations should be out of the question. If one wants to obtain a better understanding of the actual compromise agreed upon one once more needs to scrutinize the allies' transaction costs in addition to threat.

TRANSACTION COSTS AND THE WESTERN POWERS' COMPROMISE

To restate the hypothesis, threatened countries confronting high transaction costs should seek significant structural commitments. Conversely, countries experiencing lower transaction costs, ceteris paribus, should be protective of their freedom of action. As will be seen, the United States not only perceived a lesser threat than the West Europeans but also encountered substantially lower transaction costs, which explains why it sought to defend its autonomy.

First, as expected, one can see the lower degree of uncertainty in the post-1945 international arena associated with a bipolar world in the behavior of the Western countries. Given that there were only two Great Powers in 1945, the United States and the Soviet Union, there were few alliance options. A country that had chosen to ally with the United States was unlikely to defect from its security arrangement since there were no other partners available that could make more attractive offers—with the possible exception of the USSR.

Since a rift between the two Great Powers was forming already toward the end of 1945, a decision as to who would side with whom had to be made early on. The United Kingdom, squarely in the western camp, concluded that it should collaborate closely with France to ensure that France—seeking security against a resurgent Germany—would not ask the Soviet Union for help.[70] Given the uncertainty of relations with the USSR, the United Kingdom had to word its treaty with France carefully so as not to offend "Germany [which] might in the long run have to be brought into a future Western European system,"[71] or to give the USSR the impression that the treaty could be directed against it. Hence, with the Treaty of Dunkirk the British accomplished several goals. They decreased the uncertainty surrounding French behavior by pulling the French away from the USSR; they obtained an ally in the event of renewed German aggression; and they gained French support should the USSR pursue its hostile tactics.

France, in addition to being troubled by its inability to discern Soviet intentions, suffered greatly from the uncertainty surrounding German behavior.[72] Due to its geographic closeness to Germany, France was in desperate need of allies and certainly welcomed the British treaty offer. Yet France also sought U.S. assistance. Aside from requesting an immediate U.S. military guarantee, it urged the creation of some type of institutional framework that would facilitate the combined military planning of the Western powers, increase the costs of opportunism, and provide additional safeguards.[73]

The United States, far removed from Germany and militarily much stronger than any of the West European countries, had little reason to fear a resurgent Germany. In fact, the United States only experienced moderate uncertainty regarding the type of challenge posed by the Soviets. There was the possibility of miscalculation,[74] misperception, or misunderstanding, which never can be ruled out. But, by 1948, the Americans had gained greater insights concerning the intentions of the Kremlin. Moreover, given that the United States was the only country capable of defending Western Europe against Soviet belligerence, the United States did not have to worry about possible defections from the rank of its allies.

To summarize, even though bipolarity narrowed the range of alliance options, the West Europeans, plagued by a substantial degree of uncertainty regarding immediate Soviet and future German intentions, sought a binding security commitment from the United States to assure that the latter would play a continuing role in safeguarding European security. The United States, on the other hand, experiencing only moderate uncertainty with respect to Soviet behavior, initially merely provided financial aid to its allies and was not willing to curtail its autonomy any further until an upgrade from political to military threat made such action necessary. Thus, as in the Napoleonic period, exposure to transactional risks seems to be of great importance in determining institutional choice. Again, high uncertainty and great vulnerability to opportunism appear to cause a need for strong commitments.

Second, compared to the early nineteenth century, cooperation efforts benefited from a much more sophisticated state of technology. Since the days of Napoleon—when communication largely occurred via courier—miles of telephone lines had been laid; television made it possible to engage in a "direct and immediate exchange of views";[75] and, in the area of transportation, an elaborate network of railroads, roads, and airfields had been created. Even though World War II destroyed a substantial part of this improved infrastructure and the Europeans, in the short run, would face significant rebuilding costs, it was clear that, once restored, these devices could be counted on to reduce transaction costs considerably. And, by making the detection of cheating or defecting more likely, the new infrastructure could be expected to diminish the allies' vulnerability to opportunism.

The number of countries seeking cooperation, consequently, played a much smaller role. Whereas in the Napoleonic days each additional ally further exacerbated the coordination costs of the other members of the security arrangement, in the post-1945 period additional allies affected the level of transaction costs much less noticeably.

Knowing that—once brought back to its prewar level—the state of technology would be unlikely to result in high transaction costs, the Americans were mainly interested in helping Europe back on its feet. Via the Marshall Plan they therefore gave financial aid to their allies and sought to postpone more binding commitments as long as possible.

Third, focusing on heterogeneity one finds that, although there were marked cultural differences, the allies' varying backgrounds in the late 1940s seem to have had little effect on transaction costs. In the case of NATO, twelve "[n]ations, each with their traditions, customs, languages, history, misconceptions, and ways of living"[76] sought to coordinate their security provisions. But, except for occasional communication problems, the different backgrounds seem to have played a minor role in cooperation efforts. This is not to suggest that there were no feelings of distrust at the time. On the contrary, the Western powers—although to varying degrees—were suspicious of German intentions. As long as Germany were to remain subject to armament restrictions, however, its range of opportunistic behavior, and consequently transactional risks, would be limited.

As will be discussed in the next chapter, this situation began to change when an increase in threat brought about the need for German rearmament and added outright aggression to the repertoire of German behavior. Especially striking are the pronounced differences in the French and U.S. response. Whereas the French lost no opportunity to stress the Western powers' lack of cultural affinity, the United States tried to draw attention to commonalities within the North Atlantic area.

Or, while the French—fearing that Germany could become militant again and act opportunistically—insisted that the Germans could not be trusted,[77] the United States—largely unconcerned about opportunistic behavior—emphasized a shared "European cultural heritage." Hence, as will be developed in greater detail below, different exposure to transactional risks once again appears to be crucial in explaining variation in behavior. The French, most vulnerable vis-à-vis the Germans, time and again stressed the lack of a sense of trust and "we-ness," and thus the need for greater assurances. The United States, on the other hand, far removed from any real German threat, sought to downplay cultural differences and to maintain maneuverability.

A fourth factor to be looked at to ascertain the allies' transaction costs is asset specificity. One finds that the West Europeans not only sought U.S. military assistance, but, dependent on American weapons entailing both generic and highly sophisticated assets, asked for as binding a security arrangement as possible. The United States, much less concerned about opportunistic behavior on the part of its allies, sought to maintain as much sovereignty as it could without compromising its own security.

Since the end of World War II, significant advances in military technology—including jet aircraft, rockets, nuclear weapons, and other complex gadgets[78]—had been made, which had far-reaching effects. Whereas prior to the introduction of this sophisticated armament the geographic distance to one's enemy played an important role,[79] this relationship was considerably weakened by the much greater security radius of this new equipment. Smaller powers in particular became much more vulnerable since they, for the most part, could not afford this sophisticated weaponry by themselves and lacked the technical knowledge to produce it.

In fact, in the immediate post-1945 period only a few powers were capable of owning these highly complex weapons, namely the United States, the United Kingdom, and the Soviet Union. They alone possessed the special ingredients and the specialized equipment (physical assets) required to manufacture particular components. And they were the only countries with the highly trained people (human assets) necessary to develop, operate, and maintain this complex military equipment.[80]

Rendering individual defense virtually impossible,[81] these new technologies forced countries to look for allies to enhance their security. The West Europeans were in a particularly vulnerable position. Devastated by the war and threatened by the aggressive behavior of the USSR they depended on U.S. financial aid to speed up their economic recovery, direct military assistance in the form of guns, tanks, and troops, and—given the West's inferiority with respect to conventional weapons—on the U.S. nuclear umbrella.[82]

Although Churchill and Roosevelt in 1943 had discussed combining British and American efforts to produce atomic bombs and there had been exchanges of scientific ideas, "much of the industrial technology and the engineering methods" were only known to the Americans. This situation became even more pronounced with the passage of the McMahon Act in June 1946, which limited U.S. international activities severely.[83] Cooperation virtually ceased to exist and the United Kingdom slowly had to acquire the technical knowledge and physical installations necessary for the production of its own nuclear weapons.

France, "among the pioneers of atomic research before 1939,"[84] in the postwar period fell behind the United Kingdom. From 1945 until 1950 the French preoccupied themselves with the creation of an infrastructure needed for the exploitation of nuclear energy. In fact, they did not make any significant progress in the development of atomic energy for military purposes until the mid-1950s.[85]

The United States, in the immediate postwar period, therefore, clearly had the technological and military leadership.[86] It was the only Western power that possessed highly specific physical assets such as plutonium, polonium initiators, fissionable material, or modified aircrafts to carry nuclear weapons. Moreover, it had specially trained scientists, technicians, pilots, and weaponeers to produce and to handle its highly sophisticated military equipment.[87] As a result of its technological superiority, the United States could afford to take risks regarding the Soviets' superior conventional forces. Convinced that the Soviet Union would be unable to develop an atomic bomb until the mid-1950s, the United States decided to rely on strategic bombing to achieve its security objectives as cheaply as possible. As will be seen, the United States upheld this reliance on nuclear weapons until the outbreak of the Korean War forced it to rethink its war plans and to build up its conventional military capabilities.

Despite its highly specialized physical and human assets the United States, to a large extent, was spared the transactional risks normally associated with ownership of such assets. More specifically, since the production of these sophisticated weapons did not require any component the Americans did not own themselves, there was little reason to fear opportunistic behavior. A minor source of vulnerability stemmed from U.S. reliance on "certain European physical facilities."[88] That is, since even an advanced weapon like the B-29 bomber could not safely reach targets in the USSR from the United States, the Americans had to negotiate base agreements with their European allies for these long-range bombers. The United States, however, did not seem to mind giving the Europeans some leverage on its security commitments since these overseas bases would allow it to keep the enemy far removed from U.S. territory.[89]

The West Europeans, on the other hand, were much more vulnerable. Their dependence was not restricted to U.S. weapons entailing specific assets, but encompassed all types of armaments. The United Kingdom, for instance, already had to borrow U.S. equipment during World War II to make up for its own losses.[90] Other West European powers, similarly, relied on U.S. armaments for several years after the war.

> By the beginning of April, 1954, the value of military equipment shipped or planned by the United Sates for delivery to its European partners had reached about $15,000 million. The end-items supplied to NATO countries included well over a million small arms, more than twenty thousand artillery pieces and mortars, thousands of tanks and aircraft, tens of thousands of motor vehicles, to say nothing of ammunition and other equipment.[91]

Given this grave dependence on U.S. military assistance it is unlikely that the United States was very much concerned with European opportunism. On the contrary, it was understood that the West Europeans, for some time, would have to free ride on the United States until they could recover and acquire the necessary means to make a significant contribution to their own defense. In fact, the United States, at times, encouraged its allies to specialize in the production of those military goods each was most suited for[92] to achieve greater effectiveness and efficiency. That is, the United States promoted a division of labor such that it would provide nuclear weapons and strategic bombers, whereas the Europeans would be responsible for land forces and tactical air power.[93]

To summarize, particularly striking in the NATO case are the marked differences in exposure to transaction costs and risks. France, the most vulnerable of the Western powers (due to great uncertainty, a distrust of Germany, and a strong dependence on U.S. military aid), sought "ironclad assurances" from the United States to enhance French security.[94] The British, although less concerned about German opportunism, still confronted substantial uncertainty and dependence on U.S. military support, and thus also asked for great assurances. The United States, by contrast, possessing nuclear capabilities and plagued only by moderate transaction costs (due to lower uncertainty and lesser exposure to transactional risks) defended its freedom of action. Pulling together the different parts of the analysis it can thus be said that not only asymmetric threat perception led to the rejection of a more binding security arrangement, but also pronounced differences in transaction costs (see Table 5.1).

Convinced that no further time should be lost to enhance Western security, on April 4, 1949, Belgium, Canada, Denmark, France, Iceland, Italy, Luxembourg, the Netherlands, Norway, Portugal, the United

TABLE 5.1
NATO

		Level of Threat	
		Low	High
Transaction Costs	Low		U.S.
	High		U.K. Germany Benelux France

Kingdom, and the United States signed the North Atlantic Treaty consisting of a preamble and fourteen articles. Of special importance is the wording of the pledge in article 5, which reflects the negotiating parties' long struggle for a compromise.

> The Parties agree that an armed attack against one or more of them in Europe or North America shall be considered an attack against them all; and consequently they agree that, if such an armed attack occurs, each of them, in exercise of the right of individual or collective self-defence recognized by Article 51 of the Charter of the United Nations, will assist the Party or Parties so attacked by taking forthwith, individually and in concert with the other Parties, such action as it deems necessary, including the use of armed force, to restore and maintain the security of the North Atlantic area.[95]

The European powers, favoring a binding commitment all along, managed to obtain a pledge stronger than that of the Rio Treaty in that it explicitly mentioned the "use of armed force" as a possible response in the event of an attack.[96] At the same time, the United States succeeded in retaining significant autonomy over military decisions by merely promising "assistance," which could take various forms such as the dispatch of troops or only the provision of financial aid.[97]

Aside from specifying the exact nature of their pledge, the allies were interested in making a long-term commitment and in creating a structural foundation upon which they could build. Article 13 of the North Atlantic Treaty (ratified on July 25, 1949), for instance, stipulates that the signatories cannot denounce their membership for at least twenty years.[98] Article 9 calls for the creation of a council consisting of all members that would be authorized to set up any subsidiary bodies deemed necessary. And, to mention but one further treaty stipulation, the allies vowed to establish a defense committee.[99]

As will be discussed in the next chapter, within a year of its creation, NATO became much superior to traditional military coalitions. Through a high level of integration, a unified command, joint planning, and combined military training, NATO set itself apart from most previous military arrangements.[100] But it will also become clear that NATO always remained less than a supranational organization. That is, defense budgets remained national;[101] each member maintained its own forces (although there was a central command to ensure coordination); actions to be taken by individual countries continued to be determined by their national governments; and there was little delegation of authority.[102] Put differently still, in order to sign the North Atlantic Treaty the Western powers did not have to surrender a significant amount of their sovereignty, yet could voluntarily curtail their freedom of action later, if they thought this to be in their best interest.[103]

CONCLUSION

In a final analysis, NATO must be viewed as a compromise between West European and North American security interests. Given asymmetric assessments of threat and transaction costs, the Western powers favored different degrees of commitment, and thus had to settle for an arrangement that, in its initial form, approximated a traditional guarantee pact. Although the West Europeans, exposed to high threat and high transaction costs, would have preferred a more binding security apparatus, the United States, as technological and military leader, as the only power with nuclear capabilities, and as sole provider of West European military assistance, was not greatly concerned about defection on the part of its allies,[104] and thus sought to protect its freedom of action. During the NAT negotiations the United States, consequently, was not willing to make as firm a pledge as the West Europeans had asked for, but rather strove to obtain maximum security benefits (by pooling U.S. and European resources) at minimal cost to its autonomy.

When one compares the NAT discussions with security debates of the Napoleonic days, many similarities stand out. For instance, focusing on the relative causal weight of the individual measures of transaction costs, again one finds that a state's susceptibility to opportunistic behavior is crucial in determining the extent to which the state is willing to curtail its autonomy. As in the previous cases, great uncertainty and the presence of specific assets increase the risk of opportunism substantially, whereas a high degree of heterogeneity only appears to be of great concern when cultural cleavages are very pronounced and any sense of "we-ness" or trust is lacking. This is not to suggest that different language and cultural backgrounds have no impact on transaction costs, but, since these factors—much like communications and transportation—for the most part seem to affect coordination costs rather than transactional risks, they appear to be of lesser importance in deciding institutional choices.

The next chapter scrutinizes plans for a European Defense Community. Again, states can be expected to be protective of their freedom of action and thus should only surrender a substantial part of their sovereignty if they are exposed to both high threat and high transaction costs. Moreover, to bring about a significantly binding security structure, the allies' exposure to threat and transaction costs must be symmetrically high.

CHAPTER 6

The European Defense Community (EDC)

Almost immediately after the founding of NATO, and in the wake of the Korean War, the Western allies saw the need to strengthen their security provisions and to reexamine the question of German rearmament.[1] The French, seeking a very binding security arrangement, proposed a European army. Initially opposed by other countries, this proposal eventually was accepted by them only to be rejected finally by the French themselves. The result of the security debates was a strengthened NATO, that is, an outcome the French for several years had sought to avoid.

As expected, one sees in the EDC debate that France, which perceived the highest threat and experienced relatively high transaction costs, sought the most binding security arrangement. Yet one also finds that the French were only willing to curtail their sovereignty as long as they felt seriously threatened. In fact, France's conviction of an easing of tensions led to the loss of support for a very binding security structure and, ultimately, to its failure.

WESTERN SECURITY PROVISIONS
PRIOR TO THE KOREAN WAR

Although, on May 9, 1949, the USSR lifted its blockade on Berlin,[2] a period of improved East-West relations did not follow. On the contrary, on September 23, President Truman announced the detection of an atomic explosion in the Soviet Union and, on October 6, 1949, responded to this increase in Soviet military capabilities by signing a Mutual Defense Assistance Act that would facilitate cooperation among the Western allies. Furthermore, on January 27, 1950, the American president approved a plan to integrate the defense of the North Atlantic Area and released $900 million of military funds.[3] Yet it was clear to Truman that the United States, due to fiscal constraints, could not afford to finance a Western military buildup by itself[4] and that the West Europeans lacked the financial means to increase their defense spending significantly.

FROM THE KOREAN WAR
TO THE SIGNING OF THE EDC

Then, on June 25, 1950, North Korean forces attacked South Korea. This was a decisive event that forced the Western powers to rethink their security provisions. More specifically, the outbreak of the war shows how an increase in threat provided the necessary impetus to spend more money on defense,[5] to seek a more binding form of cooperation previously rejected, and to debate seriously the question of German rearmament.[6]

Convinced that the Korean War was initiated by the USSR, that it might be a first step in a series of militant acts—that it might even be a "dress rehearsal" for Europe[7]—the Western powers grew anxious about their serious military inferiority vis-à-vis the USSR. The United Kingdom announced a large-scale rearmament program,[8] the United States almost tripled its defense budget within the next three years,[9] but greater efforts were still needed to enhance western security.

France, struggling to rebuild its war-torn economy, was unable to contribute much to a rearmament program. But the French government promised to increase its defense budget and, in return, asked the United States and the United Kingdom to station troops in Europe as an additional security guarantee.[10]

Similarly, Germany realized that it would have to contribute to a common defense. Yet Adenauer was well aware of the difficult position his country was in. Not a member of NATO and still viewed as a potential enemy by most of the Western powers, the best the German government could do was to suggest to solve the question of German rearmament once and for all.[11]

For the next four years the Western allies debated how to strengthen their security provisions. Given the high level of Soviet threat it was clear that a binding security arrangement was needed and that it would have to include West Germany. There was little agreement among the allies, however, concerning the structure of such an arrangement.[12]

Terrified by the increase in Soviet belligerence and deeply troubled by the prospect of a remilitarized Germany, in the fall of 1950 France called for the founding of a European army in which the contingents of the members (including Germany) "would be incorporated . . . on the level of the smallest possible unit."[13] The United States, deeply concerned about its security interests in Western Europe as a result of the increase in Soviet hostilities, feared that the creation of such a European army (which came to be known as the European Defense Community) would take too much time, and thus proposed to integrate Germany in NATO.[14] Likewise, the United Kingdom and the Benelux countries preferred the NATO solution, arguing that, besides a much more speedy integration, a transcontinental security arrangement would provide additional safeguards due to U.S. membership.[15]

The French were not at all convinced that the NATO solution put forth by the United States would provide the best answer. Strongly opposed to German rearmament, the French felt that the degree of integration envisioned by the NATO proposal would not give adequate safeguards to warrant French acceptance. In fact, the French feared that, in the long run, Germany (once rearmed) might become militant again and act opportunistically, and then pose an even greater threat than the USSR. In a worst-case scenario the Germans might even "turn coat,"[16] that is, bandwagon, and thus the French government sought maximum control over Germany.

After careful consideration the French came to conclude that they would have to reduce their freedom of action to enhance their security. Since they could no longer prevent German rearmament, and since the creation of a German army could easily endanger their security, the French decided that Germany should be contained through further allied military integration and control.[17]

The German government, however, immediately rejected the EDC proposal. Acknowledging that the question of German rearmament would have to be solved, Chancellor Adenauer put forth two conditions that would have to be met before further progress toward the integration of Germany in the Western defense system could be made. First, he asked the United States and the United Kingdom to send enough troops to the continent so that an effective defense would become possible. Second, he demanded equality of rights, that is, full representation on all organs dealing with troop activities.[18]

Unwilling to reconcile themselves with the idea of a German national army, the French remained adamantly opposed to German integration in NATO. In fact, if Germany were to become a part of NATO, the French portended, Germany would gain equality and, after twenty years, legally obtain the right to secede.[19] Hence, the NATO solution provided no real assurance that at some point in the future France would not face a rearmed and possibly militant Germany again. Stated differently, the French feared that German integration in NATO would not provide adequate safeguards against German opportunism, and therefore were determined to prevent German rearmament unless it were to take place in a much more binding security apparatus.

While the Western allies debated the question of German rearmament they took several steps to enhance their security. One of their first tasks entailed the further integration of NATO.[20] On December 19, 1950, the North Atlantic Council appointed General Eisenhower

Supreme Allied Commander in Europe (SACEUR) and thereby created a central command.[21] To end duplication in the area of defense the Brussels Treaty powers, one day later, announced the merger of the Western Union's military organization with NATO.[22] Hence, whereas the Western alliance at its outset largely resembled a traditional guarantee pact, shortly thereafter, through the creation of various planning groups and centralized military committees, it became more structured and organized.[23]

Since the French could not afford to take further security risks (the Soviet threat remained great), yet strongly opposed a German army outside an EDC, they had to compromise and permit German divisions to be integrated on a basis of equality.[24] This concession clearly demonstrates that a strong structural commitment was more important to the French than the perpetuation of German inequality. Or, in other words, France's behavior indicates that the French were not simply interested in penalizing Germany for past belligerence, but rather sought to assure that German opportunism would be much more difficult in the future. Put differently still, by granting German equality the French proved that they were not driven by thoughts of revenge, but the need to increase their security by incorporating Germany in a sophisticated security apparatus—much like the theoretical framework advanced in this study would predict.

Not to lose further time, and hoping that in the long run the creation of an EDC would allow the United States to play a lesser role in the defense of Western Europe, the Americans began to support a European army.[25] And, once equality had been granted, German chancellor Adenauer decided to accept French plans for an EDC.

The Benelux countries, however, still refusing to surrender a significant part of their autonomy, were waiting for further safeguards.[26] Only when the United States threatened to withdraw from Europe and the British—convinced that their "world-wide responsibilities to the Commonwealth and the Empire" would forbid their joining an EDC[27]—promised to station troops in Germany was the EDC treaty finally signed.

On May 27, 1952, the Benelux countries, Italy, the Federal Republic of Germany, and France specified that Germany should provide twelve divisions to an integrated multinational army, that common programs for the armament, equipment, and supply of the European military forces were to be set up, and that a board of commissioners was to be established that would organize, recruit, and train the EDC forces.[28]

Hence, in signing the EDC treaty the members indicated their willingness to surrender a substantial amount of their autonomy to a central authority. Whereas under NATO all member nations have ceded part of their capacity, and most of their responsibility, for self-defense to a common headquarters, . . . this delegation of responsibility was carried still further in the EDC treaty, which proposed to integrate European troops into a single military formation and European armaments into a single weapons-system.[29]

Furthermore, whereas under NATO defense debates were held in the national parliaments of the various countries and defense budgets remained national, in the EDC decisions were to be made by a supranational body and there was to be a common defense budget.[30]

To summarize, the above analysis demonstrates how an increase in Soviet threat caused the Western powers to strengthen their military capabilities to offset the serious military imbalance in favor of the Soviets. Following the detection of a Soviet nuclear explosion, the United States and the British, much like realists would predict, greatly increased their defense spending. Less fortunate in that they were still caught up in rebuilding their war-torn economies, the French and the Benelux countries asked for U.S. support. And when, with the outbreak of the Korean War, the Soviet threat increased even further, the Western powers—again consistent with realist expectations—sought greater commitments from each other and discussed expanding their alliance (German rearmament) to reduce their vulnerability vis-à-vis the USSR.

Yet these drawn-out security debates also show that an examination of threat does not suffice to account for the Western powers' security choices. Although there was agreement that the increase in Soviet threat would require a binding security structure, the threat variable by itself cannot explain the discrepancy concerning the allies' security preferences.

In the paragraphs that follow, therefore, I analyze the level of transaction costs experienced by the Western powers at the time they discussed the creation of a European Defense Community. I show that transaction costs not only increased overall since the NATO debate, but differed noticeably among the allies.

TRANSACTION COSTS AND THE EDC

Examining the degree of uncertainty the Western powers confronted during the EDC negotiations, one finds that, although bipolarity prevented constant shifts in alignments that often plague a multipolar international system, the degree of uncertainty continued to be substantial and asymmetric. There were three areas of concern in particular.

First, although the outbreak of the Korean War confirmed the allies' view of the USSR as a formidable enemy, the Western powers were unsure about future Soviet intentions. Would the Korean War prove to be an isolated incident or could it be a "dress rehearsal" for Europe, as mentioned above? Would the Soviets confine warfare to the Korean peninsula or engage in similar types of aggression on the European continent?

Second, the prospect of German rearmament raised the level of uncertainty regarding Germany's future behavior substantially. By refraining to rearm up to this point, the Germans had sent a clear signal of benevolent intentions; now, however, the allies were not sure what to make of Germany's willingness to rearm. Could Germany be trusted to cooperate with the allies and play its part to enhance Western security? Or would Germany agree to rearm merely to act opportunistically later? Would Germany bandwagon, if the Soviets were to tempt it with reunification promises? Would a rearmed Germany become militant again and threaten its neighbors? At this point it was impossible to know. Yet what needs to be stressed is that the allies (much like the Swiss and the Germans in the nineteenth century) were confronted with a type of opportunism that they had given little thought to previously, namely that instead of defecting, free riding, or bandwagoning, a rearmed Germany eventually could turn against them.

Since the uncertainty regarding Germany's future behavior affected the Western powers differently, those most troubled by the possibility of renewed German militancy sought greater safeguards.[31] The United States, geographically far removed from the European continent, never feared a resurgent Germany very much.[32] The United Kingdom and the Benelux countries clearly worried about German opportunism and, as discussed above, initially sought to incorporate Germany into NATO to subject Germany to American control. France—due to its geographic closeness to and terrible past experiences with Germany—felt most keenly the uncertainty surrounding future German behavior, and thus sought to create an EDC that would prevent the formation of an independent German army. Clearly, as Germany rearmed, uncertainty about its future behavior mingled with a new kind of threat—one (from Germany) *internal* to the confederation and thus excluded from the argument I have advanced. But this threat—similar to the one posed by the Swiss cantons and the German states following the Napoleonic Wars—was merely derivative of the larger Soviet threat discussed above (that required German rearmament).[33]

A third source of uncertainty in the early 1950s stemmed from the unpredictability of future American behavior. Since the U.S. government incurred tremendous defense expenditures, and made clear that it was not willing to increase its military spending any further, the European powers feared that the United States eventually might return to isolationist policies.[34] This meant that the West European countries could face a serious security dilemma; therefore, they sought as binding a commitment from the United States as possible. Or, in other words, given the signal sent by the United States—that it was unwilling to make additional defense sacrifices—the Western allies would have liked to involve the United States in a structurally sophisticated security arrangement; but, recognizing they were hardly in a position to dictate to their much more powerful ally how to behave, the West Europeans had to settle for the stationing of American troops on the European continent.

In sum, in the early 1950s the Western powers faced high uncertainty. The outbreak of the Korean War not only caused them to worry about the next Soviet moves, but also brought the need for German rearmament, and thus gave renewed urgency to already existing concerns regarding future German intentions. Much like in the case of NATO, the Western powers felt uncertain about both immediate Soviet and more distant German behavior; yet the knowledge that Germany soon once more would possess the military means to pose a threat to the West made it all the more difficult to rely on continued German benevolence. Although there was no doubt in 1950 that (West) Germany was in the Western camp, there were no guarantees for the indefinite future. Moreover, as the above analysis has shown, the West Europeans experienced higher uncertainty than the United States (since the former had to fear a return to isolationism by the latter), which explains why the Europeans sought as firm a commitment from the Americans as possible.

By the time the Western powers discussed the creation of an EDC the state of technology had progressed even further from the days of the NATO debates so that communications as well as the shipment of troops and materials did not lead to high transaction costs. In fact, roads, airfields, railroad tracks, and train stations that had been destroyed during World War II and were being rebuilt in the immediate postwar period were expanded in the early 1950s, and thus reduced transportation costs noticeably. At the same time, changes in the field of telecommunications such as widely extended telephone lines and improved telegraph facilities kept cooperation costs and risks relatively low. Hence, although in the case of the EDC several countries sought to cooperate, there was no need for a structurally sophisticated security arrangement to offset transaction costs resulting from transportation and communications. Or the state of technology in the early 1950s was sufficiently advanced that it did not have a significant impact on the allies' choice of security arrangement.

However, if one scrutinizes the relationship between heterogeneity and security choice one comes to a different conclusion. Obviously, the degree of heterogeneity did not change much from the NAT to the EDC debates—it was high in both instances. But, the inclusion of Germany in the Western defense system, at least in the eyes of some alliance members, added substantial transactional risks and therefore raised transaction costs considerably.

France, fearing renewed German belligerence, time and time again lamented the lack of a sense of cultural affinity among the allies and continuously emphasized the great risks associated with this deficiency.[35] Since Germany had made all too clear in the past that it could not be trusted, France insisted, German rearmament would require great structural safeguards to reduce the likelihood of renewed German opportunism. The United States, on the other hand, chose to highlight the "common heritage [of the Western powers] . . . founded on the principle of democracy, individual liberty and the rule of law"[36] and, much less concerned about opportunistic behavior, sought to protect its maneuverability.

Besides forcing the Western powers to readdress the question of German rearmament, the outbreak of the Korean War prompted them to achieve greater cooperation and integration. That is, the NATO countries began to hold common maneuvers, placed their national armies under the central command of General Eisenhower, and coordinated troop training to improve military effectiveness. Under the French plan for a European army the level of integration was to be carried even further. National armies were to be replaced by military units composed of soldiers from various nationalities, and the supply, equipment, and infrastructure of the European forces were to be coordinated by a central decision-making body.

At this stage, where the members of NATO had gone beyond the mere promise of aiding each other in the event of an attack and were actually engaged in coordinating their military efforts, the large degree of heterogeneity among the allies raised their transaction costs significantly.

First, there were language problems. Although most diplomats spoke English and French, the common soldier generally did not. Hence, as was made clear at a conference on NATO military education, the members of the alliance had to "strengthen their corps of interpreters so that each combatant and technical unit [would be able to] distribute information from other member countries regularly."[37] Also, language schools had to be created to teach troops how to communicate with each other.[38]

Second, there was a need for standardization of training and personnel-related issues. For heterogeneous units to function properly military training had to be harmonized and questions regarding uniforms, promotion, pay, disciplinary action, the relationship to superiors, and so on, had to be addressed.[39] That these would not be easy tasks has been shown in previous alliances. Time and again traditions have stood in the way of harmonization and sometimes seemingly simple issues like "what to eat" or "when to break for a meal" have proven major stumbling blocks.[40]

Third, since the allies, often, were ignorant of the values, customs, and behavioral characteristics of each other, the likelihood of disagreements and conflicts increased, and thereby the need for arbitration. Particularly common appear to be problems of a social/psychological nature where soldiers from one country hold prejudices against their foreign counterparts.[41] Troops in country A, for instance, may perceive troops in country B as unreliable, or several countries may accuse soldiers of a certain nationality of being lazy, that is, not fulfilling their duties as collectively prescribed.[42]

To some degree, all of the Western powers were likely to incur costs stemming from their different cultural backgrounds. Yet France, due to its distrust of and long antagonism toward Germany, knew that it would be a likely candidate for arbitration, and thus undertook to remedy what it perceived to be the shortcomings of NATO's conflict-solving mechanisms. Since NATO decisions must be unanimous and there is no higher authority to arbitrate, France argued, change was needed to prevent paralysis should the allies fail to reach agreement on specific policies.[43] As articles 51–67 of the EDC Treaty dealing with the courts show, the French had a clear conception of what well-functioning arbitration provisions should look like.[44] For example, anticipating that there would be disagreements concerning the execution of EDC policies, article 65 grants members the right to initiate court proceedings to settle their differences and avoid stalemate.

> Any dispute between Member States arising out of the implementation of the present Treaty shall, if no other means of settlement has been found, be a proper subject for submission to the Court, either through a joint application by the parties to the dispute, or through the application of one of the parties only.[45]

Articles 54 through 56 lay out the circumstances (and the time table) under which states, the Council of Ministers, and the Assembly can appeal the Board of Commissioners' decisions or recommendations. To mention but one more legal recourse established by the EDC Treaty, article 63 spells out arbitration mechanisms.

> The Court shall be competent in the cases and under the conditions set forth in its Statute, to give rulings in virtue of an arbitration clause contained in a public or private law contract passed by the Community or on its behalf.[46]

Although it stands to reason that the need for translators, language schools, military standardization, and conflict-solving mechanisms did raise the allies' cooperation costs, these costs were clearly minor compared to say expenditures on military hardware or troop provisions. Hence, as in the German or the Swiss case, the main concern was not that heterogeneity would increase coordination costs, but that the lack of trust resulting from cultural differences would raise transactional risks.

A last factor to be looked at to ascertain the allies' transaction costs is asset specificity. The radical developments in nuclear arms which took place in the immediate post-1945 period accelerated in the early 1950s. In November 1952, the United States tested its first hydrogen bomb.[47] The United Kingdom, which in the late 1940s still lacked the trained scientists and the material resources to develop nuclear weapons, exploded its first atomic device in October 1952[48] and designed high-performance bombers to carry nuclear weapons.[49]

Although nuclear devices, atomic delivery vehicles, and jet aircraft entail highly sophisticated physical and human assets, and it would have been costly to redeploy nuclear weapons specifically designed for the European theater, the Americans and the British had little reason to fear opportunistic behavior by their allies. Since the West European countries were completely dependent on the United States and, to a lesser extent, British nuclear guarantee, it was inconceivable they would defect; hence, the British and Americans saw no need to surrender a substantial amount of their sovereignty to a more binding security apparatus.

Lacking the technological capacity (both specialized equipment and highly trained people) to develop their own nuclear deterrents, France, the Benelux countries, and West Germany were in a much more vulnerable position.[50] If the United States were to withdraw from Europe and take its nuclear umbrella with it, these countries would face serious security problems.

To make matters worse a study of the allies' conventional weapons in the early 1950s paints a similar picture of dependence.[51] Since French and Benelux industries did not recover from the war until the late 1950s, and Germany remained subject to severe armament restrictions,[52] the transfer of military equipment begun during the war continued. Particularly impressive is the long list of U.S. items handed over to the West Europeans which included 155–mm medium guns, radar, jeeps,[53] M-47 tanks,[54] F-84, F-86, F-100 planes,[55] and a variety of warships.[56]

While most West European countries were still struggling to rebuild their war-torn economies, the United States not only supplied its allies with much needed weapons, but also invested in the production of powerful new arms. To give but one example, the U.S. Navy acquired several warships displaying the "latest scientific and engineering developments" such as

> high speed turbines . . . ; light weight diesel engines; gas turbines weighing one-sixth less but delivering two-thirds more power than conventional power plants; atomic powered engines; hydrogen peroxide plants; steam catapults; and gun mountings, gun controls and weapons which are becoming separate engineering installations in themselves.[57]

Hence, whereas the United States was embracing technological advances that would enhance Western security, the French, Benelux, and West Germans continued to be dependent on American weapons entailing both highly specialized as well as generic assets these countries could not produce themselves.

The British, like the Americans (although on a smaller scale) also transferred military equipment to their European allies—mainly fighter aircraft[58] and naval vessels that the British had decided to scrap[59]—and built several new weapons entailing highly specific physical and human assets. Particularly noteworthy among these new British military designs are the previously mentioned high performance bombers[60] as well as minesweepers.[61] The latter, as the name suggests, are designed "to handle and tow gear capable of sweeping mines . . . [and] the gear required . . . is often complex, bulky, and hard to handle."[62]

> Moored mines are cleared by wire cables, usually one to each side, streamed 900 to 1,800 feet astern the sweeper. These cables are forced to the desired depth close to the ship by a hydrofoil or depressor. At the outer end, they are supported at the desired depth by floats, and other hydrofoils or otters divert them from the ship so that a wide path can be swept.[63]

Since minesweepers consist of specific physical assets, and are "essentially single-purpose ships,"[64] they lose value in their next best use—say as mail carriers or beachhead patrols.[65] Hence, one would expect the British to deploy these ships for purposes other than minesweeping only in emergencies, or when the ships have become outdated. Put differently, whereas a number of vessels could function as mail carriers or beachhead patrols, only a few would do for minesweeping—those equipped with the specialized gear necessary to accomplish this task.

Why did the United Kingdom invest in these specific naval assets and what can they tell us about the allies' security choices? Motivated by the significant losses it experienced from the mining of estuaries and harbors in the past,[66] and particularly vulnerable due to its shallow coastal waters, Britain modernized and accelerated the production of minesweepers to enhance Western naval defense against increasingly difficult to detect mines.[67] Although the newly developed British assets could benefit all Western allies, it was clear that the United States—with deeper coastal waters and its own sweepers custom-made for such terrain—would have comparatively little need for British minesweepers, and thus would not have to fear opportunistic behavior on the part of Britain. The French, by contrast, possessing only a few of these naval vessels left over from World War II, were much more dependent on British support; hence along with the Germans and the Benelux, who at the time did not own any significant mine-removal equipment of their own either, they had a strong incentive to seek a firm British commitment.

As already mentioned, France was trailing behind the United States and the British in military production, yet did make some progress developing its own weapons. In a five-year plan announced in 1950, for instance, France vowed to build 2,816 military planes,[68] and by 1955 the Caravelle and the Mirage I were in service.[69] In addition, several "destroyers of the 'Surcouf' class ha[d] been completed, . . . and the first of the 13 new anti-submarine frigates [was] also about to enter service."[70] And, a 1954 naval construction program included such items as "a large light fleet aircraft carrier . . . , three frigates of a new type, two large submarines and two killer submarines."[71] But, despite these measures, France did not manage to diminish its vulnerability significantly until the 1960s.

To sum up, since the French, Benelux, and West Germans were dependent on American and, to a lesser degree, British armament entailing highly sophisticated assets (nuclear devices, bombers, minesweepers, aircraft carriers, other naval vessels with specialized equipment, etc.) that they could not produce themselves, or could only produce in small numbers, the continental powers asked for as strong a commitment from the United States and Britain as possible and sought a structurally binding security arrangement among themselves that would leave them less vulnerable in the event of a defection by their allies. To the extent that France, the Benelux countries, and West Germany also depended on their allies for weapons with generic assets, these countries faced additional risks since there was no guarantee that the United States and the United Kingdom would continue to supply such weapons.

In the early 1950s it was already predictable that the continental powers soon would mass-produce their own weapons entailing generic assets again so that their dependence in that respect would clearly be temporary. The same, however, could not be said for military equipment consisting of specific assets. Given the much greater challenges (special ingredients, technological expertise, cost, etc.) inherent in the production of highly sophisticated weapons, it was understood that progress in this area would take place much more slowly. Thus, despite the rebuilding efforts undertaken by the French, Benelux, and Germans, for the forseeable future their security would be tied to asset-specific U.S. and British weapons so that they would remain subject to substantial transactional risks.

Tying together the various strands of the argument developed above, it can be said that the level of transaction costs not only increased overall since the late 1940s, but differed noticeably among the Western powers. France, for the reasons already mentioned, by far, experienced the highest transaction costs, which explains why France proposed the creation of the EDC and vigorously fought for its adoption. The United States, on the other hand, which did not fear opportunistic behavior on the part of its allies very much, had no reason to surrender a significant amount of its sovereignty.

The other Western powers stood between the extremes of France and the United States. Plagued by substantially lower transaction costs than her continental allies, the United Kingdom also had no need to curtail her freedom of action to the degree membership in the EDC required. The Benelux countries, facing relatively high transaction costs, yet less concerned about German opportunism and less prone to clash with Germany than France, initially favored the inclusion of Germany in NATO. Only when they had become convinced that France would not allow a NATO solution and the United States might make a firm commitment to Western European defense contingent on the ratification of the EDC treaty, did they begin to support the creation of a European army. Similarly, Germany experienced substantial transaction costs. However, mostly concerned with regaining the status of an equal power, the German government was unable to support plans for an EDC until France withdrew its demands for German inequality. That is, fearing that German soldiers would be used as cannon-fodder in a European army, Germany did not seriously contemplate joining the EDC until the French did away with stipulations indicating German inferiority.

THE LONG STRUGGLE FOR EDC RATIFICATION

It is crucial to keep in mind that on May 27, 1952, the EDC treaty was signed, not *ratified*. Although the signatories indicated their readiness to help bring about the EDC, they had to obtain approval by their parliaments before the sophisticated structural apparatus agreed upon could be built and begin to operate. As will be seen, this ratification process turned out to be much more complicated and time-consuming than envisioned.

Whereas at the outbreak of the Korean War the Western powers agreed that the USSR was posing a serious threat, this changed when Stalin died on March 5, 1953. The Soviet dictator's death led the allies to reevaluate the level of threat and, as expected, those who interpreted the policies of Stalin's successors as détente gestures were no longer willing to support the creation of a very binding security system. By contrast, those who did not see a significant change in Soviet intentions (threat) sought to push for the ratification of the EDC.[72]

Stalin's successors lost no time to create the impression that East-West relations, now that Stalin was gone, would improve substantially.[73] The Soviet leaders announced troop reductions, discussed the dissolution of Cominform,[74] and engaged in propaganda emphasizing "peaceful coexistence."[75] Furthermore, the new Kremlin leaders undertook great diplomatic efforts to persuade the Western powers that the Soviets were "digging a tunnel of friendship to the West."[76]

France reacted to these changes in Soviet behavior by procrastinating on the ratification of the EDC.[77] Convinced that the most recent Soviet moves (including the signing of the Korean armistice on July 23, 1953) signaled the Kremlin's willingness to adopt conciliatory policies toward the West, the French argued that the Soviet threat was declining considerably and therefore eliminating the need to take risks or to make unnecessary sacrifices.[78] Although the French had already signed the EDC Treaty, this meant that they reopened the question of German rearmament and once more engaged in EDC debates.[79]

The German government continued to support a European army.[80] Although it looked like the Soviet menace was decreasing, the German chancellor cautioned that it was too early to tell whether this more amicable trend would continue[81] so that the necessity to imbed Germany in a binding security arrangement still pertained. German security, in the chancellor's opinion, clearly had priority over unity since a reunified but neutral country, in the long run, had little chance of survival. In fact, by supporting the ratification of the EDC the German government hoped to restore German power and then deal with the question of German reunification from a position of strength.

The United States was most suspicious of the Kremlin's détente gestures. The government insisted that Moscow's conciliatory moves should not be interpreted as a thawing of the Cold War, but rather as moves intended to disrupt the Western alliance by creating the illusion that a common defense would no longer be necessary.[82] That is, although it was tempting to act as though the Soviet danger was decreasing (to be able to spend less money on European rearmament), U.S. authorities warned that the "Communist menace continued intact."[83]

First, there were no clear signs of a Soviet troop demobilization.[84] Second, even if the Kremlin was torn by internal power struggles,[85] there was no indication that Stalin's successors would consistently pursue more amicable policies toward the West. Moreover, given the high secrecy surrounding nuclear development—there was no way of knowing to what extent Soviet atomic capabilities had increased[86]—a great need for caution remained.

Since the United States did not want to have to choose between carrying the main burden of Western defense, or returning to isolationism should this burden become too much, it decided to put pressure on France. Secretary of State Dulles warned the French government that the American commitment to defend Western Europe could be substantially revised, should France not work toward the ratification of the EDC.[87] And, this warning was followed by the "Richards Amendment," which stipulated that half of Europe's military aid would be contingent on the adoption of the EDC.[88]

The United Kingdom also was skeptical of Moscow's alleged friendship. Afraid of the spread of communism ever since the conclusion of World War II, the British government was not persuaded by the more amicable gestures of Stalin's successors, but wrote them off as propaganda. A strong Western defense, the British claimed, remained as necessary as prior to Stalin's death, and therefore encouraged the continental powers to work toward the ratification of the EDC.

To reduce French fears of a rearmed Germany, which clearly posed the greatest obstacle to the adoption of the EDC,[89] the British made one further attempt to give assurances to France. To indicate their willingness actively to participate in the defense of the West on April 13, 1954, the British signed an agreement with the EDC countries promising to keep British troops on the continent.[90] And, three days later, Eisenhower (who had assumed the position of U.S. president in January 1953) made a similar offer.[91]

Whereas the German Bundestag voted for the ratification of the EDC on March 14, 1953,[92] and the Benelux countries—more and more convinced that they could not afford to jeopardize U.S. support by holding an anti-EDC position—were obtaining approval for the EDC by their national parliaments, in France the prospects for ratification worsened. When the United States, the United Kingdom, the USSR, and France met in Geneva on April 26, 1954, to settle the Korean problem and discuss ways to bring about peace in Indo-China,[93] France, which should have shown an interest in reaching an agreement on these issues to free up troops for a European army, merely sought to stall the negotiations.[94] This lends further support to France's conviction of a considerable easing of East-West tensions since it is inconceivable that the

French government otherwise could have preoccupied itself with the Indo-China question instead of the EDC.[95]

At the Brussels Conference on August 19, 1954, the French tried to introduce new proposals that would allow them to retain a large part of their sovereignty,[96] but these efforts were in vain. Germany, which some time ago had ratified the EDC treaty, voiced strong objections and led the French to conclude that the costs of a binding security arrangement like the EDC at this point clearly outweighed the benefits.[97] Thus, on August 29, 1954, the French Assembly voted against the ratification of the EDC and made its demise official.

THE COMPROMISE: GERMANY JOINS THE WESTERN EUROPEAN UNION AND NATO

The above discussion sheds light on why the French proposed the creation of an EDC and—seeing a significant reduction in Soviet threat—ultimately, signed its death certificate. But what became of the "grande peur"—France's fear of Germany? Did the French presume that their failure to ratify the EDC treaty would prevent German rearmament? Or were the French willing to take a big risk? That is, no longer prepared to surrender a significant part of their sovereignty did the French decide to chance ending up with their worst outcome—unrestricted German rearmament?

Several reasons speak against the first possibility—that German rearmament would not proceed. France knew the other Western powers still saw a serious Soviet threat, and thus had to anticipate that they would seek an alternative way to rearm Germany. The United States, moreover, had stressed repeatedly that an effective defense of Western Europe without Germany would be impossible, thus leaving no reason to believe that it would abandon rearmament plans.[98] And both the United States and the United Kingdom were discussing EDC alternatives a couple of months prior to the EDC's actual defeat that the French knew about.[99]

Unwilling to ratify the EDC treaty, unable to prevent German rearmament, and too weak to pursue an isolationist strategy, the best the French could do was to participate in the rearmament negotiations and hope to obtain additional safeguards. Or, in other words, no longer perceiving a serious Soviet threat and not willing to curtail their freedom of action significantly for a "watered down" EDC that they thought was unlikely to provide adequate safeguards against renewed German militarism,[100] the French decided to join their allies in new security talks.

The Western powers, fearing that Germany might be driven to ally with the USSR (bandwagon)[101] if more time were to be lost, displayed a great readiness to compromise. For several days they discussed a number of proposals outlining how to accomplish German rearmament. For instance, there was talk of bringing Germany directly into NATO,[102] or, if French concurrence could not be obtained, of proceeding under a defense agreement along the lines of the Yugoslav-Greek-Turk Pact.[103] The big breakthrough, however, occurred when the British suggested using the Brussels Treaty of 1948 as a framework for West German rearmament[104] and guaranteed to station troops on the European continent for an unlimited time. By giving the assurance that they

> [would] continue to maintain on the mainland of Europe, including Germany, the effective strength of the United Kingdom forces now assigned to SACEUR—four divisions and the tactical Air Force— . . . and undertake not to withdraw those forces against the wishes of the majority of the Brussels Treaty Powers,[105]

the British made an "unprecedented commitment" that provided France with safeguards it had sought for so long and convinced it to give up its resistance to German rearmament.[106] In the end agreement was reached that the Western European Union (WEU) should be restored within NATO,[107] that Germany would join the WEU, and thereby become a member of NATO. France thus managed to hold on to its national army and a large part of its sovereignty while receiving guarantees against a resurgent Germany.[108] And its allies, by solving the German rearmament question, enhanced their security.

But, had the French continued to view the Soviet threat as high (had Stalin not died or his successors acted less amicably), would the EDC treaty have been ratified? One might speculate that the chances for ratification would have been good since France experienced the highest transaction costs and had the greatest need for a security arrangement that would reduce these costs. Furthermore, there were no real obstacles to ratification on the part of the other Western powers. The Benelux, who also confronted substantial transaction costs and viewed EDC membership as a lesser evil than jeopardizing their security,[109] after initial objections had indicated their willingness to go along with the implementation of a European army, as had the German Bundestag when it ratified the EDC treaty. The United States and the United Kingdom, although not willing to become members of the EDC, strongly supported its creation by giving guarantees in the form of troop shipments to the European continent. Ultimately, the French thus not only conceived of the EDC but, ironically, also signed its death certificate and brought about an outcome that they for many years sought to avoid—German rearmament within NATO.

CONCLUSION

In a final analysis, the combined assessment of threat and transaction costs does a good job accounting for the Western powers' security choices in the early 1950s (see Table 6.1). Whereas an examination of threat alone yields indeterminate results, the additional study of transaction costs not only explains why the United States and the British (facing a high threat and relatively low transaction costs) could afford to maintain a large degree of autonomy, but also why the French, Benelux, and Germans had to curtail their sovereignty substantially. Confronted with high Soviet threat and trapped in the unenviable position of having to conduct their security transactions in an uncertain, culturally heterogeneous environment, while highly dependent on specific American assets, it does not come as a surprise that the French, Benelux, and Germans were in need of a binding security apparatus. Moreover, a close examination of the various indicators of transaction costs sheds light on why France, facing the highest transaction costs, conceived of the EDC and vigorously fought for its adoption, and why the Benelux countries and West Germany, also experiencing relatively high transaction costs, came to support a binding European security arrangement that—by virtue of its central control and high level of coordination—would reduce some of these costs.

The drawn-out security debates, as in previous cases, also confirm that states treasure their freedom of action. When France, due to changes in the international system (the death of Stalin and the stabilization of military operations in Korea), began to perceive a reduction in tensions, it no longer saw the need to curtail its maneuverability sub-

TABLE 6.1
The European Defense Community

		Level of Threat	
		Low	High
Transaction Costs	Low		U.S. U.K.
	High	France (1953)	Germany Benelux France (1952)

stantially, and therefore refused to ratify the EDC treaty. Put differently still, French behavior once more underlines the importance of symmetric assessments of threat and transaction costs in bringing about structurally sophisticated security arrangements. As in the Quadruple Alliance and NATO, asymmetry prevented some of the allies from making more firm commitments.

Having assessed an argument about the determinants of different degrees of institutionalization in the security realm, the next chapter summarizes the empirical findings, tests the applicability of the transaction costs model for the current period of flux in the international environment, examines the model's explanatory power for economic issues, and, finally, discusses the implications of a transaction costs argument for international relations theory.

CHAPTER 7

Conclusion:
Transaction Costs and a
Theory of Integration

The field of international relations conceptualizes autonomous, self-interested states that, in the anarchic setting of international politics, rely on self-help. And yet one finds numerous security arrangements throughout history that bear witness to frequent cooperation among states.

Although international relations scholars, for many decades, have studied various aspects of cooperative security structures (formation, duration, performance, purpose), few scholars treat them as matters of *choice*. They consequently fail to explain the different degrees of institutionalization found in these security arrangements. As shown above, both realists and proponents of economies of scale arguments focus on size to account for cooperative behavior in the international environment, but there is more to cooperation than the desire to be "bigger" or "stronger."

Given that international relations theory by itself cannot explain varying degrees of structural commitment, this book—much like Keohane, Sandler and Cauley, Martin, or Lake—argues that economic theories of organization can serve to overcome this indeterminacy. As with the creation of firms in economics, transaction costs can account for the types of international security arrangements countries choose.

What distinguishes this study from previous economic approaches is the way in which it operationalizes transaction costs. Relying on and extending Williamson's work, chapter 2 identifies four factors that determine the degree of transaction costs states confront. In addition to uncertainty and asset specificity, which Williamson emphasizes, technological developments and heterogeneity also influence transaction costs. Specifically, it is hypothesized that, given high threat, the more numerous and severe the transaction costs a state faces, the greater the likelihood it will seek firm structural guarantees to reduce these costs. Seriously threatened countries whose cooperation efforts are plagued by great uncertainty and the risks associated with asset-specific invest-ments, thus should strive for stronger commitments than seriously threatened countries whose transactions are solely plagued by the pres-ence of asset specificity. Furthermore, it is postulated that both high threat and high transaction costs are necessary to bring about a struc-turally binding security arrangement (they are separately necessary) but neither is sufficient (only jointly are they sufficient).

To test these propositions, this book focuses on security structures during the last years of the Napoleonic Wars, the period of the Congress of Vienna, and the post-1945 period with its contrasting security arrangements embodied in NATO and the EDC. In each of these peri-ods states reevaluated threat, reassessed the magnitude of transaction costs, and sought cooperative solutions to their security problems.

The cases scrutinized in chapters 3 through 6 show that states do indeed value their freedom of action, and hence are only willing to cur-tail their sovereignty when the benefits of doing so clearly outweigh the costs. Prior to Napoleon's overthrow, for instance, both the wartime nature of the alliances and relatively low transaction costs precluded more binding security arrangements. But following Napoleon's defeat, divergent patterns of commitment emerged. High transaction costs and the enormous potential power of France led the Swiss and the Germans to confederate. Countries that perceived a lesser threat—such as Austria, Prussia, Russia, and Britain—opted for informal alliances.

Much like the Napoleonic era, the post-1945 period demonstrates that the "bindingness" of security arrangements is determined by the mixture of threat and transaction costs in the international environment. Although the West Europeans—experiencing higher threat and higher transaction costs than the United States—would have preferred a more binding commitment, they hardly were in a position to dictate to the United States what form common security provisions should take. Thus, in the case of NATO, they initially had to settle for an arrangement approximating a traditional guarantee pact. Similarly, when the West-ern allies saw the need to reexamine the question of German rearma-ment in the wake of the Korean War, those that perceived the highest threat in combination with high transaction costs sought the most bind-ing security apparatus. Yet the EDC debates also make clear that these countries were only willing to curtail their freedom of action as long as the same conditions remained. Once the French perceived a reduction in Soviet threat, they withdrew their support for a very binding security arrangement and refused to ratify the EDC treaty (see Table 7.1).

The cases also shed light on the relative causal weight of the var-ious indicators of transaction costs. Of the four transaction-costs measures, the technological development of states seeking coopera-

TABLE 7.1
Threat and Transaction Costs Indicators

	Threat	Uncertainty	Technology	Heterogeneity	Asset Specificity	Symmetry
Alliance R & P	extreme	high	underdeveloped	high	low	yes
Alliance R, P, & AU	extreme	high	underdeveloped	high	low	yes
Quadruple Alliance	extreme	high	underdeveloped	high	low	no
German Confederation	high	high	underdeveloped	moderate	low	yes
Swiss Confederation	high	high	underdeveloped	high	high: site specificity	yes
Renewed Quadruple Alliance	moderate	low	underdeveloped	high	low	no
NATO	high	high	advanced	high	high: physical & human asset specificity	no
EDC	high	high	advanced	high	high: physical & human asset specificity	no

tion had the smallest effect on preferences for structural commitment. Communications and transportation technology advanced dramatically from Napoleon's time to the twentieth century, but there is no clear general impact on the preferred bindingness of security arrangements. In the early nineteenth century, underdeveloped technology did raise coordination costs, but it is clear that these costs were negligible compared to the allies' military expenditures. To the extent that a backward state of technology made it more difficult to detect undesirable behavior (as when Metternich's doublecross was aided by poor communications), technology did affect transactional risks. But, the case studies produced little evidence of any consistent relationship between underdeveloped technology and increased vulnerability to opportunism. The role of technology in raising the allies' cooperation costs—although slightly more important in the nineteenth than the twentieth century—was minor at best, when compared to other transaction costs indicators.

Cultural heterogeneity, high in all cases but one (the German confederation), led to calls for greater bindingness only fifty percent of the time. How can this inconsistency be explained? So far as cultural differences enhanced the need for language training, arbitration, or military standardization, they increased coordination costs, which were further exacerbated with each additional ally. But these costs, much like those resulting from an underdeveloped state of technology, were minor compared to the amount of money spent on troop provisions or armaments. Allies, based on this criterion alone, thus had no reason to curtail their autonomy substantially. Where cultural cleavages gave way to strong feelings of distrust (the Swiss and German cases, and the EDC), however, cooperation efforts were vulnerable to great transactional risks so that the allies, as predicted, voiced demands for structural bindingness. This finding is important. It confirms that it is the fear of being subjected to opportunism, rather than a sense of "weness" (as proponents of cultural arguments hold) that leads states to seek greater commitments.

The German case also makes clear that binding security structures are possible without highly specialized site, physical, or human ingredients. Asset specificity therefore is not a necessary condition for firm structural commitments. But the Swiss, NATO, and EDC cases show that transactions involving highly sophisticated assets do expose states to great risks. It is very difficult, if not impossible, to replace an ally possessing specific assets so that specialized components clearly increase the likelihood of substantial structural commitments.

The factor all binding security arrangements have in common is great uncertainty. Whenever states chose a binding arrangement (the

German and Swiss confederations), contemplated such action (the EDC), or when a subset of their number favored greater bindingness (NATO), a high degree of uncertainty was present which increased transactional risks—and therefore preferences for structural sophistication. This suggests that high uncertainty is important in bringing about firm structural commitments, and that in fact it may be a necessary condition for structural bindingness.

To summarize, the case studies show that the state of technology mattered the least in determining security choices. Heterogeneity was important some of the time, namely when severe cultural differences created strong distrust and higher transactional risks. High asset specificity and uncertainty, due to their direct link to opportunism, always played a crucial role in determining the degree of institutionalization. In other words, the cases demonstrate that transactional risks rather than coordination costs led to the need for binding security structures. The former were greatest in highly uncertain environments in which states distrusted each other and in which they had to rely on specific assets to enhance their security. Moreover, as the German case shows, great uncertainty and serious distrust may suffice by themselves to create demands for a confederation.

All of these observations depend, however, on symmetry. Only when allies shared symmetrically high perceptions of threat and transaction costs did binding security arrangements emerge (the Swiss and German confederations). Conversely, as the Quadruple Alliance, NATO, and the EDC reveal, asymmetry caused those countries confronting a lesser threat and fewer transactional risks to defend their freedom of action, and hence to reject a serious curtailment of their autonomy (see Table 7.2). But, even in those cases, knowledge of the actors' preferences tells us a great deal about the institutional compromises obtained. That is, although the relationship between actors' preferences and structural outcomes is not as close as when symmetry is given, a careful assessment of threat and transaction costs still sheds much light on the varying degrees of commitment sought.

Since, as discussed in the introduction, the theoretical framework laid out in this book has broad applicability to any voluntary curtailment of a state's freedom of action,[1] in the following, I demonstrate how the transaction costs model can be utilized to speculate about post–Cold War security developments. I then employ the model to account for integrative moves within the economic realm—the European Union. And, finally, examining movement from confederation to federation, I indicate how my framework may provide a first step toward making the entire process of evolution understandable in terms of theory.

TABLE 7.2
Threat and Transactional Risks

	Threat	Uncertainty	Technology	Heterogeneity	Asset Specificity	Symmetry
Alliance R & P	extreme	high risks	moderate risks	trust; small #; low risks	low risks	yes
Alliance R, P, & AU	extreme	high risks	moderate risks	trust; small #; low risks	low risks	yes
Quadruple Alliance	extreme	high risks	moderate risks	trust; small #; low risks	low risks	no
German Confederation	high	high risks	moderate risks	high distrust; large #; high risks	low risks	yes
Swiss Confederation	high	high risks	moderate risks	high distrust; large #; high risks	high risks	yes
Renewed Quadruple Alliance	moderate	low risks	moderate risks	trust; small #; low risks	low risks	no
NATO	high	high risks	low risks	moderate distrust; large #; moderate risks	high risks	no
EDC	high	high risks	low risks	high distrust; large #; high risks	high risks	no

TRANSACTION COSTS AND THE
NEW WORLD (DIS)ORDER

Due to dramatic changes in the former Soviet Union and Eastern Europe (the disintegration of the Soviet empire; the collapse of the Warsaw Pact; the restructuring of East European governments; German reunification) the international system currently is in a state of flux. The creation of new states and changes in relative power have necessarily generated a reevaluation of security needs and arrangements. Old and new states alike are reassessing the sources of threat and instability in the "New Europe" and the former Soviet Union. The changed international environment is thus likely to lead to the adjustment or replacement of extant security arrangements.

Since the rapidly changing international system, in many ways, resembles the two historical periods studied above, one should be able to make theoretically derived predictions about the present period of flux. Taking a closer look at the dramatic changes in the international environment recently witnessed, one should be able to ascertain what type of security structures one can expect to see in the near future. Or, focusing on security relations in the "New Europe," one should be able to establish whether the present combination of threat and transaction costs should lead to more binding security arrangements (formal security communities) or to less binding alliances among some states or the dissolution of alliances among others.

Clearly, different types of security arrangements can be envisioned in the "New Europe" and which type will be chosen, to a large extent, will depend on the level of perceived threat. In the following, three plausible scenarios will be outlined.

First, one could argue that, with the end of the Cold War and the disintegration of the Warsaw Pact, the threat emanating from the former Soviet Union has largely disappeared. This suggests that the rationale for NATO—to protect the West against encroachments from the East—is fading and that NATO might become obsolete. Absent any significant threat there should be no need for an Atlantic Alliance.[2]

Second, one could make the case that, although the immediate threat the Soviet Union and its former satellites posed has—as a result of the above mentioned changes in the international environment—decreased greatly, arms proliferation, ethnic conflicts, political instability, and economic hardships still give rise to security concerns.[3] What needs to be stressed is that the potential dangers lurking in the international environment affect the NATO countries differently. The United States, geographically far removed from the European continent, feels less threatened by ethnic strife in the former Yugoslavia or problems arising from failed political and economic systems in Eastern Europe or the former Soviet Union, and hence has little need for a binding security structure. The West Europeans, on the other hand, preceiving a greater threat, can be expected to continue their search for American security guarantees. However, they too should be protective of their freedom of action and stay clear of significantly binding structural commitments,[4] as long as they feel reasonably confident that present instabilities in Eastern Europe are unlikely to involve them in serious conflicts.[5]

One might expect the allies to continue to rely on NATO but adapt it to the changing international arena to preserve it as a "safety net."[6] In fact, recent institutional developments within the Atlantic Alliance—in NATO circles referred to as "internal" and "external" adaptation— appear to lend support to this position. In 1991, for instance, NATO adopted a New Strategic Concept, calling for significant cuts in military expenditures and improvements in flexibility, adaptability, and mobility to adjust to its new security challenges.[7] During the same year the allies gave rise to a North Atlantic Cooperation Council (NACC) consisting of NATO members, the states of Central and Eastern Europe, and the former Soviet Union to bring about a forum for consultation and coop- eration that would allow them to iron out their differences. In 1994, NATO extended an invitation to other Conference on Security and Cooperation (CSCE) countries to join the NACC members in a Partner- ship for Peace (PfP) to promote greater "interoperability." And NATO gave rise to a Combined Joint Task Force (CJTF) that would allow the Europeans to borrow highly specialized U.S. military equipment for mis- sions the Americans do not want to get involved in.[8]

At the same time the Europeans are taking measures to demonstrate their willingness to do more for their own defense. For example, they already have created a satellite center in Torrejon, Spain, and are nego- tiating the use of Ukranian airlift capabilities.[9] Since the mid-1990s, there also has been increased talk about a European security and defense identity (ESDI),[10] a stronger European pillar within the Atlantic Alliance, and greater burden-sharing.[11] The goal is not to duplicate costly NATO assets, but to complement them and further institutionalize U.S.-Euro- pean relations to reduce transaction costs and risks.[12]

Of all the "preventive maintenance" techniques devised by the West- ern powers to enhance their security, the issue of NATO enlargement, however, received the most attention.[13] As the theoretical framework developed in this book predicts, the country most troubled by the possi- bility of renewed instability in Eastern Europe, Germany, sought further safeguards. Convinced that its closest neighbors would have to be firmly entrenched in the Western camp, Germany persuaded its allies to extend an invitation to Poland, Hungary, and the Czech Republic to join NATO.

Yet, from the outset, it was understood that NATO membership would have to be strictly controlled. Having created a "buffer zone" with the most recent NATO entrants, absent any significant change in threat, there is little reason to believe that additional countries will be asked to join the alliance in the near future—even though for diplomatic reasons NATO speaks of an "open door" policy. On the contrary, since most East European states would be consumers rather than net producers of security, opening NATO to such candidates at this time would only exacerbate transaction costs further. And, given the unanimity rule, it is feared that the sheer number of allies would paralyze decision-making.

But by far the most important reason for restricting NATO enlargement was the need to keep damage to Russian-Western relations to a minimum. In fact, to appease Russia and to signal benevolent intentions the NATO countries proposed further cooperation in the form of a Founding Act.[14] The treaty calls for the creation of a NATO-Russia Permanent Joint Council that "will provide a mechanism for consultations, coordination and . . . , where appropriate, for joint decisions and joint action."[15] At the same time, however, the treaty leaves no doubt that both sides are eager to protect their freedom of action. The Founding Act states explicitly that neither Russia nor NATO has the right to veto actions of the other.

Finally, a third scenario assumes that the Western allies still feel seriously threatened and that the West Europeans, in particular, are deeply concerned about the high uncertainty surrounding the behavior of the Soviet successor states.[16] Will political and economic reforms be successful and bring stability to this region?[17] Or will nationalists regain power and reinstate authoritarian governments?[18] Will the Russians adhere to armament agreements or are they trying to buy time and strengthen their economy to act opportunistically later?

Given that the level of threat is perceived to be high one would expect the West Europeans to seek a strong military commitment from the United States, while, simultaneously, doing everything in their own power to enhance their security. To determine the exact nature of the allies' security provisions one once again would have to examine the extent to which cooperation efforts would be plagued by transaction costs.

If one were to speculate one might guess that transaction costs would be substantial. In addition to uncertainties surrounding the behavior of the former Soviet Republics, it is difficult to know what policies former Soviet satellite states in Eastern Europe are likely to pursue. Will they be firmly entrenched in the Western camp? Or might at least some of them turn their attention to the East, if lured by attractive offers?

Even if the East Europeans were to seek cooperation with the West, the allies' varied cultural backgrounds almost certainly would increase transaction costs significantly. More than forty years of animosity between East and West can be expected to have sown feelings of distrust that are unlikely to disappear overnight. Moreover, the sheer task of coordinating military activities among a large number of allies who do not share a native language, who possess vastly different military equipment, and who have received radically different military training, promises to be costly.

Security matters, however, are not decided in a vacuum but in conjunction with other political and economic issues. Particularly in the European case, as will be seen below, great progress has been made regarding economic integration so that cooperative structures are already in place that—provided they are not issue-specific so that their benefits cannot be transferred to other domains—should reduce the allies' transaction costs. Hence, even if the allies felt seriously threatened, based on a cost-benefit analysis there should be no need for a very binding security arrangement like a confederation. What the Europeans might do is to make use of an already existing security arrangement, NATO, but coordinate their military activities much more closely within this security apparatus, possibly by creating a strong "European pillar" within the Atlantic Alliance.[19]

In short, the three scenarios demonstrate that the transaction costs model allows one to generate theoretically derived predictions regarding European security relations. To determine which security provisions are most likely a careful analysis of the magnitude of threat and transaction costs would be needed. Absent such a study one can merely speculate that in an anarchic world in which states compete for scarce resources the first scenario appears too optimistic, and that, given the large discrepancy in military capabilities among the European countries, a security structure on the binding end of the continuum that presumes symmetrically high assessments of threat and transaction costs seems implausible.

TRANSACTION COSTS AND
EUROPEAN ECONOMIC INTEGRATION

Although employed to account for security choices in this book so far, the transaction costs argument about bindingness also applies to the economic realm. More specifically, one can envision a continuum of cooperative economic arrangements with *general trade treaties* on the less binding side of the continuum and *economic confederations* on the more binding side (See Figure 7.1). A general trade treaty entails some measure of commitment to remove some of the trade impediments between the parties involved in the agreement. A confederation, on the other hand, as already described, requires a much greater commitment in that the members of such an arrangement have to curtail aspects of their sovereignty substantially. Or, in other words, a confederation entails a much more formal relationship in which countries pledge to go far beyond the removal of tariffs and, in fact, agree to create a sophisticated structural apparatus to facilitate the removal of nontariff barriers.

As in the security realm, countries can choose among numerous economic arrangements that require different degrees of commitments and that entail the surrender of different degrees of freedom of action, that is, countries have more than just two choices. For instance, several countries can reach an agreement to create a free trade area—make the commitment to eliminate all tariffs among member states, while retaining tariffs against nonmembers. A good example is provided by the European Free Trade Association (EFTA), which, when it was founded in 1960, sought to bring about free trade with a minimum of commitment. EFTA exclusively concerned itself with the removal of restrictions on trade (excepting agricultural products), permitted its members to set their own tariffs concerning nonmembers, and kept institutionalization to a minimum.[20]

Alternatively, countries can opt for a more binding economic arrangement like a *customs union*. In this case, in addition to removing internal barriers to trade, countries would also adopt a common exter-

FIGURE 7.1
Continuum of Cooperative Economic Arrangements

general trade agreement	free trade area (EFTA)	(NAFTA)	customs union	common market (EC →)	economic confederation

freedom of action , sovereignty, autonomy, maneuverability decrease

costs of exiting the arrangement increase

likelihood of defection decreases

arrangements become more binding

nal tariff.[21] Part I of the Treaty of Rome, for instance, deals with the formation of a customs union[22] and provides a strict time frame within which the members of the European Economic Community (EEC) must have reduced internal tariffs, eliminated quantitative trade restrictions, and established uniform external tariffs.[23] Moreover, the EEC differs markedly from EFTA in that, from the outset, the EEC was much more institutionalized to realize its more ambitious goals. A Commission, for example, is responsible for negotiating external tariffs, overseeing the implementation of agreed upon tariffs and quotas, making agricultural policy, and so on. Additional governing institutions include a Council of Ministers, a Court of Justice, and an Assembly—each with clearly specified functions.[24]

Furthermore, hybrids exist such as the much fought over North American Free Trade Association (NAFTA). Like EFTA it seeks to eliminate barriers to trade and facilitate the cross-border movement of goods and services between members, yet NAFTA's objectives are more comprehensive. For instance, NAFTA also covers the agricultural sector (calling for the immediate removal of 57 percent of trade barriers in this area), contains more elaborate investment policies, and specifies more effective procedures for the implementation and the resolution of disputes by prescribing the creation of a Free Trade Commission.[25] Nevertheless, NAFTA falls short of being a customs union in that it lacks a common external tariff as well as the greater institutional sophistication of the more integrated customs union.

Similar to the military realm where the level of threat is instrumental in determining the nature and the degree of states' commitment, in the economic realm, the degree of competition (external economic threat) is important in determining what kind of commitment countries are willing to make to each other.[26] If there is little external threat, and thus countries are viable with respect to the competition they face, there is no need to surrender sovereignty. On the other hand, if competition is high, the outcomes of market-mediated interaction are likely to be suboptimal so that one would expect states to opt for binding economic arrangements that would give them greater assurances.[27] (For a summary of states' institutional choices in the economic realm, see Table 7.3.)

Yet, as in the case of security affairs, all international relations theory can explain is that competition may lead to the creation of cooperative economic structures, it cannot specify what these structures will look like. Put differently, international relations theory, by itself, cannot account for different gradations of bindingness. Again, one needs a theoretical framework that makes it possible to link hierarchical governance structures to the issue of providing protection against competition. That is, one needs to know the exact relationship between various

TABLE 7.3
Summary of the Determinants of
States' Choices in the Economic Realm

		Level of Competition	
		Low	*High*
Transaction Costs	*Low*	No cooperation	Formal, more binding institutions
	High	Informal, weakly binding institutions	Structurally sophisticated, strongly binding institutions

hierarchical arrangements and increased economic security. Without such knowledge, international relations theory, at best, suggests that a high level of competition (economic threat) may be necessary for countries to create a binding economic arrangement, but that high competition is not sufficient.

To test the above propositions this study once more returns to the post-1945 period. Examining economic developments it sketches how an optimal size argument faces problems accounting for recent integrative moves within the European Community (since Maastricht referred to as the European Union) and then outlines how a transaction costs approach fares much better.

Following World War II the European powers felt militarily threatened by the Soviets, but also found themselves economically "dwarfed" by the United States and the USSR, who "had expanded their internal markets during the previous one hundred years through the development of their own 'backyards'."[28] This serious economic competition caused the Europeans to seek cooperation and, as was the case in the military realm, those countries that experienced the greatest threat sought more binding arrangements than countries that felt less threatened.

Great Britain, due to its Commonwealth ties, was less vulnerable to economic competition than the other European countries. Thus, the British saw no need to surrender a substantial amount of their sovereignty to bring about a binding economic arrangement and chose to create a free-trade area with Sweden, Switzerland, Denmark, Norway, Portugal, and Austria.[29]

Less fortunate than the British in that they felt the shock of economic exposure much more severely, France, Germany, Italy, and the Benelux countries, on March 25, 1957, signed the Treaty of Rome to establish a common market. That is, in addition to removing internal tariffs, the member states of the European Economic Community (EEC) vowed to set common external tariffs (create a customs union), and contracted to bring about the free movement of capital, labor, and other factors of production. Thus, a Dutch financier, for instance, would be able to invest in France on the same terms as a French financier, or a German autoworker would be subject to the same working conditions in Italy as his/her Italian counterpart.

Studying European economic developments since the founding of the EEC in 1957 one finds that, as competition increased, demands for greater integration were voiced much more frequently and the structure of the EEC began to change. The membership of the organization more than doubled. The four main organs (Council of Ministers, Commission, Parliament, and Court of Justice) became more institutionalized.[30] And, in the mid-1980s, the Commission drafted a White Paper identifying approximately three hundred measures that would have to be taken to complete an internal market by the end of 1992.

To account for these developments proponents of an optimal size approach like Timothy Devinney and William Hightower typically suggest that the economies of scale for modern industrial high-tech firms require markets of a certain size.[31] The United States—by virtue of its sheer size—has a built-in advantage and the Japanese have solved their market problem by functioning as an export platform to an open American economy. To remain competitive, the Europeans have to create comparable firms and a comparable market.

Technically, European economic integration (the creation of a common external tariff and the reduction of internal tariffs) should have created an internal market and the institutional backdrop for the pursuit of the scale economies extant in modern production. However, what one finds in the European case is that economies of scale were not realized because of the existence of transaction costs. The residue of incongruent domestic policies and practices (nontariff barriers) prevented European firms from making use of scale economies. Hence, to remedy this problem, that is, to do away with transaction costs that obstruct the creation of a truly integrated market, the Europeans developed plans for "Europe 1992" that entail the harmonization of a range of practices that affect competitiveness and mobility. Since the founding of the European Economic Community,[32] with each new member (Britain, Denmark, and Ireland were added in 1973; Greece in 1981; Portugal and Spain in 1986; and Austria, Sweden, and Finland in 1995) and every new task, cooperation costs increased. And, in today's high-tech world where transactions often entail specific assets (as, for instance, in the aerospace industry), this trend is likely to continue by increasing behavioral uncertainties and the risk of opportunistic behavior.[33] Thus, as the European Union's institutional machinery proves less and less capable of coping with the numerous demands placed upon it—that is, as an ever greater amount of information needs to be processed, as frequent disputes between members require more sophisticated arbitration mechanisms, and as new voting procedures become necessary to prevent stalemate, greater centralization has to be achieved to internalize transaction costs.[34]

Economies of scale proponents, focusing strictly on size and not on the degree of institutionalization, fail to explain the integrative moves associated with Europe 1992. A transaction costs approach on the other hand, dealing with structural commitments, does shed light on why getting rid of internal tariffs and establishing a common external tariff was not enough to realize economies of scale in Europe, and hence why the elimination of nontariff barriers (as specified in the White Paper) was so important.[35]

As more and more countries seek membership in the European Union (E.U.) and place additional demands on its institutions, the Europeans can be expected to curtail their freedom of action even further to be able to cope with the high transaction costs they then are likely to confront.[36] Or, in other words, one might speculate that the EU will continue to become stronger and more centralized so that it can internalize its rapidly growing transaction costs.

Yet, recently, we have also been reminded that countries treasure their sovereignty and do not curtail their freedom of action easily.[37] The reaction to the Maastricht Treaty (signed in February 1992), calling for the further integration of macroeconomic policies in Europe (a single European currency, a common foreign and security policy, the abolition of frontier controls, a common immigration policy) is a clear affirmation of the importance of sovereignty. In this case, the proponents of greater European institutionalization (France, Italy, and the Benelux countries) suffered a major setback. In a first referendum, Denmark refused to ratify the treaty. Then, voting for a second time, the Danes decided to ratify parts of the treaty, yet, together with the British, exempted themselves from the adoption of other parts.

It is clear that progress toward greater European integration in the security realm, presently, is stalled. Since, due to the reduction in threat brought about by the end of the Cold War, there is no security basis for further integration, there is little movement toward a common foreign and security policy—as could be witnessed in Bosnia and, most recently,

Kosovo.[38] Hence, Europe is not a "superpower in the making," individual EU members maintain a substantial amount of their sovereignty, and there is no widespread desire for a United States of Europe.

While excessively ambitious visions of some integrationists are being left behind, those elements of European integration promising a reduction in transaction costs are still being pursued vigorously. Since the formulation of the White Paper most of the directives outlined have been implemented so that there are substantially fewer nontariff barriers to trade. Moreover, in the 1990s the EU member-states worked hard to meet a variety of convergence criteria[39] to bring about a monetary union by January 1, 1999, that would reduce exchange rate risks and eliminate unnecessary coordination costs. And in the economic realm decision-making is increasingly being pooled and transferred to the EU level.[40]

These recent EU developments have important implications for our understanding of international institutions and of a transaction costs model of international hierarchy. The latest integrative moves lend support to the position that institutions are developed at the level of the transaction costs problem. Thus, states can create or intensify organizational ties in one issue area (for instance economics), while leaving other domains (such as security) virtually untouched.

TRANSACTION COSTS AND FURTHER INTEGRATION: FROM CONFEDERATION TO FEDERATION

If one were to push the transaction costs argument one step further, one could hypothesize that in situations where cooperative arrangements are not sufficiently centralized to deal with the high transaction costs they face there might be a "spillover" from a confederation to a federation. Clearly, federal states such as Switzerland (1848), Germany (1871), and the United States (1787) began as confederations and evolved to federations when these countries were confronted with serious problems that raised their transaction costs. In each case one detects similar developments prior to the creation of a federation that made it imperative for these countries to cross the threshold from a confederation to a federation.

If one examines the Swiss case, for example, one finds that the Diet was capable of maintaining order only until it was confronted with serious internal challenges. After 1830, when widespread agitation developed and old differences between liberals and conservatives came to the forefront again, the Diet increasingly experienced problems settling conflicts between the feuding parties. And it was equally unsuccessful in its arbitration attempts between Protestants and Catholics. In fact, the Diet could not prevent the creation of separate cantonal leagues such as the Sonderbund (consisting of seven cantons that sought to defend the rights of Catholics), nor could it avert war between the cantons.[41]

The German Bund successfully suppressed internal disorder until 1848 when massive upheaval began to undermine its power. At that point a national constituent assembly was summoned to draft a new constitution that was to enhance the powers of the Bund, but this as well as other attempts at reform failed. The Bund then tried to arrest a power struggle between Austria and Prussia, but its mediation efforts could not prevent a seven weeks' war (1866) during which Austria was defeated. In 1867 the German Bund was replaced by the North German Bund, which, when it was extended to the whole of non-Austrian Germany in 1871, became the foundation of the German Empire.[42]

In the United States the Articles of Confederation were discarded in 1787 and replaced by the Constitution, which gave rise to a stronger central government. What accounts for this dramatic change? First, under the Articles of Confederation Congress lacked military power, and thus "as a confederation, the United States would always live in fear of foreign influence, conquest, and dismemberment."[43] Second, Congress lacked judicial power and hence could not decide disputes between state governments.[44] Finally, Congress lacked an "independent source of revenue," which made it impossible to pay foreign debts and, in the long run, to avoid armed conflict.[45]

In short, these three cases suggest that, when confronted with serious internal or external problems that increase their transaction costs, confederations give way to federations.[46] Or, in other words, if confederations are insufficiently centralized to deal with the high transaction costs they encounter (due to high uncertainty, distrust, an increased need for costly arbitration, or military cooperation), then one would expect these confederations to be replaced by political structures better equipped to handle these tasks. Put differently still, a decision to confederate precedes that of federation, and movement toward federation presumes the continued existence of those factors that gave rise to the confederation as well as the failure of the confederation to perform adequately. Hence, it is not the *existence* of cooperative structures in one area that makes greater integration in another area more likely, as integrationists and functionalists argue. On the contrary, it is the *inadequacy* (benefits cannot be transferred) or *failure* (arrangements are insufficiently centralized) of existing structures that forces countries to adopt even tighter forms of cooperation. In a final analysis it is not "habits of cooperation" that lead to greater integration but the inability of states to solve the problems they confront with the level of integration they have achieved up to that point.

HIERARCHY AMIDST ANARCHY:
WHERE TO GO FROM HERE?

This book has shown that self-interested actors create large-scale organizations (security arrangements, economic structures, etc.) to reduce threat (economic competition) and to internalize transaction costs that otherwise would plague their exchanges. Time and again states voluntarily curtail their freedom of action to bring about cooperative structures that enhance their security or economic well-being.

Based on the above analysis there is reason to believe that the same variables that allow us to account for different degrees of institutionalization are also instrumental in explaining evolutionary consequences of cooperation. Contrary to rival explanations that take an inductive approach to make sense of institutional change, however, the theoretical framework developed here allows us to deduce why institutions develop in a particular manner. That is, rather than to work from the end result backward, as scholars like Puchala, Hopkins, or Young do,[47] a focus on threat and transaction costs makes it possible to generate hypotheses concerning institutional change prior to the actual event.[48]

Even though threat and transaction costs are likely to remain important factors in explaining how cooperative international arrangements evolve, it stands to reason that additional variables may need to be looked at to get a better handle on the complex process of institutional change. Only a careful study will be able to determine which factors provide fruitful extensions of the evolutionary model sketched above. If one were to guess, "organizational costs," "institutional inertia," and the "frequency of interactions among international actors" might play a crucial role in determining how hierachical arrangements develop over time.

As Trachtman correctly points out, however, regardless of whether we are interested in explaining the creation or evolution of cooperative international structures, we do need to improve the operationalization of our core variables.[49] Since, as explained in chapter 2, there is no common metric for transaction costs, the concept remains difficult to measure and we will not get around using proxies. But what we can do is refine our indicators of asset specificity, uncertainty, and so forth, and generate new hypotheses that then can be subjected to further empirical research.

Given that the international system is in a state of flux and that numerous countries are reevaluating their security provisions and economic competitiveness, we are likely to see the adjustment or replacement of extant international institutional arrangements (and hence new test cases for a transaction costs study). Clearly, there are a number of conceivable developments. Whether we will see cooperation or conflict, and the magnitude of either, only time will tell. In the end, all we can hope for is that the self-interest of states will lead them toward a cooperative path, that is, that states will continue to create international institutions to mitigate the effects of anarchy.

NOTES

CHAPTER 1

1. Portions of this chapter first appeared as "Hierarchy amidst Anarchy: A Transaction Costs Approach to International Security Cooperation," *International Studies Quarterly* 41 (1997): 321–40, and are reprinted here with the permission of Blackwell Publishers.

2. This study subsumes the work of neorealists and structural realists in the broad category of "realism" since it is interested in laying out the main ideas of realist thought rather than to focus on the work of individual scholars.

3. See John Mearsheimer, "Back to the Future: Instability in Europe after the Cold War," reprinted in Sean Lynn-Jones, ed., *The Cold War and After: Prospects for Peace* (Cambridge: The MIT Press, 1991), pp. 141–92.

4. See Kenneth Waltz, "The Emerging Structure of International Politics," *International Security* 18.2 (1993): 44–79. Note that Waltz argues that nuclear weapons make up for some of the stability that will be lost in the transition from bipolarity to multipolarity, yet that nuclear weapons do not eliminate the importance of balancing behavior.

5. For an excellent summary of the debate between neorealists and neoliberal institutionalists, see David Baldwin, ed., *Neorealism and Neoliberalism: The Contemporary Debate* (New York: Columbia University Press, 1993).

6. See Robert Keohane, "International Liberalism Reconsidered," in John Dunn, ed., *The Economic Limits to Modern Politics* (Cambridge: Cambridge University Press, 1990), pp. 165–94. Also see Charles Lipson, "International Cooperation in Economic and Security Affairs," *World Politics* 37 (October 1984): 1–23.

7. Note that this study refrains from further categorizing scholarly writings on international institutions since such a distinction is unneccessary for the argument put forth here. That is, functionalists, neofunctionalists, transactionalists, interdependence theorists, and others, are all lumped into one category of "institutionalists." For a study that pays close attention to differences between these schools, see Clive Archer, *International Organizations* (New York: Routledge, 1992), chapter 3.

8. See David Mitrany, *A Working Peace System* (Chicago: Quadrangle Books, 1966).

9. Edward Morse, "The Transformation of Foreign Policies: Modernization, Interdependence, and Externalization," *World Politics* 22 (April 1970): 371–92.

10. See Robert Keohane, *After Hegemony: Cooperation and Discord in the World Political Economy* (Princeton: Princeton University Press, 1984).

11. Stephen Krasner, ed., *International Regimes* (Ithaca: Cornell University Press, 1983). Recently, numerous scholars also examined multilateralism as a form of organization. For special issues on multilateralism, see *International Journal* 45 (Autumn 1990); and *International Organization* 46.3 (Summer 1992). Also see Lisa Martin, "Interests, Power, and Multilateralism," *International Organization* 46.4 (Autumn 1992): 765–92; and John Ruggie, ed., *Multilateralism Matters: The Theory and Praxis of an Institutional Form* (New York: Columbia University Press, 1993).

12. For a thought-provoking discussion of how an autonomous multicentric world has emerged to compete with the state-centric world, see James Rosenau, *Turbulence in World Politics: A Theory of Change and Continuity* (Princeton: Princeton University Press, 1990).

13. For further definitions of alliances, see Stephen Walt, *The Origins of Alliances* (Ithaca: Cornell University Press, 1987), p. 1; Klaus Knorr, ed., *Historical Dimensions of National Security Problems* (Lawrence: University Press of Kansas, 1976), p. 227; Philip Burgess and David Moore, "Inter-Nation Alliances: An Inventory and Appraisal of Propositions," *Political Science Annual* 3 (1972): 351; Ole Holsti, Terrence Hopmann, and John Sullivan, *Unity and Disintegration in International Alliances* (New York: Wiley, 1973), p. 4. For a distinction between alliances and ententes, see Robert Kann, "Alliances Versus Ententes," *World Politics* 28.4 (1976): 611–21. Also see Charles Lipson, "Why Are Some International Agreements Informal?" *International Organization* 45 (1991). Note that I subsume ententes, guarantee pacts, consultation pacts, and the like, in the broad category of alliances and then merely differentiate among more flexible, informal relationships and more structured, formal relationships within alliances. This conceptualization sets me apart from the vast majority of scholars who emphasize *verbal* or *rhetorical* commitments and their loopholes, instead of *structural* commitments and the assurances the latter provide.

14. For a discussion of the term "union of states," see Murray Forsyth, *Unions of States: The Theory and Practice of Confederation* (New York: Leicester University Press, 1981), pp. 1, 7, 206. Note that Forsyth uses the terms "confederation" and "union" interchangeably.

15. Ibid., p. 16, where Forsyth argues that a confederation can be viewed as "a contract between equals to act henceforth as one." For an interesting study that shows that adherence to alliance commitments is greatest when the commitments are considered binding by prevailing international norms ("pacta sunt servanda"), see Charles Kegley and Gregory Raymond, "Alliance Norms and War: A New Piece in an Old Puzzle," *International Studies Quarterly* 26.4 (1992): 572–95.

16. Good examples of federations are Switzerland after 1848 or Canada since 1867.

17. Forsyth (1981), p. 2.

18. For an interesting discussion of the most fundamental differences between interstate and intrastate relations, see ibid., pp. 10–16. Also see Karl Deutsch et al., *Political Community and the North Atlantic Area: International Organizations in the Light of Historical Experience* (Princeton: Princeton Uni-

versity Press, 1957), p. 6, who distinguish between an *amalgamated* security community that entails the "formal merger of two or more previously independent units into a single larger unit" and a *pluralistic* security community that "retains the legal independence of separate governments." For a distinction between "alliances," "protectorates," "informal empires," and "empires," see David Lake, "Anarchy, Hierarchy, and the Variety of International Relations," *International Organization* 50.1 (Winter 1996): 1–33; and, *Entangling Relations: American Foreign Policy in Its Century* (Princeton: Princeton University Press, 1999), especially pp. 17, 27–31. Note that Lake, for the most part, focuses on "control" and "power asymmetries" and largely discusses situations in which one party gains greater decision-making authority over another (1999, p. 9). Instead of examining mutually advantages relationships, where parties voluntarily curtail their autonomy and delegate authority to a cooperative structure that benefits all, he emphasizes "subordination" and "domination." In fact, according to his model, states comparable in power do not bring about binding security structures, but ally. Hence, despite efforts to stress "the voluntary compliance of the subordinate party" (p. 10), the security relationships examined by him are mostly about control and coercion. Either the dominant party offers a "compensation package" that persuades the subordinate party not to break the relationship (p.61), or cooperation takes place "in the shadow of power" (see Robert Powell, *In the Shadow of Power: States and Strategies in International Politics* [Princeton: Princeton University Press, 1999]; cited in Lake, 1999, p. 266).

19. Note that, as Emanuel Adler and Michael Barnett in "Security Communities" (paper presented at the annual meeting of the American Political Science Association, September 1–4, 1994) correctly point out, security communities can take various forms, and hence, deserve careful scrutiny. Although "a security community does not necessitate a formal military alliance or military integration," we are told, it is "quite likely that some sort of security association is constructed" (pp. 61–62), which often entails a high level of integration.

20. A "concert," like the Concert of Europe following the Napoleonic Wars, for instance, provides an example of an informal security community that allowed the major powers to coordinate their foreign policies. Absent any permanent institutions, decisions were made by engaging in informal negotiations. For a more detailed discussion of concerts, see Charles Kupchan, "The Case of Collective Security," in George Downs, ed., *Collective Security Beyond the Cold War* (Ann Arbor: University of Michigan Press, 1994), pp. 41–67; and Charles Lipson, "Is the Future of Collective Security Like the Past?" in Downs (1994): 105–31.

21. Todd Sandler and John Forbes, "Burden Sharing, Strategy, and the Design of NATO," *Economic Inquiry* 18 (July 1980): 425–44.

22. Todd Sandler and Jon Cauley, "The Design of Supranational Structures," *International Studies Quarterly* 21.2 (June 1977): 263–64.

23. See Bruce Russet, "Components of an Operational Theory of International Alliance Formation," *Journal of Conflict Resolution* 12 (1968): 285–301. Hans Morgenthau, *Politics among Nations*, 5th ed. (New York: Knopf, 1973); and Ole Holsti, Terrence Hopmann, and John Sullivan, *Unity and Disintegra-*

tion in International Alliances (New York: Wiley, 1973). For a more recent study that looks at the "choice between unilateralism and cooperation, and among alternative forms of security cooperation," see Lake (1999, p. 9). However, as explained in note 18, in his model the dominant power seems to be the only one in a position to choose among different security structures—the weaker party is subjected to control and coercion.

24. Michael Barnett and Jack Levy, "Domestic Sources of Alliances and Alignments: The Case of Egypt, 1962–73," *International Organization* 45.3 (Summer 1991): 368–95.

25. See Michael Altfeld "The Decision to Ally: A Theory and Test," *The Western Political Quarterly* 37.4 (1984): 523–44; and James Morrow, "Alliances and Asymmetry: An Alternative to the Capability Aggression Model of Alliances," *American Journal of Political Science* 35.4 (November 1991): 904–33, who distinguishes between symmetric and asymmetric alliances.

26. See Glenn Snyder, "The Security Dilemma in Alliance Politics," *World Politics* 36.4 (1984): 461–95.

27. James Morrow, "Alliances, Credibility, and Peacetime Costs," *Journal of Conflict Resolution* 38.2 (June 1994): 270–97.

28. See Lisa Martin, "The Rational State Choice of Multilateralism," in John Ruggie, ed., *Multilateralism Matters: The Theory and Praxis of an Institutional Form* (New York: Columbia University Press, 1993), pp. 91–121.

29. Ibid., p. 117.

30. See Geoffrey Garrett, "International Cooperation and Institutional Choice: The European Community's Internal Market," in Ruggie (1993), p. 366.

31. For a summary of these scholars' writings on confederations, see Forsyth (1981), chapter 1.

32. See Sandler and Cauley (1977).

33. See Albert Breton and Anthony Scott, *The Economic Constitution of Federal States* (Toronto: University of Toronto Press, 1978).

34. See Sandler and Forbes (1980).

35. See Steve Weber, "Shaping the Postwar Balance of Power: Multilateralism in NATO," in Ruggie (1993), pp. 233–92.

36. Note that some British writers on international society assume hierarchy instead of anarchy. For more detail on this position, see Barry Buzan, "From International System to International Society: Structural Realism and Regime Theory Meet the English School," *International Organization* 47.3 (1993): 327–52; and Barry Buzan, Charles Jones, and Richard Little, *The Logic of Anarchy: Neorealism to Structural Realism* (New York: Columbia University Press, 1993). Also see John Ruggie, "Continuity and Transformation in the World Polity: Toward a Neorealist Synthesis," *World Politics* 35 (January 1983): 261–85; Richard Ashley, "The Poverty of Neorealism," *International Organization* 38 (Spring 1984): 225–86; and Nicholas Onuf, *World of Our Making: Rules and Rule in Social Theory and International Relations* (Columbia: University of South Carolina Press, 1989).

37. Staying within the realist tradition states are being treated as black boxes, that is, political debates within individual nation-states are not being

examined. For a more detailed defense of this position, see Bruce Bueno de Mesquita, "Risk, Power Distributions, and the Likelihood of War," *International Studies Quarterly* 25.4 (Dec. 1981): 543, who argues that treating states as "unitary" actors when security issues are concerned is a "reasonable assumption" and that this assumption "impl[ies] a fair degree of homogeneity of preferences."

38. See Alexander Wendt, "Constructing International Politics," *International Security* 20.1 (Summer 1995): 71. For a study that addresses similar ontological issues with respect to domestic political institutions, see William Clark, "Agents and Structures: Two Views of Preferences, Two Views of Institutions," *International Studies Quarterly* 42.2 (1998): 245–70.

39. Ibid. Also see "Anarchy Is What States Make of It: The Social Construction of Power Politics," *International Organization* 46.2 (Spring 1992): 391–425; and "Collective Identity Formation and the International State," *American Political Science Review* 88.2 (June 1994): 384–96.

40. See David Dessler, "What's at Stake in the Agent-Structure Debate?" *International Organization* 43.3 (Summer 1989): 467.

41. Given that the constructivist literature is quite large, a few examples of scholarship in this area have to suffice. For instance, see Adler and Barnett, who in "Security Communities" argue for abandoning a "rationalistic" model in favor of a "sociological" model. For a historical account of constructivism, see Timothy Dunne, "The Social Construction of International Society," *European Journal of International Relations* 1.3 (September 1995): 367–89. For a focus on norms, see Audie Klotz, "Norms Reconstituting Interests: Global Racial Equality and U.S. Sanctions against South Africa," *International Organization* 49.3 (Summer 1995): 451–78; *Norms in International Relations: The Struggle against Apartheid* (Ithaca: Cornell University Press, 1995); Friedrich Kratochwil, *Rules, Norms, and Decisions: On the Conditions of Practical and Legal Reasoning in International Relations and Domestic Affairs* (Cambridge: Cambridge University Press, 1989); Jeffrey Legro, *Cooperation under Fire: Anglo-German Restraint during World War II* (Ithaca: Cornell University Press, 1995); "Which Norms Matter? Revisiting the Failure of Internationalism," *International Organization* 51 (1997): 31–63; and Martha Finnemore and Kathryn Sikkink, "International Norms Dynamics and Political Change," *International Organization* 52.4 (1998): 887–917. On ideas, see Thomas Risse-Kappen, "Ideas Do Not Float Freely: Transnational Coalitions, Domestic Structures, and the End of the Cold War," *International Organization* 48.2 (Spring 1994): 185–214, and especially footnote 1 for a summary of the growing body of literature on ideas. For an interesting discussion of rules, see Onuf (1989); and on learning, see Jack Levy, "Learning and Foreign Policy: Sweeping a Conceptual Minefield," *International Organization* 48.2 (Spring 1994): 279–312, as well as George Breslauer and Philip Tetlock, eds., *Learning in U.S. and Soviet Foreign Policy* (Boulder, Colo.: Westview Press, 1991). For a sociological view on the politics of national security, see Peter Katzenstein, ed., *The Culture of National Security: Norms and Identity in World Politics* (New York: Columbia University Press, 1996). And, for a more recent discussion of constructivism, see Jeffrey Checkel, "The Constructivist Turn in International Relations Theory," *World Politics* 50 (1998): 324–48.

42. See Waltz (1979), p. 91.

43. For instance, see Helen Milner, "The Assumption of Anarchy in International Relations Theory," in Baldwin (1993), p. 143, who argues that "a more fruitful way to understand the international system is one that combines anarchy and interdependence."

44. See Morgenthau (1973) and Waltz (1979). Note that Wendt (1992) takes issue with the pessimistic view of realists. He insists that self-help does not logically follow from anarchy and that "[i]f states find themselves in a self-help system, this is because their practices made it that way" (p. 407). Jonathan Mercer, "Anarchy and Identity," *International Organization* 49.2 (Spring 1995): 251, disagrees with both realists (who deduce states' interests from structural factors) and constructivists (who deduce interests from social factors), and instead, focuses on cognition (social identity theory) to show that self-help is a "consequence of intergroup relations in anarchy."

45. See Joseph Grieco, "Understanding the Problem of International Cooperation: The Limits of Neoliberal Institutionalism and the Future of Realist Theory," in Baldwin (1993), p. 315.

46. See Arthur Stein, *Why Nations Cooperate: Circumstance and Choice in International Relations* (Ithaca: Cornell University Press, 1990), p. 151; and "Disequilibrium and Equilibrium Theory: Explaining War in a Theory of Peace, Explaining Alliances in a Theory of Autonomy" (paper presented at the Annual Meeting of the American Political Science Association, Washington, D.C., September 5, 1993).

47. For an interesting study of the conditions that promote or impede international cooperation, see Celeste Wallander, *Mortal Friends, Best Enemies: German-Russian Cooperation after the Cold War* (Ithaca: Cornell University Press, 1999). Also see Richard Rosecrance and Arthur Stein, eds., *The Domestic Bases of Grand Strategy* (Ithaca: Cornell University Press, 1993); and William Long, *Economic Incentives and Bilateral Cooperation* (Ann Arbor: University of Michigan Press, 1996).

48. It is useful to distinguish among three types of threats: (1) threats external to states as well as to already existing security arrangements; (2) threats internal to a specific security arrangement but external to its constituent states; and (3) threats internal to a particular state. (For this point I am indebted to an anonymous reviewer.) This study examines exclusively threats that are external to security arrangements, that is, it seeks to determine what kind of security structures states form in response to threatening behavior of states with whom they have no security ties. As will be discussed in chapter 4, the German confederation, for instance, was formed in response to a(n) (external) threat from France. Once in place, this confederation may have also prevented the culturally heterogeneous member-states from threatening each other (diffused an internal threat); however, such an observation is beyond the scope of this book.

49. See Walt (1987).

50. Ibid., p. 19.

51. See Beth Yarbrough and Robert Yarbrough, "International Institutions and the New Economics of Organization," *International Organization* 44.2 (Spring 1990): 240.

52. Note that the time constraints under which states operate also affect the kind of security arrangements they choose. The higher the level of threat, the more serious the time-constraints countries face. Hence, in situations of *extreme* threat—such as being on the brink of war—countries should be less likely to create very binding security arrangements, since severe time-constraints make elaborate institutional frameworks impossible. For a study that addresses the security challenge underlying the decision to bring about hierarchical structures, albeit only indirectly, see Lake (1999). Instead of examining the magnitude and origin of threat, he focuses on joint production economies in the production of security (pp. 44–52). This decision not to scrutinize the security setting directly prevents him from explaining why extreme threats lead to different institutional outcomes than less pressing (severe) threats.

53. See Grieco, "Understanding the Problem of International Cooperation," in Baldwin (1993), who argues that "to date it [realism] has not offered an explanation for the tendency of states to undertake their cooperation through *institutionalized* (emphasis in original) arrangements" (p. 335).

54. See Richard Bean, "War and the Birth of the Nation State," *Journal of Economic History* 33 (1973): 203–21.

55. Ibid., pp. 204–5.

56. See William McNeill, *The Pursuit of Power: Technology, Armed Force, and Society since A.D. 1000* (Chicago: University of Chicago Press, 1982): 80–116.

57. For another example of scholarly work that explains change in the relative size of states, see Charles Tilly, ed., *The Formation of National States in Western Europe* (Princeton: Princeton University Press, 1975). For a study that examines economic factors (changes in relative product and factor prices; changes in the size of markets), see Douglass North and Robert Thomas, "An Economic Theory of the Growth of the Western World," *The Economic History Review* 23.1 (1970): 1–17.

58. For the argument that size is an imperfect predictor for the survival of a specific institutional form (the territorial state), see Hendrik Spruyt, "Institutional Selection in International Relations: State Anarchy as Order," *International Organization* 48.4 (Autumn 1994): 527–57.

CHAPTER 2

1. See Waltz (1979): 89–91.

2. Ibid., pp. 105 and 117–18.

3. Kenneth Boulding, "Theoretical Systems and Political Realities: A Review of Morton A. Kaplan, System and Process in International Politics," *Journal of Conflict Resolution* 2 (December 1958): 330. Also see Thomas Schelling, *Micromotives and Macrobehavior* (New York: Norton, 1978), p. 23, who tests the explanatory power of economic theories outside of economics.

4. See Ronald Coase, "The Nature of the Firm," *Economica*, n.s., 4 (1937): 386–405; and Oliver Williamson, "The Modern Corporation: Origins, Evolution, Attributes," *Journal of Economic Literature* 19 (December 1981): 1537–68.

5. For a more detailed discussion of this position, see Coase (1937), p. 387.

6. See Williamson (1981), p. 1540; also see p. 1544, where he explains that a transaction occurs "when a good or service is transferred across a technologically separable interface."

7. Coase (1937): 390–91.

8. See Ernest Englander, "Technology and Oliver Williamson's Transaction Cost Economics," *Journal of Economic Behavior and Organization* 10 (1988): 340. Note that the real determining factor whether coordination takes place through the market or through organizations is the *net balance* of organization and transaction costs. However, since in the security realm organization costs do not play a decisive role—countries can be expected to pay even high setup costs for an organization they envision to enhance their security noticeably—the following analysis neglects organization costs and merely focuses on transaction costs. Or, put differently, it is argued that organization costs are not security related, whereas transaction costs are.

9. Coase (1937): 394–95.

10. See David Teece, "Transactions Cost Economics and the Multinational Enterprise," *Journal of Economic Behavior and Organization* 7 (1986): 23.

11. See Frank Knight, *Risk, Uncertainty and Profit* (1922): 267–68, cited in Coase (1937), p. 399. Note that Knight's book was reprinted in 1965 by Harper & Row. Also see Jack Hirshleifer and John Riley, *The Analytics of Uncertainty and Information* (New York: Cambridge University Press, 1992).

12. See Teece (1986), p. 24, who argues that the specialized governance structure of the firm shields and protects transactions.

13. See Chester Barnard, *The Functions of the Executive* (Cambridge: Harvard University Press, 1938). Also, see Herbert Simon, *Administrative Behavior*, 2nd ed., (New York: Macmillan, [1947] 1961), p. xxiv, who refers to man as "intendedly rational, but only limitedly so."

14. See Williamson (1981), p. 1545.

15. See Williamson, *The Economic Institutions of Capitalism* (New York: The Free Press, 1985), p. 47. Note that he defines opportunism as "self-interest seeking with guile."

16. See Williamson (1981), p. 1545; Williamson (1985), p. 45.

17. See Williamson, *Markets and Hierarchies: Analysis and Anti-Trust Implications: A Study in the Economics of Internal Organization* (New York: The Free Press, 1975), pp. 4, 7.

18. See Williamson (1985), pp. 61–63.

19. See Kenneth Arrow, "The Organization of Economic Activity: Issues Pertinent to the Choice of Market Versus Nonmarket Allocation," in *The Analysis and Evaluation of Public Expenditures: The PPB System*, vol. 1. U.S. Joint Economic Committee, 91st Congress, 1st Session (U.S. Government Printing Office, 1969), pp. 59–73. Note that Arrow defines transaction costs as "the costs of running the economic system." For a summary of Arrow's transaction costs discussion, see Williamson (1981), p. 1541.

20. For a more detailed discussion of each of these components of transaction costs, see Williamson (1985), pp. 20–21.

21. Ibid., p. 19. Also see William Ouchi, "Markets, Bureaucracies, and Clans," *Administrative Science Quarterly* 25 (March 1980): 130, who defines transaction costs as "any activity which is engaged in to satisfy each party to an exchange that the value given and received is in accord with his or her expectations." Moreover, see James Robins, "Organizational Economics: Notes on the Use of Transaction-Cost Theory in the Study of Organizations," *Administrative Science Quarterly* 32 (1987): 69.

22. See Williamson, "Transaction-Cost Economics: The Governance of Contractual Relations," *The Journal of Law and Economics* 22.2 (October 1979): 246, 249.

23. Ibid., p. 239. Also see Benjamin Klein, Robert Crawford, and Armen Alchian, "Vertical Integration, Appropriable Rents, and the Competitive Contracting Process," in Louis Putterman, ed., *The Economic Nature of the Firm* (Cambridge: Cambridge University Press, 1986), who associate transaction-specific investments with "appropriable quasi-rents."

24. Williamson (1981), p. 1548.

25. Williamson (1985), p. 54.

26. See Englander (1988), p. 345; also see Williamson (1979), p. 239.

27. For a more detailed discussion of the concept of a "fundamental transformation," see Williamson (1985), p. 61; Yarbrough and Yarbrough (1990), pp. 245–46.

28. See Williamson (1985), p. 59.

29. See Williamson (1981), p. 1549; and (1985), p. 60.

30. A public good (e.g., clean air) is nonrival if the consumption by one person does not diminish the consumption possibilities of another person. Furthermore, a public good is nonexcludable if the benefits of the good, once provided, cannot be withheld from anyone. For an interesting discussion of how well various weapons fulfill these "publicness" requirements, see Sandler and Forbes (1980).

31. According to Sandler and Forbes (1980), for deterrence to be nonexcludable "an attack upon any ally [must be perceived as] inflict[ing] unacceptable damage on the other allies" (p. 427). Yet, as the two scholars suggest, it is at least conceivable that the damage to the interests of nuclear powers arising from an attack on their allies may be within tolerable limits.

32. Note that there are theories of the firm other than transaction cost theories. For an excellent discussion of the nature of the firm, see Thrainn Eggertsson, *Economic Behavior and Institutions* (New York: Cambridge University Press, 1990).

33. See Waltz (1979), p. 111.

34. See Keohane (1984), p. 107.

35. See Beth Yarbrough and Robert Yarbrough, *Cooperation and Governance in International Trade: The Strategic Organizational Approach* (Princeton: Princeton University Press, 1992); James Caporaso, "International Relations Theory and Multilateralism: The Search for Foundations," in Ruggie (1993): 51–90; Jeffry Frieden, "International Investment and Colonial Control: A New Interpretation," *International Organization* 48 (1994): 559–93; Andrew Moravcsik, "Preferences and Power in the European Community: A Liberal

Intergovernmentalist Approach," in Simon Bulmer and A. Scott, eds., *Economic and Political Integration in Europe: Internal Dynamics and Global Context* (Oxford: Blackwell Publishers, 1994): 29–80, and *The Choice for Europe: Social Purpose and State Power from Messina to Maastricht* (Ithaca: Cornell University Press, 1998); Joel Trachtman, "Reflections on the Nature of the State: Sovereignty, Power and Responsibility," *United States Law Journal* 20 (1994), and "The Theory of the Firm and the Theory of the International Economic Organization: Toward Comparative Institutional Analysis," *Northwestern Journal of International Law and Business* 17 (1996–97): 470–555.

36. See chapter 1.

37. Lake (1999); and Sandler and Cauley (1977).

38. Lake (1999), p. 7.

39. See Sandler and Cauley (1977), p. 267.

40. Ibid., pp. 260–62.

41. It needs to be reemphasized that this study focuses exclusively on the *creation* of security arrangements, *not* their *durability*. Hence, factors like internal threat and organization costs that may be of great concern for the durability of security structures are beyond the scope of this study.

42. See Kenneth Boulding, *Conflict and Defense: A General Theory* (New York: Harper & Row, 1962): 229–31, and pp. 245–47, for a more detailed discussion of the law of diminishing strength ("the further, the weaker") as well as the "loss-of-strength gradient" (the amount by which the strength of a country diminishes per mile movement away from home). For a study that uses geographic proximity as an indicator of threat, see Walt (1987), pp. 23–24.

43. For an interesting historical treatment of the "loss-of-strength gradient," see Boulding (1962), pp. 269–73. Also see Albert Wohlstetter, "Illusions of Distance," *Foreign Affairs* 46.2 (1968): 252, who argues that, in spite of significant technological changes, the geographic distance between countries has not lost its importance, but rather, that the effects of distance have become more complex. For a study that employs the "aggressive intentions" of states as well as their "offensive power" as additional indicators of threat, see Walt (1987), pp. 24–26. Yet, since an examination of intentions often is largely speculative, and since in many instances it cannot be clearly established whether weapons are offensive or defensive, or whether the offense or defense has the advantage, these concepts remain too vague to be of much use. For a critique of offense/defense theories, see Jack Levy, "The Offensive/Defensive Balance of Military Technology: A Theoretical and Historical Analysis," *International Studies Quarterly* 28.2 (1984): 219–38.

44. Ole Holsti, Terrence Hopmann, and John Sullivan in *Unity and Disintegration in International Alliances* (New York: Wiley, 1973) seek to ascertain the amount of threat in the international system by differentiating between years in which wars of a certain magnitude occurred and those in which no wars or wars of a lesser magnitude occurred. Yet this operationalization of threat is problematic in that it does not allow for the fact that the level of threat can be high even if war does not occur.

45. See Williamson (1985), pp. 56–59. Note that the distinction between the two types of uncertainty does not matter for the argument developed here.

46. For a discussion of this interaction effect between uncertainty and asset specificity, ibid., pp. 59–60.

47. See Waltz (1979, p. 168), who argues that, in a multipolar world, there are too many powers for any one of them to determine clearly who one's ally or enemy is, yet not enough powers to minimize the effects of opportunism. Also note that Waltz (1979, p. 165) claims that behavioral uncertainties increase as the number of states becomes larger.

48. For an excellent discussion of the possibility of countries misperceiving each others' intentions, see Robert Jervis, *Perception and Misperception in International Politics* (Princeton: Princeton University Press, 1976).

49. Williamson (1979), p. 239.

50. Williamson (1981), p. 1546.

51. Given that the likelihood of opportunism declines with greater hierarchy, once sophisticated security apparati are in place, states might decide to invest in additional specific assets. In that case, asset specificity would result from cooperation rather than give rise to it. However, since I am interested in explaining the founding moment of different cooperative structures, rather than their evolution, "after the fact" developments (Lake, 1999, p. 9) are beyond the scope of this study.

52. Ibid.

53. See Williamson (1979), p. 242.

54. As discussed above it is assumed that the costs of exiting a confederation are higher than those of exiting an alliance, and hence that opportunistic behavior should be less likely in a confederation.

55. See Williamson (1979), p. 242; and (1981), p. 1546, where he argues that physical asset specificity exists in situations where "specialized dies are required to produce a component."

56. Ibid; for a good discussion of how, when physical asset specificity arises, both buyer and supplier are "locked into" their transaction, see Williamson (1981), p. 1546.

57. Again it is assumed that the high exit costs of this particular type of security system significantly reduce the potential for opportunistic behavior, although they cannot completely eliminate it.

58. Ibid.

59. For various examples of investments in specific human assets, see Williamson (1979), pp. 242–44.

60. Williamson (1985), pp. 47–49, 64–67.

61. The frequency of transactions, although crucial in the economic realm, is of little importance for security relations. That is, countries that are threatened are primarily interested in assuring their survival, rather than contemplating whether—at a later point in time—they will be able to recover the setup costs of a binding security arrangement.

62. Since the twentieth century saw much greater sophistication with respect to transportation and communication devices, when compared to the nineteenth century, there should be a noticeable reduction in transaction costs.

63. See Waltz (1979), who claims that "the diversity of parties increases the difficulty of reaching agreements" (p. 136).

64. Note that since scholars who adopt a sociological framework to make sense of international relations ignore state size and strength as indicators of heterogeneity, I will do so as well to facilitate a comparison between sociological (cultural) and economic approaches.

65. See Harold Guetzkow, "Isolation and Collaboration: A Partial Theory of Inter-Nation Relations," *Journal of Conflict Resolution* 1 (1957): 48–68; and Deutsch (1957).

66. Ibid.; also see Morgenthau (1973), who acknowledges the importance of cultural similarities for the creation of alliances, yet argues that power considerations are more important than cultural considerations. For a more recent discussion of cultural arguments, see Emanuel Adler, "Cognitive Evolution: A Dynamic Approach for the Study of International Relations and Their Progress," in Emanuel Adler and Beverly Crawford, eds., *Progress in Postwar International Relations* (New York: Columbia University Press, 1991), pp. 43–88; and Wendt (1992).

67. For more detail on this position, see Emanuel Adler and Michael Barnett, "Governing Anarchy: A Research Agenda for the Study of Security Communities," *Ethics and International Affairs* 10 (1996): 66.

68. See Lynne Zucker, "Production of Trust: Institutional Sources of Economic Structure, 1840 to 1920" (UCLA: Mimeo., 1984), who defines trust as "a set of expectations shared by all those involved in an exchange" (p. 4).

69. This is not to say that states do not reevaluate their security during the early stages of war. However, since security arrangements have to be in operation for some time to determine their performance, the likelihood of realignments is greater during later stages of war or in immediate postwar periods.

70. Clearly, other cases such as the Union of American Colonies, the Australian colonies, Canada (prior to the federation of 1867), or the United Arab Emirates could be scrutinized, if it were not for time and resource constraints.

71. See Gary King, Robert Keohane, and Sidney Verba, *Designing Social Inquiry: Scientific Inference in Qualitative Research* (Princeton: Princeton University Press, 1994), pp. 143–44. For the warning that selection on the dependent variable biases the sample, see Barbara Geddes, "How the Cases You Choose Affect the Answers You Get: Selection Bias in Comparative Politics," *Political Analysis* 2 (1990): 131–52.

72. For a more detailed discussion, see Adam Przeworski and Henry Teune, *The Logic of Comparative Social Inquiry* (New York: Wiley, 1970), p. 43; for a "structured, focused comparison," see Alexander George, "Case Studies and Theory Development: The Method of Structured, Focused Comparison," in P. G. Lauren, ed., *Diplomacy: New Approaches in History, Theory, and Policy* (London: Collier Macmillan, 1979), pp. 43–68.

73. As pointed out in chapter 1, constructivists might provide an alternative explanation for states' security choices. However, since an evaluation of the explanatory power of ideational forces would require careful scrutiny of such factors as actors' ideas, norms, identities, and so on, no systematic assessment of sociological approaches can be made in this book.

74. Note that this sets my study apart from Lake's "decision theoretic work." Whereas he, almost exclusively, focuses on the actions of the dominant

state (the United States)—largely ignoring the other "polities" in this "voluntary" security relationship—I do not assume that the actions of other players can be anticipated, but do investigate them.

CHAPTER 3

1. For a good overview of the vast literature on the Napoleonic period, see Donald Howard, ed., *Napoleonic Military History: A Bibliography* (New York: Garland, 1986); Jack Meyer, *An Annotated Bibliography of the Napoleonic Era: Recent Publications, 1945–1985* (New York: Greenwood Press, 1987).

2. For a chronological overview of the Napoleonic period, see Hermann Kinder and Werner Hilgemann, *Dtv-Atlas zur Weltgeschichte*, vol. 2 (Munich: Deutscher Taschenbuch Verlag, 23rd ed., 1989), pp. 23–40. For a more detailed account of the events leading up to Napoleon's Russian campaign, see Willy Andreas, *Das Zeitalter Napoleons und die Erhebung der Völker* (Heidelberg: Quelle & Meyer, 1955).

3. Edward Gulick, *Europe's Classical Balance of Power* (New York: Norton, 1967), p. 97.

4. Ibid., p. 98.

5. Clemens Metternich, *Memoirs of Prince Metternich: 1773–1815*, vol. 1, translated by Mrs. Alexander Napier (New York: Harper & Brothers, 1881), p. 647.

6. C. S. B. Buckland, *Metternich and the British Government from 1809 to 1813* (London: Macmillan, 1932), p. 179.

7. Derek McKay and H. M. Scott, *The Rise of the Great Powers 1648–1815* (New York: Longman, 1983), p. 334.

8. Georges Lefebvre, *Napoleon: From Tilsit to Waterloo, 1807–1815* (New York: Columbia University Press, 1969), p. 148.

9. Metternich (1881), p. 656.

10. Henry Kissinger, *A World Restored: Metternich, Castlereagh and the Problems of Peace 1812–22* (Boston: Houghton Mifflin, 1973), p. 7; and Gunther Rothenberg, *Napoleon's Great Adversaries: The Archduke Charles and the Austrian Army, 1792–1814* (Bloomington: Indiana University Press, 1982).

11. Metternich makes this position clear in a letter to the Emperor Francis on March 26, 1811; see Metternich (1881), p. 640.

12. Michael Broers, *Europe under Napoleon: 1799–1815* (London: Arnold, 1996), p. 236.

13. Buckland (1932), p. 179. Also see Lefebvre (1969), p. 153.

14. Harold Nicolson, *The Congress of Vienna: A Study in Allied Unity, 1812–1822* (New York: Harcourt, Brace & Co., 1946), p. 15.

15. Charles Breunig, *The Age of Revolution and Reaction: 1789–1850* (New York: Norton, 1970), p. 105.

16. Gulick (1967), p. 111.

17. Rothenberg (1982), p. 177.

18. This meant that Austria had to renege on its promise of neutrality to Russia; see Buckland (1932).

19. Ben Jones, *Napoleon: Man and Myth* (New York: Holmes & Meier, 1977), p. 46; also see Anthony De Luca, *Personality, Power and Politics* (Cambridge, Mass.: Schenkman Publishing, 1983), p. 7.

20. William McNeill, *The Pursuit of Power* (Chicago: University of Chicago Press, 1982), p. 198.

21. A. W. Ward and G. P. Gooch, eds., *Cambridge Modern History*, vol. 9 (Cambridge: Cambridge University Press, 1934), p. 488.

22. McKay and Scott (1983), p. 334.

23. Ward and Gooch (1934), p. 498.

24. Ibid., p. 507.

25. Nicolson (1946), p. 15.

26. Metternich (1881), p. 98.

27. Lefebvre (1969), p. 327.

28. Kissinger (1973), p. 31.

29. Lefebvre (1969), p. 331.

30. Gulick (1967), p. 110.

31. McKay and Scott (1983), p. 334.

32. See Kissinger (1973), p. 60.

33. For a detailed discussion of the concept of a "defensive positionalist," see Joseph Grieco, *Cooperation among Nations: Europe, America, and Non-Tariff Barriers to Trade* (Ithaca: Cornell University Press, 1990), pp. 10, 28, 39, and 49.

34. In 1803 Prussia declared neutrality. In the Treaty of Schoenbrunn (December 12, 1805) Prussia gave up its neutrality and allied with France, which promised to give Prussia Hanover in exchange. When Napoleon broke his promise, Prussia allied with Russia and Saxony, but the allies were beaten by Napoleon in 1806. After the settlement at Tilsit Prussia needed time to recover.

35. See Martin van Creveld, *Technology and War: From 2000 B.C. to the Present* (New York: The Free Press, 1991), p. 155, who explains that "the speed at which messages could be transmitted over the system depended on the weather as well as on the length of the messages themselves." Also see Holland Rose, *The Personality of Napoleon* (New York: Putnam's Sons, 1912), p. 213.

36. See van Creveld (1991), p. 114. Also note that in such a technologically backward world, as an anonymous reader correctly pointed out, reputation may have played a role in compensating for poor communication. But still the costs associated with opportunistic behavior would have been high due to delays in detecting such behavior.

37. The obvious exception was Britain. Since Castlereagh had not yet left Britain, he depended on written accounts of meetings.

38. Rose (1912), p. 213.

39. Clive Trebilcock, *The Industrialization of the Continental Powers: 1780–1914* (New York: Longman, 1981).

40. Jones (1977) argues that armies did not use new weapons until the Crimean War in 1854 (p. 47).

41. Ibid. Also see Michael Glover, *The Napoleonic Wars: An Illustrated History 1792–1815* (New York: Hippocrene Books, 1979), who explains that the type of musket used was introduced around 1700 and that the weaponry was very "static" at the time (p. 10).

42. See Franklin Ford, *Europe 1780–1830* (New York: Longman, 1989), p. 254.

43. Jones (1977), p. 48.

44. Note that there is no mention of site specificity in the literature.

45. Steven Ross, *European Diplomatic History 1789–1815: France against Europe* (New York: Anchor Books, 1969), p. 328.

46. Ward and Gooch (1934), p. 517.

47. Gulick (1967), p. 98.

48. McKay and Scott (1983), p. 336. Also see Lefebvre (1969), p. 324.

49. Metternich (1881), p. 103.

50. Buckland (1932), p. 519. Note that Austria's fears were magnified by her vulnerable geographic position.

51. Metternich (1881), p. 107. For a list of such terms see Gulick (1967), p. 119.

52. Lefebvre (1969), p. 327.

53. For a more detailed account of the events leading to the failure of the Congress of Prague, see Andreas (1955), pp. 535–42. Also see Gulick (1967), pp. 117–26.

54. Ibid., p. 126; also see Ward and Gooch (1934) who estimate the number of allied soldiers at 860,000 men (p. 522).

55. Nicolson (1946), p. 53.

56. Ward and Gooch (1934), p. 522.

57. See Gulick (1967) who gives several reasons for the lack of British influence on the continent: (1) poor contact (geographical distance made it difficult for Castlereagh to communicate); (2) confusion in Britain's representation (three ambassadors with no clear delineation of authority); (3) as a maritime power Britain had not yet assumed a military role in Germany; (4) Castlereagh's initial unwillingness to link British subsidies directly to specific elements of his foreign policy (pp. 132–33). Also see A. W. Ward and G. P. Gooch, eds., *Cambridge History of British Foreign Policy*, vol. 1 (New York: 1922), who attribute the delays in sending messages from Britain to the continent to contrary winds (p. 423).

58. McNeill (1982), p. 215. Also see Broers (1970) who explains that by then Britain was able to finance half a million coalition troops and to "[link] together all the disparate centres of resistance to Napoleon" (p. 236).

59. See Kissinger (1973), pp. 51 and 67.

60. Ibid., p. 58.

61. Ibid., p. 104.

62. I am indebted to an anonymous reviewer for stressing this point.

63. For more detail, see Van Creveld (1991), p. 145.

64. See Andreas (1955), p. 561.

65. For more detail, see Gulick (1967), p. 134.

66. Nicolson (1946), p. 71.

67. See Gulick (1967), p. 148.

68. C. K. Webster, *The Congress of Vienna: 1814–1815* (London: Thames & Hudson, 1963), p. 51.

69. For a discussion of various articles as well as the treaty text for articles V through XVI, see Gulick (1967), pp. 151–60.

70. Ibid., p. 152.

71. See Andreas (1955), p. 567. Also see Gulick (1967), pp. 148, 152.

72. Joel Wiener, ed., *Great Britain: Foreign Policy and the Span of Empire 1689–1971: A Documentary History*, vol. 1 (New York: Chelsea House Publishers, 1972), p. 209.

73. See Kissinger (1973), p. 131.

74. For a more detailed discussion of the balance-of-power thinking imbedded in the Treaty of Chaumont, see Gulick (1967), pp. 155–59.

75. For more detail, see Kissinger (1973), pp. 6, 13, 36, and 59.

76. See George Modelski, "The Long Cycle of Global Politics and the Nation-State," *Comparative Studies in Society and History* 20 (April 1978): 227. Also see A. F. K. Organski, "The Power Transition," in *World Politics*, 2nd ed. (New York: Knopf, 1968), p. 355.

77. William Langer, ed., *An Encyclopedia of World History* (London: Harrap & Co., 1972), p. 649.

78. Gulick (1967), p. 179.

79. Langer (1972), p. 650.

80. Ibid.

81. Gulick (1967), p. 265.

82. Ward and Gooch (1934), p. 616.

83. Langer (1972), p. 651.

CHAPTER 4

1. Forsyth (1981), p. 44.

2. See Peter Burg, *Die Deutsche Trias in Idee und Wirklichkeit* (Stuttgart: Franz Steiner Verlag, 1989), p. 14.

3. Forsyth (1981), pp. 44–45.

4. McKay and Scott (1983), p. 340.

5. Burg (1989), p. 14.

6. Ibid., pp. 19–20.

7. McKay and Scott (1983), p. 340.

8. See L. C. B. Seaman, *From Vienna to Versailles* (New York: Harper & Row, 1963), p. 5

9. Ibid.

10. Ibid

11. Ludwig Bentfeldt, *Der Deutsche Bund Als Nationales Band: 1815–1866* (Göttingen: Musterschmidt, 1985), p. 26. Also see Metternich (1881), p. 100.

12. Paul Schroeder, *Metternich's Diplomacy at Its Zenith: 1820–1823* (Austin: University of Texas Press, 1982), p. 8.

13. Peter Burg, *Der Wiener Kongreß: Der Deutsche Bund im europäischen Staatensystem* (Munich: Deutscher Taschenbuch Verlag, 1984), p. 144.

14. Walter Phillips, *The Confederation of Europe* (London: Longmans, Green & Co., 1920), p. 101.

15. Ward and Gooch (1934), p. 345.

16. Henry Kissinger (1973), p. 235.

17. Burg (1989) provides an excellent summary of the European powers' goals following Napoleon's defeat (p. 21). For a discussion of the territorial redistribution, in particular the debates surrounding the future of Poland and Saxony, see Gulick (1967) and Burg (1984).

18. See Andreas (1955), p. 615.

19. See Burg (1984), p. 52.

20. Burg (1989), pp. 21–22.

21. See C. K. Webster, *The Foreign Policy of Castlereagh: 1815–1822* (London: Bell & Sons, 1925), p. 116.

22. Ibid.

23. See Burg (1989), p. 22.

24. Ibid., pp. 23–24.

25. For more detail on Stein's proposal as well as numerous other proposals made by German statesmen, see Burg (1984), pp. 73–75.

26. These districts were derived from geographical divisions of the old German Empire; ibid., p. 76.

27. Ibid.

28. Bavaria and Württemberg sought a distribution of votes such that no German state would have an automatic majority.

29. Burg (1984), p. 77. For an account of the dispute over the disposal of Poland and Saxony, also see Gulick (1967).

30. For a more detailed account of the various positions, see Burg (1984), pp. 78–79.

31. Ibid., p. 93.

32. The possibility that some German states might be seen as a threat, and not merely a source of uncertainty, clouds the argument presented here, but does not contradict it. On the contrary, it fits the general pattern of threat leading to greater preferences for bindingness.

33. Forsyth (1981), p. 46.

34. Ibid., for a list of the German city republics.

35. See Hajo Holborn, *A History of Modern Germany 1648–1840* (New York: Knopf, 1969), pp. 367–68.

36. Andreas Kärnbach, "Die Deutsche Frage: Die Gründung des Deutschen Bundes auf dem Wiener Kongreß," in *Information für die Truppe*, vol. 4 (1990), p. 94.

37. G. Barraclough, *The Origins of Modern Germany* (Oxford: Blackwell, 1966), pp. 406 and 387.

38. Although the level of threat increased noticeably with Napoleon's return there was no *extreme* threat, since the European powers were not yet at war and, since—as a result of the terms worked out in the Quadruple Alliance—the armies of the Great Powers could be employed quickly.

39. See Burg (1984), p. 57.

40. Ibid., p. 149. Also see Bentfeldt (1985), who argues that the creation of a German confederation was in the interest of all of Europe (p. 26).

41. Ibid.

42. See Gulick (1967) and Webster (1931), p. 116.

43. Burg (1989), p. 25; and (1984), p. 80.

44. Note that on May 15, 1820, the Federal Act was supplemented by the Final Act of Vienna.

45. Forsyth (1981), p. 48.

46. This right to make alliances—as long as they would not threaten the confederation's security or interfere with any of its treaties—is important in that it symbolizes that the "confederal" body's powers regarding external matters were not exclusive. Or, put differently, the right to ally shows that the members of the confederation still possessed international rights alongside the confederal structure (ibid., p. 50).

47. Ibid., p. 49.

48. See Burg (1984), pp. 91–92, for an excellent discussion of the numerous proposals put forth by the negotiating parties.

49. Bentfeldt (1985), p. 103.

50. Forsyth (1981), p. 49.

51. Ibid.

52. Ibid., p. 50.

53. Ibid.

54. Andreas (1955), p. 618.

55. See Burg (1984), who argues that Austria and Prussia were European powers first and only secondarily members of the Bund, and thus could be expected to subordinate their German policies to their European political goals (p. 152).

56. Ibid., p. 58.

57. Forsyth (1981, p. 21) points out that the newly created arrangement possessed its own territory, arbitral procedures, rudimentary laws, and assembly.

58. Peter Dürrenmatt, *Schweizer Geschichte*, vol. 1 (Zurich: Schweizer Verlagshaus AG, 1976), p. 218.

59. Ernst Feuz, *Schweizer Geschichte* (Zurich: Schweizer Spiegel Verlag, 1941), p. 74.

60. Forsyth (1981), p. 23.

61. Ernst Bohnenblust, *Geschichte der Schweiz* (Zurich: Eugen Rentsch Verlag, 1974), p. 357.

62. Forsyth (1981, p. 25) characterizes the situation as an "astonishing attempt to transform an association of oligarchically governed states at one stroke into a single, unitary state."

63. See Wilhelm Öchsli, "Die politische Einigung der Schweiz im neunzehnten Jahrhundert," in M. Feldmann and H. G. Wirz, eds., *Schweizer Kriegsgeschichte*, vol. 10 (Zurich: Ernst Kuhn Verlag, 1917), p. 8.

64. Ibid., p. 9; also see Forsyth (1981), p. 25.

65. Öchsli (1917), p. 9.

66. Forsyth (1981), p. 25.

67. Dürrenmatt (1976), p. 521.

68. See Markus Feldmann, *Hundert Jahre Schweizer Wehrmacht* (Bern: Verlag Hallwag, 1939), p. 324.

69. Bohnenblust (1974), p. 391.

70. See Feldmann (1939), p. 325.

71. Ibid.

72. Ibid., p. 326. Feldmann explains that on March 15, 1815, the number of Swiss soldiers was raised to thirty thousand since the Tagsatzung had received word that Napoleon's troops were getting closer to the Swiss border.

73. Öchsli (1917), pp. 12–13; also see Feldmann (1939), p. 332.

74. Bohnenblust (1974), p. 363.

75. See Forsyth (1981) who explains that the French had raised six former French- and Italian-speaking allies of the Swiss Confederation to full cantonal status in 1803, and that the Swiss not only endorsed these changes in 1815, but also admitted three further French-speaking communities into their confederation (p. 26).

76. For a more detailed account, see E. Bonjour et al., *A Short History of Switzerland* (Oxford: Oxford University Press, 1955), p. 195.

77. Note that again the internal threat was merely derivative of the larger French threat.

78. Bonjour (1955), p. 9.

79. Andre Siegfried, *Switzerland: A Democratic Way of Life* (New York: Duell, Sloan, and Pearce, 1950), p. 147 (italics in original). Also see, Georg Thürer, *Free and Swiss: The Story of Switzerland* (Coral Gables: University of Miami Press, 1971), pp. 69–70.

80. Ibid., chapter 3.

81. Charles Gilliard, *A History of Switzerland* (London: George Allen & Unwin, 1955), pp. 41–42; and Thürer (1971), p. 61.

82. For a detailed account of the various battles fought, in particular the first and second Villmergen War, see Bonjour (1955), pp. 191–97.

83. Ibid., p. 230.

84. Ibid., p. 12.

85. Thürer (1971), p. 23.

86. Ibid.

87. Ibid., p. 30.

88. Ibid.

89. See Klaus Lankheit, "Ein einzig Volk von Brüdern: 700 Jahre Schweizer Eidgenossenschaft," in *Information für die Truppe* 9 (1991): 61. Since the cities supplied the rural areas with goods in exchange for protection, one could argue that human asset specificity did exist in this case (people in the cities specialized in being artisans or merchants whereas people in the countryside specialized in being mercenaries). However, geographic factors, in most instances, appear to provide much more compelling reasons for why the various cantons joined the confederation when they did.

90. Thürer (1971), p. 33.

91. Gilliard (1955), p. 26.

92. Bonjour (1955), p. 13.

93. Ibid.

94. For a listing of the major Swiss mountain passes as well as an interesting account of the various connections between them, see Bonjour (1955), pp. 2 and 10–11, respectively.

95. Uri, as described above, for instance, most likely was perceived to be of greater geostrategic importance than say Zug. However, the latter also occupied a strategic position by separating Zurich from Schwyz and Lucerne.

96. Öchsli (1917), pp. 10-11.

97. Forsyth (1981), p. 26.

98. Öchsli (1917), pp. 12–13.

99. See Bohnenblust (1974), p. 213.

100. Feldmann (1939) explains that the capability of self-defense is a prerequisite for the recognition of neutrality (p. 53).

101. Ibid., p. 54.

102. Öchsli (1917), p. 14.

103. Forsyth (1981) makes clear that this newly created army was financed by quota payments and that the Diet decided upon the organization, mobilization, and use of the troops (p. 27).

104. Dürrenmatt (191976), p. 563; and Bohnenblust (1974), p. 401.

105. Forsyth (1981), p. 27.

106. Ward and Gooch (1934), p. 667. Also see Langer (1972), p. 650. Aside from the reinstatement of her former borders Austria received Lombardy and Venetia, the Illyrian provinces, Salzburg, the Tyrol, and Galicia; Prussia received Posen, Danzig, Swedish Pomerania, Rügen, the former Prussian possessions in Westphalia, Neuchatel, and the greater part of Saxony.

107. Ernst Molden, *Zur Geschichte des österreichisch-russischen Gegensatzes* (Vienna: Verlag von Seidel & Sohn, 1916), p. 26. For a list of the fortresses created and the amount of indemnities paid, see Ward and Gooch (1934), p. 659; and Langer (1972), p. 652.

108. Harold Temperley and Lillian Penson, *Foundations of British Foreign Policy* (Cambridge: Cambridge University Press, 1938), p. 36. Also see A. W. Ward and D. Litt, *The Period of Congresses* (New York: Macmillan, 1919), p. 69; and Joel Wiener, ed., *Great Britain: Foreign Policy and the Span of Empire 1689–1971: A Documentary History*, vol. 1 (New York: Chelsea House, 1972), p. 241.

109. C. K. Webster, "The Pacification of Europe, 1813–1815," in A. W. Ward and G. P. Gooch, eds., *Cambridge History of British Foreign Policy*, vol. 1 (New York: Macmillan, 1922), p. 516. Also see Wiener (1972), p. 242.

110. See Walter Bussmann, "Europa von der Französischen Revolution zu den nationalstaatlichen Bewegungen des 19. Jahrhunderts," *Handbuch der Europäischen Geschichte* 5 (1981).

111. See Ward and Litt (1919), p. 70. Also note that in addition to renewing the Quadruple Alliance, on September 26, 1815, the European statesmen signed the Holy Alliance—an informal pact composed by Alexander I. Since this pact was largely of ideological and religious rather than political importance it will not be examined in any detail here. Suffice it to say that the Russian tsar suggested that the signatories of the Holy Alliance base their international relations on the "precepts of . . . holy religion, . . . justice, charity and peace," and that the European rulers never thought of the alliance as an important diplomatic instrument but merely signed it to appease the tsar (see Gulick, 1967, p. 286). Also see Hildegard Schäder, *Autokratie und Heilige Allianz* (Darmstadt,

Germany: Wissenschaftliche Buchgesellschaft, 1963), who suggests that Alexander thought of himself as inferior, and thus wanted to compensate by accomplishing something great in the European arena (p. 62).

112. Hans Schmalz, "Versuche einer gesamteuropäischen Organisation 1815–1820," in Werner Näf, ed., *Berner Untersuchungen zur Allgemeinen Geschichte*, vol. 10 (Aarau, Switzerland: Verlag Sauerländer, 1940), p. 22.

113. Kissinger (1973), p. 283, points out that continental and British foreign policy goals became increasingly incompatible.

CHAPTER 5

1. *NATO: Facts and Figures* (Brussels: NATO Information Service, 1981), p. 13.

2. John Gaddis, *The United States and the Origins of the Cold War, 1941–1947* (New York: Columbia University Press, 1972), p. 263.

3. Henry Stimson, "The Challenge to Americans," *Foreign Affairs* 26.1 (1947): 8.

4. Geoffrey Warner, "The United States and the Origins of the Cold War," *International Affairs* 46.3 (1970): 533.

5. Hastings Ismay, *NATO: The First Five Years, 1949–1954* (Utrecht: Bosch, 1954), p. 4. Also see *NATO: Facts and Figures* (1981), p. 14.

6. Robert Osgood, *NATO: The Entangling Alliance* (Chicago: University of Chicago Press, 1962), p. 29. For a discussion of British military capabilities, see Alfred Goldberg, "The Military Origins of the British Nuclear Deterrent," *International Affairs* 40.4 (1964), who claims that between 1945 and 1950 the Royal Air Force found itself in a condition of "accelerated rundown" (p. 602).

7. Andre Beaufre, *NATO and Europe* (New York: Alfred Knopf, 1966), p. 12.

8. Richard Best, *Cooperation with Like-Minded Peoples* (New York: Greenwood Press, 1986), pp. 61–64. Also see Warner (1970), p. 543.

9. Beaufre (1966), p. 99. Also see John Baylis, "Britain and the Dunkirk Treaty: The Origins of NATO," *Journal of Strategic Studies* 5.2 (1982): 237; and John Foster Dulles, "Policy for Security and Peace," *Foreign Affairs* 32.3 (1954): 356.

10. Burkhart Mueller-Hillebrand, "Nationale Armee oder Europa-Armee?" *Wehrwissenschaftliche Rundschau* 3 (April 1953): 165.

11. See Osgood (1962), p. 23.

12. Gaddis (1972), p. 284.

13. Walter Poole, "From Conciliation to Containment: The Joint Chiefs of Staff and the Coming of the Cold War, 1945–1946," *Military Affairs* 42.1 (1978): 13; and Peter Lane, *Europe since 1945* (London: Batsford Academic & Educational, 1985), p. 58.

14. John Gaddis, "Was the Truman Doctrine a Real Turning Point?" *Foreign Affairs* 52.2 (1974): 388; also see Lane (1985), who discusses how Stalin sought to establish a "cordon sanitaire" in Eastern Europe (pp. 40–54).

15. See Melvyn Leffler, "Strategy, Diplomacy, and the Cold War: The United States, Turkey, and NATO, 1945–1952," *The Journal of American History* 71.4 (1985): 810.

16. Poole (1978), p. 13; and Lane (1985), p. 77.

17. Gaddis (1974), p. 391. Also see, Walter Millis, *The Forrestal Diaries* (New York: Viking Press, 1951), p. 212; and George Kennan, "Containment Then and Now," *Foreign Affairs* 65.4 (1987): 885.

18. *NATO: Facts and Figures* (1981), pp. 14–15.

19. Harry S. Truman Papers, reprinted in Thomas Etzold and John Gaddis, eds., *Containment: Documents on American Policy and Strategy, 1945–1950* (New York: Columbia University Press, 1978), p. 66.

20. Gaddis (1972), p. 284.

21. Thomas Wolfe, *Soviet Power and Europe, 1945–1970* (Baltimore: Johns Hopkins University Press, 1970), p. 18.

22. See Timothy Ireland, *Creating the Entangling Alliance: The Origins of the North Atlantic Treaty Organization* (Westport, Conn.: Greenwood Press, 1981), pp. 4–5.

23. Ibid., p. 222.

24. Phil Williams, *North Atlantic Treaty Organization*, vol. 8 (New Brunswick, N.J.: Transaction Publishers, 1994), p. xii.

25. Baylis (1982), p. 237.

26. Sean Greenwood, "Return to Dunkirk: The Origins of the Anglo-French Treaty of March 1947," *Journal of Strategic Studies* 6.4 (1983): 62.

27. Baylis (1982), pp. 238–44.

28. Alan Henrikson, "The Creation of the North Atlantic Alliance," in John Reichart and Steven Sturm, eds., *American Defense Policy*, 5th ed. (Baltimore: Johns Hopkins University Press, 1982), p. 299.

29. Baylis (1982), p. 236.

30. Lawrence Kaplan, "After Forty Years: Reflections on NATO as a Research Field," in Francis Heller and John Gillingham, eds., *NATO: The Founding of the Atlantic Alliance and the Integration of Europe* (New York: St. Martin's Press, 1992), p. 18.

31. *NATO: Facts and Figures* (1981), p. 324.

32. For a more detailed discussion of this point, see George Kennan, *Russia, the Atom and the West* (New York: Harper & Brothers, 1958), p. 18; Bernard Montgomery, *The Memoirs of Field-Marshal the Viscount Montgomery of Alamein* (London: Collins Press, 1958), p. 450; and Ireland (1981), p. 66.

33. Millis (1951), p. 350.

34. Henrikson (1982), p. 298.

35. Escott Reid, "The Miraculous Birth of the North Atlantic Alliance," *NATO Review* 28 (December 1980): 12–13.

36. Ibid., p. 13.

37. Theodore Achilles, "US Role in Negotiations that Led to Atlantic Alliance," *NATO Review* 27 (August 1979): 12 (part 1).

38. John Baylis, "Britain, the Brussels Pact and the Continental Commitment," *International Affairs* 60.4 (1984): 622. The same argument is also made by Achilles (1979), p. 12 (part 1).

39. Montgomery (1958), p. 501.

40. Henrikson (1982), p. 301.

41. Millis (1951), p. 387.

42. Henrikson (1982), p. 301.

43. Escott Reid, *Time of Fear and Hope: The Making of the North Atlantic Treaty, 1947–1949* (Toronto: McClelland & Stewart, 1977), p. 18.

44. Henrikson (1982), p. 302.

45. Wichard Woyke, "Foundation and History of NATO, 1948–1950," in Norbert Wiggershaus and Roland Förster, eds., *The Western Security Community, 1948–1950* (Oxford: Berg Publishers, 1993), pp. 258–59.

46. Ireland (1981), pp. 103–4. Also see *Foreign Relations of the United States (FRUS)* 1948, vol. 3, by the U.S. Department of State. Here Ambassador Caffrey explains in a telegram: "As the French Government sees it, the Western democracies are faced with (1) an eventual threat, which is Germany; (2) an actual threat, which is the Soviet Union; (3) an immediate threat, which is Soviet action in Germany" (pp. 142–43).

47. Woyke (1993), p. 258.

48. Baylis (1984), pp. 626–27.

49. *NATO: Facts and Figures* (1981), p. 19.

50. For the exact wording of the Rio Treaty, see Frederick Hartmann, ed., *Basic Documents of International Relations* (New York: McGraw-Hill, 1951), pp. 287–94. Particular attention should be paid to article III, which contains the mutual assistance pledge. The Brussels Treaty text is reprinted in Margret Carlyle, ed., *Documents on International Affairs, 1947–1948* (London: Oxford University Press, 1952), pp. 225–29. Here the pledge is given in article IV.

51. See Wolfe (1970), who estimates that the United States had 1.4 million troops compared to 2.8 million Soviet troops (p. 11). Also see Matthew Evangelista, "Stalin's Postwar Army Reappraised," *International Security* 7.3 (1982/83), who puts the number of Soviet troops at 4 million (p. 113). Evangelista cautions that the measures used in some reports clearly are wrong. For instance, a comparison of Soviet and Western divisions, he argues, is problematic in that Soviet divisions are "much smaller in manpower and lack the extensive logistical and support services of Western divisions" (pp. 110–38).

52. Millis (1951), p. 395.

53. John Erickson, "The 'Military Factor' in Soviet Policy," *International Affairs* 39.2 (1963): 216.

54. Osgood (1962), p. 33. Also see, Henrikson (1982), p. 300; and Nicholas Henderson, *The Birth of NATO* (Boulder, Colo.: Westview Press, 1983), p. 25.

55. Secrecy, the participants thought, was essential since it would not only keep the USSR uninformed, but also give each participant greater flexibility to negotiate and to compromise (see Reid, 1977, p. 79).

56. Cees Wiebes and Bert Zeeman, "The Pentagon Negotiations March 1948: The Launching of the North Atlantic Treaty," *International Affairs* 59.3 (1983): 356. Also see Henrikson (1982), p. 303.

57. Henrikson (1982), p. 304.

58. Ibid.

59. Donald McLachlan, "Rearmament and European Integration," *Foreign Affairs* 29.2 (1951): 284.

60. Reid (1977), p. 126.

61. Osgood (1962), p. 24.

62. Avi Shlaim, "Britain, the Berlin Blockade and the Cold War," *International Affairs* 60.1 (1983/84): 4.

63. Secretary of State Marshall and U.S. Ambassador to Moscow, Smith, doubted that Berlin could be retained in the long run, and thus questioned whether the United States should aid Berlin (see Wilfried Loth, "The Formation of the Blocs: Structures of the East-West Conflict, 1948–1950," in Wiggershaus and Förster, [1993], p. 14); and Henrikson (1982, p. 305), who suggests that the United States seems to have exercised caution in the hope of avoiding public controversy until after the presidential elections in November.

64. Shlaim (1983/84), p. 5.

65. Ibid., pp. 7–8.

66. See Wiebes and Zeeman (1983, p. 362), who make clear that Kennan also has come around indicating his willingness to give up resistance.

67. Osgood (1962), p. 32.

68. For instance, the NSC reported on November 23, 1948:

Present intelligence estimates attribute to Soviet armed forces the capability of overrunning in about six months all of Continental Europe and the Near East as far as Cairo, while simultaneously occupying important continental points in the Far East. Meanwhile Great Britain could be subjected to severe air and missile bombardment.

See *FRUS*, 1948, vol. 1, part 2, pp. 663–69, reprinted in Thomas Etzold and John Lewis Gaddis, eds., *Containment: Documents on American Policy and Strategy, 1945–1950* (New York: Columbia University Press, 1978), pp. 206–7. For a similar assessment by Kennan, see *FRUS*, 1948, vol. 3, p. 285, reprinted in Reid (1977), p. 15.

69. Ibid., p. 47.

70. John Baylis, "British Wartime Thinking about a Post-war European Security Group," *Review of International Studies* 9.4 (1983): 270.

71. Baylis (1982), p. 244.

72. See Melvyn Leffler, *A Preponderance of Power: National Security, the Truman Administration, and the Cold War* (Stanford: Stanford University Press, 1992), p. 280.

73. Henderson (1983), p. 51.

74. Leffler (1992), p. 220.

75. Beaufre (1966), p. 94.

76. Russel Ritchey, "Military Education," *NATO's Fifteen Nations* 6.6 (1962): 88.

77. Alfred Cobban, "Security and Sovereignty in French Foreign Policy," *International Journal* 8 (Summer 1953): 177.

78. Müller-Hillebrand (1953), p. 165. Also see Richard Rosecrance, *Defense of the Realm: British Strategy in the Nuclear Epoch* (New York: Columbia University Press, 1968) for a discussion of British military achieve-

ments such as the "procurement of the Canberra, the Centurion tank, and the Hunter" (p. 22).

79. See Chester Wilmot, "Britain's Strategic Relationship to Europe," *International Affairs* 29.4 (1953): 413.

80. As Charles Spofford, "Toward Atlantic Security," *International Affairs* 27.4 (1951): 436, puts it,

> the men from Mars who fly the high altitude jet fighters of today not only have to be superbly trained, but the ground crews who stand behind them must be experts in the maintenance and repair of complicated and delicate instruments in a number of highly specialized fields.

81. Herve Alphand, "The 'European Policy' of France," *International Affairs* 29.2 (1953): 145.

82. Eberhard Pikart, "The Military Situation and the Idea of Threat," in Wiggershaus and Förster (1993), p. 276.

83. J. A. Jukes, "Nuclear Energy: A Survey of Britain's Position," *International Affairs* 32.3 (1956): 274.

84. Wolf Mendl, "The Background of French Nuclear Policy," *International Affairs* 41.1 (1965): 22.

85. Ibid., p. 23.

86. Jennifer Laurendeau, "The Politics of NATO Defense Policy: Lessons of the EDC Debate, 1950–1954," *Center for Science & International Affairs Working Papers*, No. 88–1 (Harvard University, April 1988), p. 37.

87. David Rosenberg, "U.S. Nuclear Stockpile: 1945–1950," *Bulletin of Atomic Scientists* 38 (May 1982): 28–29.

88. Wolfgang Krieger, "American Security Policy in Europe before NATO," in Heller and Gillingham (1992), p. 119.

89. Ibid.

90. Montgomery (1958), p. 449.

91. Ismay (1954), p. 136; and Paul Garbutt, *Naval Challenge 1945–1961: The Story of Britain's Post-War Fleet* (London: MacDonald, 1961), p. 3.

92. Osgood (1962), p. 46.

93. Woyke in Wiggershaus and Förster (1993), p. 267. As Till Geiger and Lorenza Sebesta, "National Defense Policy and the Failure of Military Integration in NATO: American Military Assistance and Western European Rearmament, 1949–1954," in Francis Heller and John Gillingham, *The United States and the Integration of Europe: Legacies of the Postwar Era* (New York: St. Martin's Press, 1996), p. 256, correctly point out, the United States, due to its postwar demobilization, "lacked ground and tactical air forces to respond conventionally to a Soviet attack in Central Europe," which explains its sole reliance on nuclear deterrence.

94. Klaus Schwabe, "The Origins of the United States' Engagement in Europe, 1946–1952," in Heller and Gillingham (1992), p. 173.

95. Reid (1977), p. 265.

96. The Rio Treaty stipulates that "each one of the Contracting Parties may determine the immediate measures which it may individually take in fulfillment of the obligation" so that the use of armed force is, at best, implicit. For the treaty text, see Hartmann (1951), p. 289.

97. Henrikson (1982), p. 310.

98. *NATO Handbook* (Brussels: NATO Office of Information and Press, 1995), p. 234.

99. Ibid., p. 233.

100. Ismay (1954), p. 14.

101. Edward Fursdon, *The European Defence Community: A History* (London: Macmillan, 1980), p. 197.

102. Charles Spofford, "NATO's Growing Pains," *Foreign Affairs* 31.1 (1952), argues that "except for the command functions vested in the military, no individual or agency of NATO up to the Council itself has any delegated power of authority" (p. 96).

103. Fursdon (1980), p. 193.

104. There were no other alliance options. In leaving NATO the West Europeans could have only attempted to defend themselves (which would have been suicidal at that point) or they could have gone over to the Soviet side (bandwagon), but that seemed implausible.

CHAPTER 6

1. An earlier version of this chapter originally appeared as "Hierarchy amidst Anarchy: A Transaction Costs Approach to International Security Cooperation," *International Studies Quarterly* 41 (1997): 321–40, and is reprinted here with the permission of Blackwell Publishers.

2. The blockade was canceled since it had become clear to the Soviets that they could not force the Western powers to retreat from Berlin.

3. *NATO: Facts and Figures* (1981), p. 326.

4. In "Was the Truman Doctrine a Real Turning Point?" *Foreign Affairs* 52.2 (1974), John Gaddis argues that Truman believed the United States could not afford to spend more than $15 billion a year on defense (p. 395). Also see Warner Schilling, "The Politics of National Defense: Fiscal 1950," in Warner Schilling, Paul Hammond, and Glenn Snyder, eds., *Strategy, Politics, and Defense Budgets* (New York: Columbia University Press, 1962), who claims that there was a "fixed limit to what could be spent" (p. 102). Truman feared that excess spending would lead to economic ruin, and thus ruled out the possibility of increasing taxes or allowing for a larger deficit.

5. Samuel Wells Jr., "Sounding the Tocsin: NSC 68 and the Soviet Threat," *International Security* 4.2 (1979), argues that "had the Korean War not occurred, the United States probably would not have expanded its military power as advocated by NSC 68" (p. 157).

6. See Clarence Walton, "Background for the European Defense Community," *Political Science Quarterly* 68 (March 1953): 52; and Hajo Holborn, "American Foreign Policy And European Integration," *World Politics* 6.1 (1953): 8.

7. Jean Monnet, *Memoires* (Paris: Fayard, 1976), p. 295, reprinted in Fursdon (1980), p. 68.

8. Alfred Goldberg, "The Military Origins of the British Nuclear Deterrent," *International Affairs* 40.4 (1964): 613.

9. Leffler (1992), p. 451.

10. Osgood (1962), p. 71.

11. Fursdon (1980), p. 68.

12. There was also disagreement *within* various countries regarding security policy. In Germany the Christian Democrats favored the creation of a binding security arrangement that would restore power and prestige to their country, whereas the Social Democrats opposed such an arrangement, arguing that the switch from complete disarmament to rearmament would occur too fast. Yet, as Waltz makes clear, while "each state arrives at policies and decides on actions according to its own internal processes, . . . its decisions are shaped by the very presence of other states as well as by interactions with them" (1979, p. 65). And, at any rate, this study treats states as unitary actors for purposes of theory development.

13. C. G. D. Onslow, "West German Rearmament," *World Politics* 3.4 (1951): 467.

14. Ibid., p. 462.

15. See *FRUS* (1951), vol. 3, part 1, p. 850. Also see Fursdon (1980), p. 97.

16. See *FRUS* (1950), vol. 3, p. 384, reprinted in Klaus Maier, "Die EVG in der Außen-und Sicherheitspolitik der Truman-Administration," in Hans-Erich Volkmann and Walter Schwengler, eds., *Die Europäische Verteidigungsgemeinschaft: Stand und Probleme der Forschung* (Boppard, Germany: Boldt, 1985), p. 39.

17. Wilhelm Meier-Dörnberg, "Politische und militärische Faktoren bei der Planung des deutschen Verteidigungsbeitrages im Rahmen der EVG," in Hans-Erich Volkmann and Walter Schwengler, eds., *Die Europäische Verteidigungsgemeinschaft: Stand und Probleme der Forschung* (Boppard, Germany: Boldt, 1985), p. 271; and *FRUS* (1950), vol. 1, p. 34.

18. Carlo Schmid, "Germany and Europe," *International Affairs* 27.3 (1951): 310.

19. Fursdon (1980), p. 94.

20. James Huston, *One for All: NATO Strategy and Logistics through the Formative Period (1949–1969)* (Newark: University of Delaware Press, 1984), p. 38; and Charles Cogan, *Forced to Choose: France, the Atlantic Alliance, and NATO—Then and Now* (Westport, Conn.: Praeger, 1997), especially chapters 5–6.

21. Osgood (1962), p. 72; and Reid (1977), p. 238.

22. *NATO: Facts and Figures* (1981), p. 327; Onslow (1951), pp. 479–80.

23. Norbert Wiggershaus, "Außenpolitische Voraussetzungen für den Westdeutschen Verteidigungsbeitrag," in Alexander Fischer, ed., *Wiederbewaffnung in Deutschland nach 1945* (Berlin: Duncker & Humblot, 1986) argues that the Western alliance, which was held together by not much more than a North Atlantic Treaty (NAT), finally changed into a North Atlantic Treaty Organization (NATO) (p. 69).

24. Osgood (1962), p. 85.

25. Fursdon (1980), p. 120; and Osgood (1962), p. 92. Also see the Acheson-Lovett memo of July 30, 1951, in *FRUS* (1951), vol. 3, part 1, pp. 849–52.

26. Fursdon (1980), p. 120. Also see *FRUS* (1952–54), vol. 5, part 1, pp. 668 and 673.

27. Wilmot (1953), p. 416.

28. Osgood (1962), p. 92. For further details on the structure of the EDC, see Fursdon (1980), pp. 163 and 193.

29. Daniel Lerner, "Reflections on France in the World Arena," in Daniel Lerner and Raymond Aron, eds., *France Defeats EDC* (New York: Praeger, 1957), p. 212.

30. See Fursdon (1980), p. 193.

31. Note that, even in this case, threat and uncertainty remain distinct variables. Although all of the Western powers were uncertain about Germany's intentions, they differed in their perceptions of threat.

32. Robert McGeehan, *The German Rearmament Question* (Urbana: University of Illinois Press, 1971), p. 262.

33. The possibility that Germany might itself be seen as a threat and not merely a source of uncertainty clouds the argument presented here, but does not contradict it. On the contrary, it fits the general pattern of threat leading to greater preferences for bindingness.

34. Cobban (1953), p. 177.

35. Ibid.; and *FRUS* (1950), vol. 3, p. 384.

36. See the preamble of the North Atlantic Treaty reprinted in the *NATO Handbook* (Brussels: NATO Office of Information and Press, 1995), p. 231.

37. Ritchey (1962), p. 122; also see Wilhelm Meier-Dörnberg, "Integration und Kontrolle: Die Europäische Verteidigungsgemeinschaft (EVG)," *Information für die Truppe* 10 (1990): 64.

38. A good example provides the language school of the Bundeswehr in Euskirchen which is discussed in Reinhard Luschert's "Fremdsprachenschule: Das Bundessprachenamt in Hürth," *Luftwaffe* 1 (1978): 3–4.

39. Ritchey (1962), p. 122; and Meier-Dörnberg (1990), p. 64.

40. Ibid. Also see Paul Klein, "Ende der Nationalarmee? Die Bundeswehr auf dem Weg zur Multinationalität," *Information für die Truppe* 10/11 (1995): 96.

41. Ibid., p. 93.

42. Ibid.

43. Alphand (1953), p. 146.

44. For an excellent interpretive analysis of the EDC Treaty, see Fursdon (1980), pp. 150–88. For the section dealing with the court system, see pp. 159–60.

45. For the English translation of *The European Defence Community Treaty, Paris, May 1952* presented to the British Parliament in April 1954, see Cmd. 9127 (London: Her Majesty's Stationery Office, 1954).

46. Ibid., article 63.

47. Richard Gott, "The Evolution of the Independent British Deterrent," *International Affairs* 39.2 (1963): 238.

48. Osgood (1962), p. 89.

49. Goldberg (1964b) p. 600.

50. Osgood (1962), p. 131; and Wolf Mendl, "The Background of French Nuclear Policy," *International Affairs* 41.1 (1965): 31. Also recall that the Germans were prohibited from producing certain types of arms—among them nuclear weapons—by the peace settlements following World War II.

51. Due to poor documentation an accurate assessment of non-nuclear weapons in the late 1940s and early 1950s is difficult. For an interesting discussion of some of the problems encountered in collecting data on military equipment from that period, see Wolfgang Heisenberg and Dieter Lutz, eds., *Sicherheitspolitik kontrovers: Konventionelle Militärpotentiale NATO/WP 1949–1986 aus offenen Quellen* (Bonn: Bundeszentrale für Politische Bildung, 1990), pp. 23–28. *Jane's Fighting Ships* (London: Sampson Low, Marston & Co.) gives a detailed account of naval equipment since 1897; but most armament yearbooks do not begin to compile data until much later. For example, see the Institute for Strategic Studies's *The Military Balance*, which began in 1959; the Stockholm International Peace Research Institute's *SIPRI Yearbook of World Armaments and Disarmament* (New York: Humanities Press, 1970) beginning in 1968/69; or the United States Arms Control and Disarmament Agency's *World Military Expenditures and Arms Transfers*, beginning in 1966.

52. See David Large, "Grand Illusions: The United States, the Federal Republic of Germany, and the European Defense Community, 1950–1954," in Jeffry Diefendorf et al., eds., *American Policy and the Reconstruction of West Germany, 1945–1955* (Cambridge: Cambridge University Press, 1993, p. 388), who explains that Germany had to refrain from producing aircraft, warships, and ABC (atomic, biological, and chemical) weapons.

53. H. G. Thursfield, ed., *Brassey's Annual: The Armed Forces Year-Book, 1950* (New York: Macmillan, 1950), p. 178. Also see, Jan Feldman, "Collaborative Production Of Defense Equipment within NATO," *Journal of Strategic Studies* 7.3 (1984): 284; and Friedrich Wiener, ed. *Taschenbuch der Landstreitkräfte: Die Armeen der NATO-Staaten*, vol. 1 (Munich: Lehmanns Verlag, 1974), p. 309.

54. Dieter Ose, "Lebendige Integration: Deutschland 40 Jahre in der NATO," *Information für die Truppe* 10/11 (1995): 77.

55. Charles Christienne and Pierre Lissarague, *A History of French Military Aviation*, translated by Francis Kianka (Washington, D.C.: Smithsonian Institution Press, 1986), p. 444.

56. See Paul Garbutt, *Naval Challenge 1945–1961: The Story of Britain's Post-War Fleet* (London: MacDonald, 1961), p. 3.

57. *Jane's Fighting Ships* (1954–55), p. iv.

58. Thursfield (1950), p. 293.

59. *Jane's Fighting Ships* (1949–50), p. v.

60. For a more detailed discussion, see A. G. T. James, *The Royal Air Force: The Past 30 Years* (London: MacDonald & Jane's, 1976), p. 52.

61. I am indebted to an anonymous reviewer for drawing attention to this category of ships the British were building in great numbers in the 1950s. As Robert Gardiner in *Conway's All the World's Fighting Ships 1947–1982, Part I: The Western Powers* (London: Conway Maritime Press, 1983) points out, between 1950 and 1958 the Royal Navy produced 120 coastal minesweepers (p. 127).

62. Richard Miller, "Minesweepers," *Naval Review* 5 (1967): 210.

63. Ibid., p. 219.

64. Ibid., p. 210.

65. Ibid., p. 218.

66. Gardiner (1983), p. 127.

67. As Miller (1967) makes clear, especially problematic are "magnetic-influence" and "acoustic-influence" mines (p. 219).

68. Christienne and Lissarague (1986), p. 444.

69. Ibid., p. 448.

70. For a more detailed discussion of French naval developments, see *Jane's Fighting Ships* (1954–55), p. vi.

71. Ibid.

72. Note that the allies were facing the same *objective* conditions—with the exception of some variation in geographic exposure to Soviet expansionism—but that they differed in their *perception* of threat. And, although scholars have developed sophisticated assessments of subjective threat (content analysis of politicians' statements, factor analysis of elite opinion data, and so on; see R. Cottam, *Foreign Policy Motivation: A General Theory and a Case Study* [Pittsburgh: Pittsburgh University Press, 1977]; R. Herrmann, "Perceptions and Foreign Policy Analysis," in D. Sylvan and S. Chan, eds., *Foreign Policy Decision Making* [New York: Praeger Publishers, 1984]) such examinations lie outside the framework of systemic theories. As Waltz (1979, p. 69) correctly points out, "within a system, a theory explains recurrences and repetitions, not change." If one wants to account for particular policies of states (specific outcomes) rather than patterns of behavior, one must focus on domestic-level explanations. It is for this reason, indeed, that one should *expect* perceptual variations in assessments of the variables (such as threat) identified here.

73. McGeehan (1971), p. 232; and Raymond Aron, "Historical Sketch of the Great Debate," in Lerner and Aron, eds., *France Defeats EDC* (New York: Praeger Publishers, 1957), p. 8.

74. Osgood (1962), p. 99.

75. Cobban (1953), p. 178.

76. Philip Mosely, "The Kremlin's Foreign Policy Since Stalin," *Foreign Affairs* 32.1 (October 1953): 20. For a more detailed account of the Kremlin's conciliatory moves, see p. 22.

77. Wilmot (1953), p. 411; and Hamilton Armstrong, "The Grand Alliance Hesitates," *Foreign Affairs* 32.1 (1953): 54.

78. See Cobban (1953), p. 179; and Schwabe in Heller and Gillingham (1992), p. 142.

79. Since this study treats states as unitary actors the various views held by the French people are beyond its scope. For excellent accounts of the domestic debates, see Jean Stoetzel, "The Evolution of French Opinion," in Lerner and Aron (1957), pp. 81–85; Aron in Lerner and Aron (1957), p. 7; and Jacques Fauvet, "Birth and Death of a Treaty," in Lerner and Aron (1957), p. 128.

80. For a discussion of the view held by the German Social Democrats, see Emlyn Williams, "The German Federal Republic Today," *International Affairs* 28.4 (1952): 429; and Wilmot (1953), p. 411.

81. Armstrong (1953) claims that Western statesmen warned that the conciliatory moves by Stalin's successors were no real change in intentions, but merely a new strategy (p. 48).

82. Ibid.

83. Hamilton Armstrong, "Postscript to E.D.C.," *Foreign Affairs* 33.1 (1954): 18.

84. Mosely (1953), p. 29.

85. Ibid., pp. 28–30.

86. Osgood (1962) explains that the USSR exploded its first hydrogen bomb in August 1953. The mere knowledge that the Soviets possessed a hydrogen bomb undermined the United States' confidence in its own deterrent capabilities significantly (p. 104). Yet most troubling was that, although U.S. nuclear specialists studied Soviet nuclear developments, they had no way of verifying their results.

87. Fursdon (1980), p. 197. Also see a memo of the 187th meeting of the NSC, March 5, 1954 (reprinted in *FRUS* [1952–54], vol. 5, part 1, p. 889), where Defense Secretary Wilson remarked that "he was sick and tired of seeing the United States pulling France's chestnuts out of the fire."

88. Osgood (1962), p. 95. For the text of the Richards Amendment see, *FRUS* (1952–54), vol. 5, part 1, pp. 796–97; p. 974.

89. See Armstrong (1954) who explains that the French could not see the Soviet danger beyond the German danger (p. 21).

90. Fursdon (1980), p. 253.

91. Armstrong (1954), p. 20.

92. Fursdon (1980), p. 212.

93. *NATO: Facts and Figures* (1981), p. 329.

94. France raised enough objections to the suggestions made by the other conference members that it managed to postpone an armistice agreement until July 21. For a more detailed discussion, see Fursdon (1980), p. 260.

95. Also see a memorandum by the Second Secretary of the U.S. Embassy in France, Herz, in which he explains that the danger of Soviet aggression was less and less frequently mentioned in France "because of the basic fact that in 1954 the fear of Russia was less than in 1953, when it was less than in 1952 and much less than in 1951 and 1950" (see *FRUS* [1952–54], vol. 5, part 1, p. 1112).

96. Fursdon (1980), p. 281.

97. Recall that, due to the concessions the French had to make to get the Germans to sign the EDC Treaty (allow for German equality rather than to insist on very small German contingents) the initial proposal had been significantly weakened so that, in French eyes, the EDC had lost much of its appeal. Also see Edward Fursdon, "The Role of the European Defense Community in European Integration," in Heller and Gillingham (1992), p. 238.

98. Hajo Holborn, "American Foreign Policy and European Integration," *World Politics* 6.1 (1953): 20.

99. See *FRUS* (1952–54), vol. 5, part 1, pp. 994 and 1077.

100. In France's opinion the main defects of the EDC were the lack of British participation, the substantial concessions made to Germany, and the loss of a national army.

101. Rolf Steininger, "Das Scheitern der EVG und der Beitritt der Bundesrepublik zur NATO," *Aus Politik und Zeitgeschichte* 17 (April 1985): 5.

102. *FRUS* (1952–54), vol. 5, part 2, p. 1164.

103. For more detail on this proposal, see ibid., pp. 1161 and 1166.

104. Geoffrey Warner, "The United States and the Rearmament of West Germany, 1950–54," *International Affairs* 61.2 (1985) suggests that "the paternity of this plan is disputed," but that Eden clearly promoted it (p. 285).

105. *FRUS* (1952–54), vol. 5, part 2, p. 1362.

106. See Warner (1985), p. 286. Also note that, on September 29, 1954, Dulles wrote to Eisenhower "this was regarded . . . as an historical decision tying England to the continent in a way which has never been done before" (*FRUS* [1952–54], vol. 5, part 2, p. 1366).

107. Osgood (1962), p. 95.

108. See Nathan Leites and Christian de la Malene, "Paris From EDC to WEU," *World Politics* 9.2 (January 1957): 197.

109. A refusal to join the EDC, the Benelux countries knew, would alienate the United States, and thus endanger a strong U.S. commitment to Western Europe's defense.

CHAPTER 7

1. Lake (1999) also claims to "develop a general theory of security relationships" (p. 4). Hence, his model should be able to explain the creation of a structurally sophisticated security arrangement (like a confederation) by sovereign consenting states of comparable power and influence. Or, put differently, he should be able to account for strong commitments made by states in mutually beneficial relationships, and not merely in power asymmetries.

2. Ted Gallen Carpenter, *Beyond NATO: Staying Out of Europe's Wars* (Washington: Cato Institute, 1994).

3. See John Lewis Gaddis, "Toward The Post-Cold War World," *Foreign Affairs* 70.2 (Spring 1991), who argues that the end of the Cold War did not bring an end to threats but rather a diffusion of them (p. 113). Also see Sam Nunn, "The Course for NATO," *The Atlantic Council of the US Bulletin* 8.1 (1997).

4. See Arnulf Baring, *Deutschland was nun?* (Berlin: Siedler Verlag, 1991), p. 120; and Gale Mattox and Bradley Shingleton, eds., *Germany at the Crossroads: Foreign and Domestic Policy Issues* (Boulder, Colo.: Westview Press, 1992).

5. Jan Zielonka, "Europe's Security: A Great Confusion," *International Affairs* 67.1 (1991): 131.

6. Stanley Sloan, "NATO's Future in a New Europe: An American Perspective," *International Affairs* 63.3 (1990): 511; and "US Perspectives on NATO's Future," *International Affairs* 71.2 (1995). Also see Charles Glaser, "Why NATO Is Still Best: Future Security Arrangements in Europe," *International Security* 18 (1993): 5–50; Philip Gordon, "Recasting the Atlantic Alliance," *Survival* 38.1 (1996); and Ronald Asmus, Richard Kugler, and Stephen Larrabee, "Building a New NATO," *Foreign Affairs* 72 (1993).

7. For a more detailed discussion, see "The Alliance's Strategic Concept," *NATO Office of Information and Press* (Brussels: November 1991).

8. For a more detailed discussion, see Andreas Kintis, "NATO-WEU: An Enduring Relationship," *European Foreign Affairs Review* 3.4 (1998).

9. Dmitriy Danilov and Stephan De Spiegeleire, "From Decoupling to Recoupling: A New Security Relationship between Russia and Western Europe?" *Chaillot Paper* 31 (Paris: Institute for Security Studies, Western European Union, 1998).

10. Kintis (1998), p. 541.

11. James Sperling and Emil Kirchner, *Recasting the European Order* (Manchester, U.K.: Manchester University Press, 1997).

12. Robert Art, "Why Western Europe Needs the United States and NATO," *Political Science Quarterly* 111.1 (1996).

13. Robert Kennedy and William Edgar, "Why NATO Should Enlarge Now," *The Atlanta Papers*, no. 2 (1997). Also see Nunn (1997); and R. G. Hürner, "The Enlargement of NATO: A Survey of the Many-Faceted Russian Position," *Le Monde Atlantique*, no. 63 (February 1997).

14. Andrew Pierre and Dimitri Trenin, "Developing NATO-Russian Relations," *Survival* 39.1 (1997); Leon Goure, "NATO Expansion and Russia: How Will Their Relations Change?" in Stephen Blank, ed., *From Madrid to Brussels: Perspectives on NATO Enlargement* (Washington, D.C.: Center for Strategic and International Studies, 1997), pp. 49–72; and Mildred Neely, ed., "U.S. Senate Vote on NATO Enlargement: 'Reason to Celebrate,' But What about Russia?" *Foreign Media Reaction Daily Digest* (USIA: Office of Research and Media Reaction, May 7, 1998), pp. 1–10.

15. See the "Founding Act on Mutual Relations, Cooperation and Security between the North Atlantic Treaty Organization and the Russian Federation," *NATO Office of Information and Press* (May 1997), p. 5.

16. Grigory Yavlinsky, "Russia's Phony Capitalism," *Foreign Affairs* 77.3 (1998): 67–79.

17. Gail Lapidus, ed., *The New Russia: Troubled Transformation* (Boulder, Colo.: Westview Press, 1995); Clifford Gaddy and Barry Ickes, "Russia's Virtual Economy," *Foreign Affairs* 77.5 (1998): 53–67; Pauline Luong, "The Current Economic Crisis in Russia Is Neither," *Program on New Approaches to Russian Security Policy Memo Series* (PONARS), Memo No. 35 (1998); Martin Malia," Russia's Retreat from the West," *New York Times* (September 3, 1998); Michael McFaul, "A Precarious Peace: Domestic Politics in the Making of Russian Foreign Policy," *International Security* 22.3 (1998): 5–35; William Odom, "Our Russian Illusions, Crushed by Reality," *Washington Post* (September 6, 1998). Also see Yavlinsky (1998, p. 71), who explains that "the Russian market is still veering toward the corporatist, criminalist, oligarchic path."

18. Lawrence Kaplan, *NATO and the United States: The Enduring Alliance* (New York: Twayne Publishers, 1994, updated edition), p. 181; and Matthew Evangelista, "Short-Term Compromises and Long-Term Dangers for Russian-American Security Cooperation," *Program on New Approaches to Russian Security Policy Memo Series (PONARS)*, Memo No. 6 (1997).

19. For a more detailed discussion of Western Europe's security policy, see Mathias Jopp, Reinhardt Rummel, and Peter Schmidt, *Integration and Security in Western Europe: Inside the European Pillar* (Boulder, Colo.: Westview Press, 1991).

20. For more detail on the All-European Free Trade Area negotiations, see Emile Benoit, *Europe at Sixes and Sevens* (New York: Columbia University Press, 1961), p. 71. For the actual treaty text, see the Council of Europe, *European Yearbook*, vol. 7 (The Hague: Martinus Nijhoff, 1960), pp. 662–727.

21. See Joan Spero, *The Politics of International Economic Relations*, 3rd ed. (New York: St. Martin's Press, 1985), p. 399.

22. It needs to be stressed that the Treaty of Rome envisaged more than the creation of a customs union, namely the creation of a customs union in the broader context of a European common market.

23. See Clive Archer and Fiona Butler, *The European Community: Structure and Process* (New York: St. Martin's Press, 1992), who stress that the customs union was realized prior to the 1970 completion date, specified in the Treaty of Rome (p. 46). Also see Benoit (1961), p. 19.

24. For a discussion of the various functions of the primary EEC institutions, see Benoit (1961), pp. 9–19.

25. For the full text of NAFTA, see *The NAFTA*, vol. 1 (Washington, D.C.: U.S. Government Printing Office, 1993).

26. Other motives for economic cooperation might be the desire to increase a country's wealth or the need to strengthen an already existing alliance to enhance the allies' chances to prevail in a military competition with an adversary. For more detail on the latter, see Joanne Gowa, "Bipolarity, Multipolarity, and Free Trade," *American Political Science Review* 83.4 (1989): 1245–56. Also see Lars Skalnes, "Allies and Rivals: Politics, Markets, and Grand Strategy," Ph.D. diss., University of California, Los Angeles, 1992; and "Grand Strategy and Foreign Economic Policy: British Grand Strategy in the 1930s," *World Politics* 50.4 (1998).

27. See Robert Keohane, "The Demand for International Regimes," in Stephen Krasner, ed., *International Regimes* (Ithaca: Cornell University Press, 1983); and Beth Yarbrough and Robert Yarbrough, "Dispute Settlement in International Trade: Regionalism and Procedural Coordination," in Edward Mansfield and Helen Milner, eds., *The Political Economy of Regionalism* (New York: Columbia University Press, 1997).

28. Forsyth (1981), p. 176.

29. These countries founded the European Free Trade Association (EFTA) in 1960.

30. See Neill Nugent, *The Government and Politics of the European Community*, 2nd ed. (Durham, N.C.: Duke University Press, 1991); and James Lee Ray, *Global Politics*, 5th ed. (Boston: Houghton Mifflin, 1992).

31. See, for instance, Timothy Devinney and William Hightower, *European Markets after 1992* (Lexington, Mass.: D.C. Heath & Co, 1991), who, in addition to focusing on external pressure to explain EC reforms, also examine internal pressure by various interest groups.

32. Note that, in 1967, the European Economic Community, the European Atomic Energy Community, and the European Coal and Steel Community were merged into a single organization, the European Community (EC).

33. For a transaction costs analysis of three different EU industrial sectors (automobiles, pharmaceuticals, and airbus), see Katja Weber, "Varying Degrees of Institutionalization in the European Union: Going Beyond the Neofunction-

alist/Intergovernmentalist Debate," Georgia Tech Center for International Business Education and Research Working Papers, No. 97–007, March 1998.

34. See Douglas North, *Institutions, Institutional Change and Economic Performance* (New York: Cambridge University Press, 1990), p. 127. For a study that focuses on "increasing levels of cross-border transactions" to account for European level cooperation, see Wayne Sandholtz and Alec Sweet Stone, eds., *European Integration and Supranational Governance* (Oxford: Oxford University Press, 1998).

35. Note that Geoffrey Garrett and Barry Weingast, "Ideas, Interests, and Institutions: Constructing the European Community's Internal Market," in Judith Goldstein and Robert Keohane, eds., *Ideas and Foreign Policy: Beliefs, Institutions, and Political Change* (Ithaca: Cornell University Press, 1993), suggest "integrat[ing] interests and ideas" to obtain a better understanding of "the evolution and operation of the EC's internal market" (p. 177); also see Andrew Moravcsik, "Negotiating the Single European Act: National Interests and Conventional Statecraft in the European Community," *International Organization* 45.1 (1991), who, in addition to focusing on the interests of states, stresses the importance of relative bargaining power.

36. Many of the newly created East European democracies are interested in EU membership and applied for admission; see Robert Keohane and Stanely Hoffmann, "Institutional Change in Europe in the 1980s," in Keohane and Hoffmann, eds., *The New European Community: Decisionmaking and Institutional Change* (Boulder, Colo.: Westview Press, 1991). For a more detailed account of the debate between proponents of "widening" versus "deepening," see Jacques Delors, "Europe's Ambitions," in John Rourke, ed, *Taking Sides: Clashing Views on Controversial Issues in World Politics*, 4th ed. (Guilford, Conn.: The Dushkin Publishing Group, 1992); Paolo Liebl, "The Illusions of 'Euro-Optimism,'" in Rourke (1992); Angelo Codevilla, "The Euromess," *Commentary* (February 1993); and Walter Goldstein, "Europe after Maastricht," *Foreign Affairs* 72.5 (Winter 1992/93).

37. Gerald Schneider, Patricia Weitsman, and Thomas Bernauer, eds., *Towards a New Europe: Stops and Starts in Regional Integration* (Westport, Conn.: Praeger Publishers, 1995).

38. See Tomas Valasek, "European Defense: Slumbering No More?" *Weekly Defense Monitor* 3.19 (Center for Defense Information, May 13, 1999), who discusses European policy differences toward the Balkans. While the British were determined to put an end to ethnic conflict in Kosovo, he explains, Greece ignored NATO's calls for a voluntary oil embargo on Yugoslavia. And, whereas Germany sent fighter planes, Italy sought a halt in the bombings.

39. For a more detailed discussion of these criteria, see Pascal Fontaine, *Europe in Ten Lessons* (Luxembourg: Office for Publications of the European Communities, 1992), pp. 20–21. Of the fifteen EU member-states eleven adopted the EURO on January 1, 1999. The United Kingdom, Denmark, and Sweden met the criteria, but chose to postpone entry into the monetary union. Greece was the only EU country that was too weak economically to join.

40. See Martin Holland, *European Community Integration* (New York: St. Martin's Press, 1993), pp. 87–88.

41. For a more detailed account of the events that led to the creation of a federal state in Switzerland, see Forsyth (1981), pp. 28–29.

42. Ibid., pp. 52–53.

43. See Frederick Marks III, *Interdependence on Trial: Foreign Affairs and the Making of the Constitution* (Wilmington, Del.: Scholarly Resources, 1986), p. 143.

44. Ibid., p. 3.

45. Ibid., pp. 15 and 45.

46. This presumes that the confederation has not been weakened to the point where it is no longer able to make this adjustment. It is at least conceivable that confederations that have been seriously weakened simply dissolve.

47. For inductive approaches to regime change, see Donald Puchala and Raymond Hopkins, "International Regimes: Lessons from Inductive Analysis," in Krasner (1983), pp. 61–91; and Oran Young, "Regime Dynamics: The Rise and Fall of International Regimes," in Krasner (1983), pp. 93–113.

48. For an application of deductive logic to account for regime change, see Robert Keohane, "The Demand for International Regimes," in Krasner (1983), pp. 141–71.

49. Trachtman (1996/97), p. 554.

BIBLIOGRAPHY

Abs, Hermann. 1955. "Germany and the London and Paris Agreements." *International Affairs* 31 (April): 167–73.

Acheson, Dean. 1969. *Present at the Creation: My Years in the State Department.* New York: Norton.

Achilles, Theodore. 1979. "US Role in Negotiations That Led to Atlantic Alliance." *NATO Review* 27 (August): 11–14 (part 1).

———. 1979. "US Role in Negotiations That Led to Atlantic Alliance." *NATO Review* 27 (October): 16–19 (part 2).

Adair, Robert. 1821. *The Declaration of England against the Acts and Projects of the Holy Alliance.* London: James Ridgway (microfilm).

Adler, Emanuel. 1991. "Cognitive Evolution: A Dynamic Approach for the Study of International Relations and Their Progress." In Emanuel Adler and Beverly Crawford, eds. *Progress in Postwar International Relations.* New York: Columbia University Press.

Adler, Emanuel and Michael Barnett. 1994. "Security Communities." Paper presented at the Annual Meeting of the American Political Science Association, New York, September 1–4.

———. 1996. "Governing Anarchy: A Research Agenda for the Study of Security Communities." *Ethics and International Affairs* 10: 63–98.

Alphand, Herve. 1953. "The 'European Policy' of France." *International Affairs* 29.2: 141–48.

Altfeld, Michael. 1984. "The Decision to Ally: A Theory and Test." *The Western Political Quarterly* 37.4: 523–44.

Andreas, Willy. 1955. *Das Zeitalter Napoleons und die Erhebung der Völker.* Heidelberg: Quelle & Meyer.

Archer, Clive. 1992. *International Organizations.* New York: Routledge.

Armstrong, Hamilton. 1953. "The Grand Alliance Hesitates." *Foreign Affairs* 32.1: 48–67.

———. 1954. "Postscript to E.D.C." *Foreign Affairs* 33.1: 17–27.

Aron, Raymond. 1957. "Historical Sketch of the Great Debate." In Lerner and Aron, eds. *France Defeats EDC.* New York: Praeger.

Arrow, Kenneth. 1969. "The Organization of Economic Activity: Issues Pertinent to the Choice of Market versus Nonmarket Allocation." In *The Analysis and Evaluation of Public Expenditure: The PPB System.* Vol. 1. U.S. Joint Economic Committee, 91st Congress, 1st Session, U.S. Government Printing Office, 59–73.

Art, Robert. 1996. "Why Western Europe Needs the United States and NATO." *Political Science Quarterly* 111.1: 1–39.

Artz, Frederick. 1934. *Reaction and Revolution: 1814–1832*. New York: Harper & Brothers.

Ashley, Richard. 1984. "The Poverty of Neorealism." *International Organization* 38.1: 225–86.

Asmus, Ronald, Richard Kugler, and Stephen Larrabee. 1993. "Building a New NATO." *Foreign Affairs* 72: 28–40.

The Atlantic Community: An Introductory Bibliography. 1961. 2 vols. Leyden: Sijthoff.

Auswärtiges Amt. 1953. *Europa: Dokumente zur Frage der Deutschen Einigung*. Bonn: Verlag Bonner Universitäts-Buchdruckerei.

Baldwin, David, ed. 1993. *Neorealism and Neoliberalism: The Contemporary Debate*. New York: Columbia University Press.

Barclay, Roderick. 1975. *Ernest Bevin and the Foreign Office, 1932–1969*. London: Author.

Baring, Arnulf. 1991. *Deutschland Was Nun?* Berlin: Siedler Verlag.

Barnard, Chester. 1938. *The Functions of the Executive*. Cambridge, Mass.: Harvard University Press.

Barnett, Michael and Jack Levy. 1991. "Domestic Sources of Alliances and Alignments: The Case of Egypt, 1962–73." *International Organization* 45.3: 367–95.

Barraclough, G. 1966. *The Origins of Modern Germany*. Oxford: Blackwell.

Baylis, John. 1982. "Britain and the Dunkirk Treaty: The Origins of NATO." *Journal of Strategic Studies* 5.2: 236–47.

———. 1983. "British Wartime Thinking about a Post-war European Security Group." *Review of International Studies* 9.4: 265–81.

———. 1984. "Britain, the Brussels Pact and the Continental Commitment." *International Affairs* 60.4: 615–29.

Bean, Richard. 1973. "War and the Birth of the Nation State." *Journal of Economic History* 33: 203–21.

Beaufre, Andre. 1966. *NATO and Europe*. New York: Alfred Knopf.

Bell, Coral. 1963. *Negotiation from Strength: A Study in the Politics of Power*. New York: Alfred Knopf.

Bellers, Jürgen and Erwin Häckel. 1990. "Theorien internationaler Integration und internationaler Organisationen." *Politische Vierteljahresschrift* (special issue) 21: 286–310.

Benoit, Emile. 1961. *Europe at Sixes and Sevens*. New York: Columbia University Press.

Bentfeldt, Ludwig. 1985. *Der Deutsche Bund Als Nationales Band: 1815–1866*. Göttingen: Musterschmidt.

Best, Richard. 1986. *Cooperation with Like-Minded Peoples*. New York: Greenwood Press.

Bladen, Christopher. 1970. "Size of Alliances: Introduction." In Julian Friedman, Christopher Bladen, and Steven Rosen, eds. *Alliance in International Politics*. Boston: Allyn & Bacon.

Bohnenblust, Ernst. 1974. *Geschichte der Schweiz*. Zurich: Eugen Rentsch Verlag.

Bonjour, E. et al. 1955. *A Short History of Switzerland*. Oxford: Oxford University Press.

Boulding, Kenneth. 1958. "Theoretical Systems and Political Realities: A Review of Morton Kaplan, *System and Process in International Politics.*" *Journal of Conflict Resolution* 2.4: 329–34.

——. 1962. *Conflict and Defense: A General Theory.* New York: Harper & Row.

Boyce, Myrna. 1918. "The Diplomatic Relations of England with the Quadruple Alliance 1815–1830." *Studies in the Social Sciences* 7.1: 5–76.

Breslauer, George and Philip Tedlock, eds. 1991. *Learning in U.S. and Soviet Foreign Policy.* Boulder, Colo.: Westview Press.

Breton, Albert and Anthony Scott. 1978. *The Economic Constitution of Federal States.* Toronto: University of Toronto Press.

Breunig, Charles. 1970. *The Age of Revolution and Reaction: 1789–1850.* 2nd ed. New York: Norton.

Broers, Michael. 1996. *Europe under Napoleon: 1799–1815.* London: Arnold.

Buckland, C. S. B. 1932. *Metternich and the British Government from 1809 to 1813.* London: Macmillan.

Bueno de Mesquita, Bruce. 1981. "Risk, Power Distributions, and the Likelihood of War." *International Studies Quarterly* 25.4: 541–68.

Bueno de Mesquita, Bruce and David Singer. 1973. "Alliances, Capabilities, and War." *Political Science Annual* 4: 237–80.

Bullen, Roger and M. E. Pelly, eds. 1986. *Documents on British Policy Overseas: 1950–1952.* Series 2 (vol. 1). London: Her Majesty's Stationery Office.

Burg, Peter. 1984. *Der Wiener Kongreß; Der Deutsche Bund im europäischen Staatensystem.* Munich: Deutscher Taschenbuch Verlag.

——. 1989. *Die Deutsche Trias in Idee und Wirklichkeit.* Stuttgart: Franz Steiner Verlag.

Burgess, Philip, and David Moore. 1972. "Inter-Nation Alliances: An Inventory and Appraisal of Propositions." *Political Science Annual* 3: 339–83.

Burt, Richard and Geoffrey Kemp. 1974. *Congressional Hearings on American Defense Policy: 1947–1971: An Annotated Bibliography.* Lawrence: University Press of Kansas.

Bussmann, Walter. 1981. "Europa von der Französischen Revolution zu den nationalstaatlichen Bewegungen des 19. Jahrhunderts." In *Handbuch der Europäischen Geschichte* 5: 1–186.

Buzan, Barry. 1993. "From International System to International Society: Structural Realism and Regime Theory Meet the English School." *International Organization* 47.3: 327–52.

Buzan, Barry, Charles Jones, and Richard Little. 1993. *The Logic of Anarchy: Neorealism to Structural Realism.* New York: Columbia University Press.

Byrnes, James. 1947. *Speaking Frankly.* New York: Harper and Brothers.

Calleo, David. 1987. *Beyond American Hegemony: The Future of the Atlantic Alliance.* New York: Basic Books.

Calvocoressi, Peter. 1955. *Survey of International Affairs, 1952.* London: Oxford University Press.

Caporaso, James. 1993. "International Relations Theory and Multilateralism: The Search for Foundations." In John Ruggie, ed. *Multilateralism Matters: The Theory and Praxis of an Institutional Form.* New York: Columbia University Press.

Carlyle, Margaret, ed. 1952. *Documents on International Affairs, 1947–1948*. London: Oxford University Press.

Carpenter, Ted. 1994. *Beyond NATO: Staying Out of Europe's Wars*. Washington, D.C.: Cato Institute.

Cartwright, D. and F. Harary. 1956. "Structural Balance: A Generalization of Heider's Theory." *Psychological Review* 63: 277–93.

Chalmers, Malcolm. 1990. "Beyond the Alliance System." *World Policy Journal* 7.2: 215–50.

Chandler, Alfred. 1966. *Strategy and Structure: Chapters in the History of the Industrial Enterprise*. New York: Doubleday.

Charmley, John. 1985. "Duff Cooper and Western European Union, 1944–47." *Review of International Studies* 11: 53–64.

Checkel, Jeffrey. 1998. "The Constructivist Turn in International Relations Theory." *World Politics* 50: 324–48.

Christensen, Thomas and Jack Snyder. 1990. "Chain Gangs and Passed Bucks: Predicting Alliance Patterns in Multipolarity." *International Organization* 44.2: 137–68.

Christienne, Charles and Pierre Lissarague. 1986. *A History of French Military Aviation*. Translated by Francis Kianka. Washington, D.C.: Smithsonian Institution Press.

Clark, William. 1998. "Agents and Structures: Two Views of Preferences, Two Views of Institutions." *International Studies Quarterly* 42.2: 245–70.

Clay, Lucius. 1950. *Decision in Germany*. Garden City, N.Y.: Doubleday.

———. 1974. *The Papers of General Lucius D. Clay, Germany 1945–1949*. Bloomington: Indiana University Press.

Coase, Ronald. 1937. "The Nature of the Firm." *Economica*, n.s., 4: 386–405.

Cobban, Alfred. 1953. "Security and Sovereignty in French Foreign Policy." *International Journal* 8 (Summer): 172–80.

Codevilla, Angelo. 1993. "The Euromess." *Commentary* (February). Reprinted in John Rourke, ed. 1994. *Taking Sides: Clashing Views on Controversial Issues in World Politics*. 5th ed. Guilford, Conn.: The Dushkin Publishing Group.

Cogan, Charles. 1997. *Forced to Choose: France, the Atlantic Alliance, and NATO—Then and Now*. Westport, Conn.: Praeger Publishers.

Collester, Bryan. 1979. *The European Communities: A Guide to Information Sources*. Detroit: Gale Research Company.

Collins, Irene. 1964. *The Age of Progress*. London: Edward Arnold.

Condit, Kenneth. 1979. *The History of the Joint Chiefs of Staff: The Joint Chiefs of Staff and National Policy, 1947–1949*. Vol. 2. Wilmington, Del.: Michael Glazier.

Cook, Don. 1989. *Forging the Atlantic Alliance: NATO, 1945–1950*. New York: Arbor House.

Cornides, Wilhelm and Hermann Volle. 1952. "Atlantikpakt und Europäische Verteidigungsgemeinschaft." *Europa-Archiv* 20 (July): 5020–40.

Cottam, R. 1977. *Foreign Policy Motivation: A General Theory and a Case Study*. Pittsburgh: Pittsburgh University Press.

Council of Europe. 1960. *European Yearbook*. Vol. 7. The Hague: Martinus Nijhoff.

Craig, Gordon. 1961. *Europe Since 1815*. New York: Holt, Rheinhart & Winston.

Danilov, Dmitriy and Stephan De Spiegeleire. 1998. "From Decoupling to Recoupling: A New Security Relationship between Russia and Western Europe?" *Chaillot Paper* 31. Paris: Institute for Security Studies, Western European Union.

Davis, William. 1926. *Europe Since Waterloo*. New York: Century Company.

Delmas, Claude. 1980. "France and the Creation of the Atlantic Alliance." *NATO Review* 28 (August): 21–25.

Delors, Jacques. 1992. "Europe's Ambitions." In John Rourke, ed. *Taking Sides: Clashing Views on Controversial Issues in World Politics*. 4th ed. Guilford, Conn.: The Dushkin Publishing Group.

De Luca, Anthony. 1983. *Personality, Power, and Politics*. Cambridge: Schenkman Publishing Co.

Dessler, David. 1989 "What's at Stake in the Agent-Structure Debate." *International Organization* 43.3: 441–73.

Deutsch, Karl, Sidney Burrell, Robert Kahn, Maurice Leem Jr., Martin Lichterman, Raymond Lindgren, Francis Lowenheim, and Richard van Wagenen. 1957. *Political Community and the North Atlantic Area: International Organizations in the Light of Historical Experience*. Princeton: Princeton University Press.

Deutsch, Karl and David Singer. 1964. "Multipolar Power Systems and International Stability." *World Politics* 16 (April): 390–406.

Devinney, Timothy and William Hightower. 1991. *European Markets after 1992*. Lexington, Mass.: D.C. Heath & Co.

Dinerstein, Herbert. 1965. "The Transformation of Alliance Systems." *American Political Science Review* 59: 589–601.

Dürrenmatt, Peter. 1976. *Schweizer Geschichte*. Vol. 1. Zurich: Schweizer Verlagshaus AG.

Dulles, John Foster. 1954. "Policy for Security and Peace." *Foreign Affairs* 32.3: 353–64.

Duncan, George and Randolph Siverson. 1982. "Flexibility of Alliance Partner Choice in a Multipolar System." *International Studies Quarterly* 26.4: 511–38.

Dunne, Timothey. 1995. "The Social Construction of International Society." *European Journal of International Relations* 1.3: 367–89.

Eliot, George. 1949. "Military Organization under the Atlantic Pact." *Foreign Affairs* 27.4: 640–50.

Ely, Louis. 1949. *The Red Army Today*. Harrisburg, Pa.: Military Service Publishing Co.

Englander, Ernest. 1988. "Technology and Oliver Williamson's Transaction Cost Economics." *Journal of Economic Behavior* 10: 339–53.

Enthoven, Alain and K. Wayne Smith. 1971. *How Much Is Enough? Shaping the Defense Program, 1961–1969*. New York: Harper & Row.

Erickson, John. 1963. "The 'Military Factor' in Soviet Policy." *International Affairs* 39.2: 214–26.

Etzold, Thomas and John Lewis Gaddis, eds. 1978. *Containment: Documents on American Policy and Strategy, 1945–1950*. New York: Columbia University Press.

The European Defense Community Treaty: Paris, May 27, 1952. 1954. (English translation presented to the British Parliament in April 1954). Cmd. 9127. London: Her Majesty's Stationery Office.

Evangelista, Matthew. 1982/83. "Stalin's Postwar Army Reappraised." *International Security* 7.3: 110–38.

———. 1997. "Short-Term Compromises and Long-Term Dangers for Russian-American Security Cooperation." *Program on New Approaches to Russian Security Policy Memo Series (PONARS).* Memo No. 6.

Fauvet, Jacques. 1957. "Birth and Death of a Treaty." In Daniel Lerner and Raymond Aron, eds., *France Defeats EDC.* New York: Praeger.

Fedder, Edwin. 1968. "The Concept of Alliance." *International Studies Quarterly* 12.1: 65–86.

Feldman, Jan. 1984. "Collaborative Production of Defense Equipment within NATO." *Journal of Strategic Studies* 7.3: 282–300.

Feldmann, Markus. 1939. *Hundert Jahre Schweizer Wehrmacht.* Bern: Verlag Hallwag.

Feuz, Ernst. 1941. *Schweizer Geschichte.* Zurich: Schweizer Spiegel Verlag.

Finnemore, Martha and Kathryn Sikkink. 1998. "International Norms Dynamics and Political Change." *International Organization* 52.4: 887–917.

Fleming, D. F. 1961. *The Cold War and Its Origins, 1917–1950.* Garden City, N.Y.: Doubleday.

Fontaine, Pascal. 1992. *Europe in Ten Lessons.* Luxembourg: Office for Publications of the European Communities.

Ford, Franklin. 1989. *Europe 1780–1830.* New York: Longman.

Forsyth, Murray. 1981. *Unions of States: The Theory and Practice of Confederation.* New York: Leicester University Press.

Frieden, Jeffry. 1994. "International Investment and Colonial Control: A New Interpretation." *International Organization* 48: 559–93.

Friedman, Julian, Christopher Bladen, and Steven Rosen, eds. 1970. *Alliance in International Politics.* Boston: Allyn & Bacon.

Fursdon, Edward. 1980. *The European Defence Community: A History.* London: Macmillan.

——— . 1992. "The Role of the European Defense Community in European Integration." In Francis Heller and John Gillingham, eds. *NATO: The Founding of the Atlantic Alliance and the Integration of Europe.* New York: St. Martin's Press.

Gaddis, John. 1972. *The United States and the Origins of the Cold War, 1941–1947.* New York: Columbia University Press.

——— . 1974. "Was the Truman Doctrine a Real Turning Point?" *Foreign Affairs* 52.2: 386–402.

———. 1982. *Strategies of Containment: A Critical Appraisal of Postwar American National Security Policy.* New York: Oxford University Press.

———. 1991. "Toward the Post-Cold War World." *Foreign Affairs* 70.2: 102–22.

Gaddis, John and Paul Nitze. 1980. "NSC 68 and the Soviet Threat Reconsidered." *International Security* 4.4: 164–76.

Gaddy, Clifford and Barry Ickes. 1998. "Russia's Virtual Economy." *Foreign Affairs* 77.5: 53–67.

Garbutt, Paul. 1961. *Naval Challenge 1945–1961: The Story of Britain's Post-War Fleet.* London: MacDonald.

Gardiner, Robert, ed. 1983. *Conway's All the World's Fighting Ships 1947–1982, Part I: The Western Powers.* London: Conway Maritime Press.

Garnett, John. 1968. "The United States and Europe: Defense, Technology and the Western Alliance." *International Affairs* 44.2: 282–88.

Garrett, Geoffrey. 1992. "International Cooperation and Institutional Choice: The European Community's Internal Market." *International Organization* 46.2: 533–60.

Garrett, Geoffrey and Barry Weingast. 1993. "Ideas, Interests, and Institutions: Constructing the European Community's Internal Market." In Judith Goldstein and Robert Keohane, eds. *Ideas and Foreign Policy: Beliefs, Institutions, and Political Change.* Ithaca: Cornell University Press.

Garthoff, Raymond. 1965. "The Military Establishment." *East Europe* (September): 2–12.

Geddes, Barbara. 1990. "How the Cases You Choose Affect the Answers You Get: Selection Bias in Comparative Politics." *Political Analysis* 2: 131–50.

Geiger, Till and Lorenza Sebesta. 1996. "National Defense Policy and the Failure of Military Integration in NATO: American Military Assistance and Western European Rearmament, 1949–1954." In Francis Heller and John Gillingham, eds. *The United States and the Integration of Europe: Legacies of the Postwar Era.* New York: St. Martin's Press.

George, Alexander. 1979. "Case Studies and Theory Development: The Method of Structured, Focused Comparison." In P. G. Lauren, ed. *Diplomacy: New Approaches in History, Theory, and Policy.* London: Collier Macmillan.

Gilliard, Charles. 1955. *A History of Switzerland.* London: George Allen & Unwin.

Glaser, Charles. 1993. "Why NATO Is Still Best: Future Security Arrangements for Europe." *International Security* 18.1: 5–50.

Glover, Michael. 1978. *The Napoleonic Wars: An Illustrated History 1792–1815.* New York: Hippocrene Books.

Goldberg, Alfred. 1964a. "The Atomic Origins of the British Nuclear Deterrent." *International Affairs* 40.3: 409–29.

———. 1964b. "The Military Origins of the British Nuclear Deterrent." *International Affairs* 40.4: 600–18.

Goldstein, Walter. 1992–93. "Europe after Maastricht." *Foreign Affairs* 71.5: 117–32.

Gordon, Colin. 1978. *The Atlantic Alliance: A Bibliography.* New York: Nichols.

Gordon, Philip. 1996. "Recasting the Atlantic Alliance." *Survival* 38.1: 32–57.

Gott, Richard. 1963. "The Evolution of the Independent British Deterrent." *International Affairs* 39.2: 238–52.

Goure, Leon. 1997. "NATO Expansion and Russia: How Will Their Relations Change?" In Stephen Blank, ed. *From Madrid to Brussels: Perspectives on NATO Enlargement.* Washington, D.C.: Center for Strategic and International Studies.

Gowa, Joanne. 1989. "Bipolarity, Multipolarity, and Free Trade." *American Political Science Review* 83.4: 1245–56.

Graebner, Norman. 1969. "Cold War Origins and the Continuing Debate: A Review of Recent Literature." *Journal of Conflict Resolution* 13.1: 123–32.

Greenwood, Sean. 1983. "Return to Dunkirk: The Origins of the Anglo-French Treaty of March 1947." *Journal of Strategic Studies* 6.4: 49–65.

Grieco, Joseph. 1993. "Understanding the Problem of International Cooperation: The Limits of Neoliberal Institutionalism and the Future of Realist Theory." In David Baldwin, ed. *Neorealism and Neoliberalism: The Contemporary Debate.* New York: Columbia University Press.

Guetzkow, Harold. 1957. "Isolation and Collaboration: A Partial Theory of Inter-Nation Relations." *Journal of Conflict Resolution* 1: 48–68.

Gulick, Edward. 1955. *Europe's Classical Balance of Power.* Ithaca: Cornell University Press.

Hammond, Thomas, ed. 1982. *Witnesses to the Origins of the Cold War.* Seattle: University of Washington Press.

Harbutt, Fraser. 1981/82. "American Challenge, Soviet Response: The Beginning of the Cold War, February-May, 1946." *Political Science Quarterly* 96.4: 623–39.

Hartmann, Frederick, ed. 1951. *Basic Documents of International Relations.* New York: McGraw-Hill.

Head, H. M. 1951. "European Defence." *International Affairs* 27.1: 1–9.

Healy, Brian and Arthur Stein. 1973. "The Balance of Power in International History." *Journal of Conflict Resolution* 17.1: 33–61.

Heisenberg, Wolfgang and Dieter Lutz, eds. 1990. *Sicherheitspolitik kontrovers: Konventionelle Militärpotentiale NATO/WP 1949–1986 aus offenen Quellen.* Bonn: Bundeszentrale für Politische Bildung.

Henderson, Sir Nicholas. 1983. *The Birth of NATO.* Boulder, Colo.: Westview Press.

Henrikson, Alan. 1982. "The Creation of the North Atlantic Alliance." In John Reichart and Steven Sturm, eds. *American Defense Policy.* Baltimore: Johns Hopkins University Press.

Herrmann, R. 1984. "Perceptions and Foreign Policy Analysis." In D. Sylvan and S. Chan, eds. *Foreign Policy Decision Making.* New York: Praeger.

Herzfeld, Hans. 1950. *Die Moderne Welt: 1789–1945.* Braunschweig, Germany: Westermann Verlag.

Hirshleifer, Jack and John Riley. 1992. *The Analytics of Uncertainty and Information.* New York: Cambridge University Press.

Holborn, Hajo. 1953. "American Foreign Policy and European Integration." *World Politics* 6.1: 1–30.

Holland, Martin. 1993. *European Community Integration.* New York: St. Martin's Press.

Holsti, K. J. 1967. *International Politics: A Framework for Analysis.* Englewood Cliffs, N.J.: Prentice Hall.

Holsti, Ole, Terrence Hopmann, and John Sullivan. 1973. *Unity and Disintegration in International Alliances.* New York: Wiley.

Howard, Donald, ed. 1986. *Napoleonic Military History: A Bibliography.* New York: Garland.

Hudson, Daryl. 1977. "Vandenberg Reconsidered: Senate Resolution 239 and American Foreign Policy." *Diplomatic History* 1 (Winter): 46–63.

Hürner, R. G. 1997. "The Enlargement of NATO: A Survey of the Many-Faceted Russian Position." *Le Monde Atlantique* 63 (February): 3–57.

Huston, James. 1984. *One for All: NATO Strategy and Logistics through the Formative Period (1949–1969)*. Newark, Del.: University of Delaware Press.

Institute for Strategic Studies. 1959. *The Soviet Union and the NATO Powers: The Military Balance*. London.

International Journal. 1990. (Special issue on multilateralism) 45 (Fall).

International Organization. 1992. (Special issue on multilateralism) 46.3.

Ireland, Timothy. 1981. *Creating the Entangling Alliance: The Origins of the North Atlantic Treaty Organization*. Westport, Conn.: Greenwood Press.

Ismay, Hastings. 1954. *NATO: The First Five Years, 1949–1954*. Utrecht: Bosch.

James, A. G. T. 1976. *The Royal Air Force: The Past 39 Years*. London: Mac-Donald and Jane's.

Jane's Fighting Ships. 1897. London: Sampson Low, Marstow & Co.

Jervis, Robert. 1978. "Cooperation under the Security Dilemma." *World Politics* 30.3: 167–214.

Jones, Ben. 1977. *Napoleon: Man and Myth*. New York: Holmes and Meier.

Jopp, Mathias, Reinhardt Rummel, and Peter Schmidt. 1991. *Integration and Security in Western Europe: Inside the European Pillar*. Boulder, Colo.: Westview Press.

Jukes, J. A. 1956. "Nuclear Energy: A Survey of Britain's Position." *International Affairs* 32.3: 273–82.

Kärnbach, Andreas. 1990. "Die Deutsche Frage: Die Gründung des Deutschen Bundes auf dem Wiener Kongreß." In *Information für die Truppe* 4: 90–96.

Kann, Robert. 1976. "Alliances versus Ententes." *World Politics* 28.4: 611–21.

Kaplan, Lawrence. 1980. *A Community of Interests: NATO and the Military Assistance Program, 1948–1951*. Washington, D.C.: Office of the Secretary of Defense Historical Office.

———. 1984. *The United States and NATO: The Formative Years*. Lexington: The University Press of Kentucky.

———. 1992. "After Forty Years: Reflections on NATO as a Research Field." In Francis Heller and John Gillingham, eds. *NATO: The Founding of the Atlantic Alliance and the Integration of Europe*. New York: St. Martin's Press.

———. 1994. *NATO and the United States: The Enduring Alliance*. New York: Twayne Publishers. Updated edition.

Kaplan, Morton. 1957. *System and Process in International Politics*. New York: Wiley.

———. 1979. *Towards Professionalism in International Theory: Macrosystem Analysis*. New York: Free Press.

Katzenstein, Peter, ed. 1996. *The Culture of National Security: Norms and Identity in World Politics*. New York: Columbia University Press.

Kegley, Charles and Gregory Raymond. 1992. "Alliance Norms and War: A New Piece in an Old Puzzle." *International Studies Quarterly* 26.4: 572–95.

Kennan, George. 1951. "America and the Russian Future." *Foreign Affairs* 29.3: 351–70.

———. 1958. *Russia, the Atom and the West.* New York: Harper & Brothers.

———. 1967. *Memoirs, 1925–1950.* Boston: Little, Brown.

———. 1972. *Memoirs, 1950–1963.* Boston: Little, Brown.

———. 1987a. "The Sources of Soviet Conduct." *Foreign Affairs* 65.4: 852–68.

———. 1987b. "Containment Then and Now." *Foreign Affairs* 65.4: 885–90.

Kennedy, Paul. 1987. *The Rise and Fall of the Great Powers: Economic Change and Military Conflict from 1500 to 2000.* New York: Random House.

Kennedy, Robert and William Edgar. 1997. "Why NATO Should Enlarge Now." *The Atlanta Papers* 2. Center for Interntional Strategy, Technology, & Policy, Georgia Institute of Technology.

Keohane, Robert. 1984. *After Hegemony: Cooperation and Discord in the World Political Economy.* Princeton: Princeton University Press.

———. 1990. "International Liberalism Reconsidered." In John Dunn, ed. *The Economic Limits to Modern Politics.* Cambridge: Cambridge University Press.

———. 1983. "The Demand for International Regimes." In Stephen Krasner, ed. *International Regimes.* Ithaca: Cornell University Press.

Keohane, Robert and Stanley Hoffmann, eds. 1991. *The New European Community: Decisionmaking and Institutional Change.* Boulder, Colo.: Westview Press.

Keohane, Robert and Joseph Nye Jr. 1987. "Power and Interdependence Revisited." *International Organization* 41.4: 725–53.

Kim, Kyung-Won. 1970. *Revolution and International System.* New York: New York University Press.

Kinder, Hermann and Werner Hilgemann. 1989. *Dtv-Atlas zur Weltgeschichte.* Vol. 2, 23rd ed. Munich: Deutscher Taschenbuch Verlag.

King, Gary, Robert Keohane, and Sidney Verba. 1994. *Designing Social Inquiry: Scientific Inference in Qualitative Research.* Princeton: Princeton University Press.

King, James, Jr. 1960. "NATO: Genesis, Progress, Problems." In Gordon Turner and Richard Challener, eds. *National Security in the Nuclear Age.* New York: Praeger.

Kintis, Andreas. 1998. "NATO-WEU: An Enduring Relationship." *European Foreign Affairs Review* 3.4: 537–62.

Kircheisen, F. 1902. *Bibliography of Napoleon.* London: Sampson Low, Marston & Co.

Kissinger, Henry. 1973. *A World Restored: Metternich, Castlereagh and the Problems of Peace 1812–22.* Boston: Houghton Mifflin.

Klein, Benjamin, Robert Crawford, and Armen Alchian. 1986. "Vertical Integration, Appropriable Rents, and the Competitive Contracting Process." In Louis Putterman, ed. *The Economic Nature of the Firm.* Cambridge: Cambridge University Press.

Klotz, Audie. 1995a. "Norms Reconstituting Interests: Global Racial Equality and U.S. Sanctions against South Africa." *International Organization* 49.3: 451–78.

———. 1995b. *Norms in International Relations: The Struggle against Apartheid.* Ithaca: Cornell University Press.

Klüber, Johann. 1845. *Wichtige Urkunden für den Rechtszustand der deutschen Nation.* Mannheim: Verlag von Friedrich Bassermann. (Reprinted in Aachen: Scientia Verlag, 1977).

Knorr, Klaus, ed. 1959. *NATO and American Security.* Princeton: Princeton University Press.

Kolko, Joyce and Gabriel Kolko. 1972. *The Limits of Power: The World and United States Foreign Policy, 1945–1954.* New York: Harper & Row.

Krasner, Stephen, ed. 1983. *International Regimes.* Ithaca: Cornell University Press.

———. 1984. "Approaches to the State: Alternative Conceptions and Historical Dynamics." *Comparative Politics* 16.2: 223–46.

Kratochwil, Friedrich. 1989. *Rules, Norms, and Decisions: On the Conditions of Practical and Legal Reasoning in International Relations and Domestic Affairs.* Cambridge: Cambridge University Press.

Krieger, Wolfgang. 1992. "American Security Policy in Europe before NATO." In Francis Heller and John Gillingham, eds. *NATO: The Founding of the Atlantic Alliance and the Integration of Europe.* New York: St. Martin's Press.

Krushchev, N. S. 1960. "Disarmament Is the Path toward Strengthening Peace and Ensuring Friendship among Peoples." *Pravda* (January 15). Quoted in Thomas Wolfe. 1970. *Soviet Power and Europe: 1945–1970.* Baltimore: Johns Hopkins Press.

Kupchan, Charles. 1994. "The Case of Collective Security." In George Downs, ed. *Collective Security Beyond the Cold War.* Ann Arbor: University of Michigan Press.

LaFeber, Walter. 1976. *America, Russia, and the Cold War 1945–1975.* 3rd ed. New York: Wiley.

Lake David. 1996. "Anarchy, Hierarchy, and the Variety of International Relations." *International Organization* 50.1: 1–33.

———. 1999. *Entangling Relations: American Foreign Policy in Its Century.* Princeton: Princeton University Press.

Lane, Peter. 1985. *Europe Since 1945.* London: Batsford Academic & Educational.

Lange, Halvard. 1950. "European Union: False Hopes and Realities." *Foreign Affairs* 28.3: 441–50.

Langer, William, ed. 1972. *An Encyclopedia of World History.* London: Harrap & Co.

Lankheit, Klaus. 1991. "Ein einzig Volk von Brüdern: 700 Jahre Schweizer Eidgenossenschaft. In *Information für die Truppe* 9: 58–67.

Lapidus, Gail, ed. 1995. *The New Russia: Troubled Transformation.* Boulder, Colo.: Westview Press.

Large, David. 1993. "Grand Illusions: The United States, the Federal Republic of Germany, and the European Defense Community, 1950–1954." In Jeffry Diefendorf et al., eds. *American Policy and the Reconstruction of West Germany, 1945–1955.* Cambridge: Cambridge University Press.

Laurendeau, Jennifer. 1988. "The Politics of NATO Defense Policy: Lessons of the EDC Debate, 1950–1954." *Center for Science & International Affairs Working Papers.* No. 88-1 (April). Harvard University.

Lefebvre, Georges. 1969. *Napoleon: From Tilsit to Waterloo, 1807–1815.* New York: Columbia University Press.

Leffler, Melvyn. 1985. "Strategy, Diplomacy, and the Cold War: The United States, Turkey, and NATO, 1945–1952." *Journal of American History* 71.4: 807–25.

———. 1992. *A Preponderance of Power: National Security, the Truman Administration, and the Cold War.* Stanford: Stanford University Press.

Legro, Jeffrey. 1995. *Cooperation under Fire: Anglo-German Restraint during World War II.* Ithaca: Cornell University Press.

———. 1997. "Which Norms Matter? Revisiting the Failure of Internationalism." *International Organization* 51: 31–63.

Leites, Nathan and Christian De La Malene. 1957. "Paris from EDC to WEU." *World Politics* 9.2: 193–219.

Lerner, Daniel and Raymond Aron, eds. 1957. *France Defeats EDC.* New York: Praeger.

Levy, Jack. 1984. "The Offensive/Defensive Balance of Military Technology: A Theoretical and Historical Analysis." *International Studies Quarterly* 28.2: 219–38.

———. 1994. "Learning and Foreign Policy: Sweeping a Conceptual Minefield." *International Organization* 48.2: 279–312.

Liebl, Paolo. 1992. "The Illusions of 'Euro-Optimism.'" In John Rourke, ed. *Taking Sides: Clashing Views on Controversial Issues in World Politics.* 4th ed. Guilford, Conn.: The Dushkin Publishing Group.

Lipgens, Walter, ed. 1980. *Sources for the History of European Integration, 1945–1955: Archives of the Countries of the Community.* Leyden: Sijthoff.

Lippmann, Walter. 1987. "The Cold War." *Foreign Affairs* 65.4: 869–84.

Lipson, Charles. 1984. "International Cooperation in Economic and Security Affairs." *World Politics* 37: 1–23.

———. 1991. "Why Are Some International Agreements Informal?" *International Organization* 45: 495–538.

———. 1994. "Is the Future of Collective Security Like the Past?" In George Downs, ed. *Collective Security Beyond the Cold War.* Ann Arbor: University of Michigan Press.

Liska, George. 1962. *Nations in Alliance: The Limits of Interdependence.* Baltimore: Johns Hopkins University Press.

Long, William. 1996. *Economic Incentives and Bilateral Cooperation.* Ann Arbor: University of Michigan Press.

Loth, Wilfried. 1993. "The Formation of the Blocs: Structures of the East-West Conflict, 1948–1950." In Norbert Wiggershaus and Roland Förster, eds. *The Western Security Community, 1948–1950.* Oxford: Berg Publishers.

Luong, Pauline. 1998. "The Current Economic Crisis in Russia is Neither." *Program on New Approaches to Russian Security Policy Memo Series* (PONARS). Memo No. 35.

Luschert, Reinhard. 1978. "Fremdsprachenschule: Das Bundessprachenamt in Hürth." *Luftwaffe* 1: 3–4.

Mackintosh, Malcolm. 1967. *Juggernaut: A History of the Soviet Armed Forces*. London: Secker & Warburg.

Maier, Klaus. 1985. "Die EVG in der Außen-und Sicherheitspolitik der Truman-Administration." In Hans-Erich Volkmann and Walter Schwengler, eds. *Die Europäische Verteidigungsgemeinschaft: Stand und Probleme der Forschung*. Boppard, Germany: Militärgeschichtliches Forschungsamt.

Malia, Martin. 1998. "Russia's Retreat from the West." *New York Times* (September 3).

Markham, Felix. 1954. *Napoleon and the Awakening of Europe*. London: The English Universities Press.

Marks, Frederick III. 1986. *Interdependence on Trial: Foreign Affairs and the Making of the Constitution*. Wilmington, Del.: Scholarly Resources.

Martin, Lisa. 1992. "Interests, Power, and Multilateralism." *International Organization* 46.4: 765–92.

———. 1993. "The Rational State Choice of Multilateralism." In John Ruggie, ed. *Multilateralism Matters: The Theory and Praxis of an Institutional Form*. New York: Columbia University Press.

Mattox, Gale and Bradley Shingleton, eds. 1992. *Germany at the Crossroads: Foreign and Domestic Policy Issues*. Boulder, Colo.: Westview Press.

McDonald, Brooke and Richard Rosecrance. 1985. "Alliance and Structural Balance in the International System." *Journal of Conflict Resolution* 29.1: 57–82.

McFaul, Michael. 1998. "A Precarious Peace: Domestic Politics in the Making of Russian Foreign Policy." *International Security* 22.3: 5–35.

McGeehan, Robert. 1971. *The German Rearmament Question*. Urbana: University of Illinois Press.

McKay, Derek and H. M. Scott. 1983. *The Rise of the Great Powers 1648–1815*. New York: Longman.

McLachlan, Donald. 1951. "Rearmament and European Integration." *Foreign Affairs* 29.2: 276–86.

McNeill, William. 1982. *The Pursuit of Power*. Chicago: University of Chicago Press.

Mearsheimer, John. 1991. "Back to the Future: Instability in Europe after the Cold War." In Sean Lynn-Jones, ed. *The Cold War and After: Prospects for Peace*. Cambridge: The MIT Press.

Meier-Dörnberg, Wilhelm. 1985. "Politische und militärische Faktoren bei der Planung des deutschen Verteidigungsbeitrages im Rahmen der EVG." In Hans-Erich Volkmann and Walter Schwengler, eds. *Die Europäische Verteidigungsgemeinschaft: Stand und Probleme der Forschung*. Boppard, Germany: Militärgeschichtliches Forschungsamt.

———. 1986. "Die Europäische Verteidigungsgemeinschaft." In Alexander Fischer, ed. *Wiederbewaffnung in Deutschland nach 1945*. Berlin: Duncker & Humblot.

Memoirs of the Rt Hon Sir Anthony Eden—Full Circle. 1960. London: Cassell.

Mendl, Wolf. 1965. "The Background of French Nuclear Policy." *International Affairs* 41.1: 22–36.

Mercer, Jonathan. 1995. "Anarchy and Identity." *International Organization* 49.2: 229–52.

Metternich, Clemens. 1881. *Memoirs of Prince Metternich: 1773–1815.* Vol. 1. Translated by Mrs. Alexander Napier. New York: Harper & Brothers.

Meyer, Jack. 1987. *An Annotated Bibliography of the Napoleonic Era: Recent Publications, 1945–1985.* New York: Greenwood Press.

Middleton, Drew. 1953. "NATO Changes Direction." *Foreign Affairs* 31.3: 427–40.

Militärgeschichtliches Forschungsamt. 1975. *Aspekte der deutschen Wiederbewaffnung bis 1955.* Boppard, Germany.

———. *Anfänge westdeutscher Sicherheitspolitik 1945–1956: Von der Kapitulation bis zum Pleven-Plan.* Vol. 1. Munich: Oldenbourg-Verlag.

———. *Anfänge westdeutscher Sicherheitspolitik 1945–1956: Die EVG Phase.* Vol. 2. Munich: Oldenbourg-Verlag.

Miller, Richard. 1967. "Minesweepers." *Naval Review* 5: 209–29.

Millis, Walter. 1951. *The Forrestal Diaries.* New York: Viking Press.

Milner, Helen. 1993. "The Assumption of Anarchy in International Relations Theory." In David Baldwin, ed. *Neorealism and Neoliberalism: The Contemporary Debate.* New York: Columbia University Press.

Modelski, George. 1963. "The Study of Alliances: A Review." *Journal of Conflict Resolution* 7.4: 769–76.

Moe, Terry. 1984. "The New Economics of Organization." *American Journal of Political Science* 78.4: 739–77.

Molden, Ernst. 1916. *Zur Geschichte des österreichisch-rußischen Gegensatzes.* Vienna: Verlag von Seidel & Sohn.

Mollet, Guy. 1954. "France and the Defense of Europe: A French Socialist View." *Foreign Affairs* 32.3: 365–73.

Monnet, Jean. 1976. *Memoires.* Paris: Fayard.

Montgomery, Bernard. 1958. *The Memoirs of Field-Marshal the Viscount Montgomery of Alamein.* London: Collins Press.

Moravcsik, Andrew. 1991. "Negotiating the Single European Act: National Interests and Conventional Statecraft in the European Community." *International Organization* 45.1: 19–56.

———. 1994. "Preferences and Power in the European Community: A Liberal Intergovernmentalist Approach." In Simon Bulmer and A. Scott, eds. *Economic and Political Integration in Europe: Internal Dynamics and Global Context.* Oxford: Blackwell Publishers.

———. 1998. *The Choice for Europe: Social Purpose and State Power from Messina to Maastricht.* Ithaca: Cornell University Press.

Morgenthau, Hans. 1959. "Alliances in Theory and Practice." In Arnold Wolfers, ed. *Alliance Policy in the Cold War.* Baltimore: Johns Hopkins University Press.

———. 1973. *Politics among Nations.* 5th ed. New York: Alfred Knopf.

Morrow, James. 1991. "Alliances and Asymmetry: An Alternative to the Capability Aggregation Model of Alliances." *American Journal of Political Science* 35.4: 904–33.

———. 1994. "Alliances, Credibility, and Peacetime Costs." *Journal of Conflict Resolution* 38.2: 270–97.

Morse, Edward. 1970. "The Transformation of Foreign Policies: Modernization, Interdependence, and Externalization." *World Politics* 22: 371–92.

Mosely, Philip. 1953. "The Kremlin's Foreign Policy since Stalin." *Foreign Affairs* 32.1: 20–33.

———. 1961. "Soviet Myths and Realities." *Foreign Affairs* 39 (April): 341–54.

Müller-Hillebrand, Burkhart. 1953. "Nationale Armee Oder Europa-armee?" *Wehrwissenschaftliche Rundschau* 3 (April): 165–68.

Müller, Klaus, ed. 1986. *Quellen zur Geschichte des Wiener Kongresses: 1814/1815.* Darmstadt, Germany: Wissenschaftliche Buchgesellschaft.

Munro, Dana. 1952. "The First Years of the Cold War." *World Politics* 4.4: 536–547.

Mushaben, Joyce. 1988. "A Search For Identity: The 'German Question' in Atlantic Alliance Relations." *World Politics* 40.3: 395–417.

Näf, Werner. 1928. *Zur Geschichte der Heiligen Allianz.* Bern: Paul Haupt Verlag.

———. 1974. *Die deutsche Bundesakte und der schweizerische Bundesvertrag von 1815.* Bern: Verlag Herbert Lang.

The NAFTA. Vol. 1. 1993. Washington, D.C.: U.S. Government Printing Office.

NATO Information Service. 1969. *NATO: Tatsachen und Dokumente.* Brussels: NATO Information Service.

———. 1981. *NATO: Facts and Figures.* Brussels: NATO Information Service.

———. 1983. *NATO and the Warsaw Pact: Force Comparisons.* Brussels: NATO Information Service.

———. 1989. *NATO: Facts and Figures.* Brussels: NATO Information Service.

———. 1991. *The Alliance's Strategic Concept.* Brussels: NATO Office of Information and Press.

———. 1997. *Founding Act on Mutual Relations, Cooperation and Security between the North Atlantic Treaty Organization and the Russian Federation.* Brussels: NATO Office of Information and Press.

Neely, Mildred, ed. 1998. "U.S. Senate Vote on NATO Enlargement: 'Reason to Celebrate,' But What about Russia?" *Foreign Media Reaction Daily Digest.* U.S. Information Agency, Office of Research and Media Reaction.

Nicolson, Harold. 1946. *The Congress of Vienna: A Study in Allied Unity: 1812–1822.* New York: Harcourt, Brace and Company.

Noack, Paul. 1977. *Das Scheitern Der Europäischen Verteidigungsgemeinschaft.* Düsseldorf, Germany: Droste Verlag.

North, Douglass. 1981. *Structure and Change in Economic History.* New York: Norton.

———. 1990. *Institutions, Institutional Change and Economic Performance.* Cambridge: Cambridge University Press.

North, Douglass and Robert Thomas. 1970. "An Economic Theory of the Growth of the Western World." *The Economic History Review* 23.1: 1–17.

Norton, August, Robert Friedlander, Martin Greenberg, and Donald Rowe. 1985. *NATO: A Bibliography and Research Guide.* New York: Garland.

Nuggent, Neill. 1991. *The Government and Politics of the European Union.* 2nd ed. Durham, N.C.: Duke University Press.

Nunn, Sam. 1997. "The Course for NATO." *The Atlantic Council of the US Bulletin* 8.1: 1–5.

Oberländer, Erwin. 1981. "Rußland von Paul I. bis zum Krimkrieg, 1796–1855." In *Handbuch der Europäischen Geschichte* 5: 616–76.

Öchsli, Wilhelm. 1917. "Die politische Einigung der Schweiz im neunzehnten Jahrhundert." In M. Feldmann and H. G. Wirz, eds. *Schweizer Kriegsgeschichte* 10. Zurich: Ernst Kuhn Verlag.

Odom, William. 1998. "Our Russian Illusions, Crushed by Reality." *Washington Post* (September 6).

Olson, Mancur. 1971. *The Logic of Collective Action: Public Goods and the Theory of Groups*. Cambridge, Mass.: Harvard University Press.

Onslow, C. G. D. 1951. "West German Rearmament." *World Politics* 3.4: 450–85.

Onuf, Nicholas. 1989. *World of Our Making: Rules and Rule in Social Theory and International Relations*. Columbia: University of South Carolina Press.

Ose, Dieter. 1995. "Lebendige Integration: Deutschland 40 Jahre in der NATO." *Information für die Truppe* 10/11: 72–80.

Osgood, Robert. 1962. *NATO: The Entangling Alliance*. Chicago: University of Chicago Press.

———. 1968. *Alliances and American Foreign Policy*. Baltimore: Johns Hopkins University Press.

Ouchi, William. 1980. "Markets, Bureaucracies, and Clans." *Administrative Science Quarterly* 25: 129–41.

Palmer, Alan. 1984. *An Encyclopedia of Napoleon's Europe*. New York: St. Martin's Press.

Park, William. 1986. *Defending the West: A History of NATO*. Brighton, U.K.: Wheatsheaf Books.

Petersen, Nikolaj. 1982. "Who Pulled Whom and How Much? Britain, the United States and the Making of the North Atlantic Treaty." *Millennium* 11.2: 93–114.

———. 1986. "Bargaining Power among Potential Allies: Negotiating the North Atlantic Treaty, 1948–49." *Review of International Studies* 12: 187–203.

Pfaltzgraff, Robert, Jr. 1965. "Alternative Designs for the Atlantic Alliance." *Orbis* 9 (Summer): 358–77.

Phillips, Walter. 1920. *The Confederation of Europe*. London: Longmans, Green & Co.

Pierre, Andrew and Dimitri Trenin. 1997. "Developing NATO-Russian Relations." *Survival* 39.1: 5–18.

Pikart, Eberhard. 1993. "The Military Situation and the Idea of Threat." In Norbert Wiggershaus and Roland Förster, eds. *The Western Security Community, 1948–1950*. Oxford: Berg Publishers.

Pinkney, David, ed. 1969. *Napoleon: Historical Enigma*. Lexington, Mass.: D.C. Heath & Co.

Pollard, Sidney. 1981. *The Integration of the European Economy since 1815*. University Association for Contemporary European Studies. London: George Allen & Unwin.

Poole, Walter. 1978. "From Conciliation to Containment: The Joint Chiefs of Staff and the Coming of the Cold War, 1945–1946." *Military Affairs* 42.1: 12–16.

———. 1980. *The History of the Joint Chiefs of Staff: The Joint Chiefs of Staff and National Policy: 1950–1952*. Vol. 4. Wilmington, Del.: Michael Glazier.

Powell, Robert. 1999. *In the Shadow of Power: States and Strategies in International Politics*. Princeton: Princeton University Press.

Puchala, Donald and Raymond Hopkins. 1983. "International Regimes: Lessons from Inductive Analysis." In Stephen Krasner, ed. *International Regimes*. Ithaca: Cornell University Press.

Przeworski, Adam and Henry Teune. 1970. *The Logic of Comparative Social Inquiry*. New York: Wiley.

Quester, George. 1977. *Offense and Defense in the International System*. New York: Wiley.

Ray, James. 1992. *Global Politics*. 5th ed. Boston: Houghton Mifflin.

Rearden, Steven. 1984. *The Formative Years, 1947–1950: History of the Office of the Secretary of Defense*. Vol. 1. Washington, D.C.: Office of the Secretary of Defense.

Reid, Escott. 1977. *Time of Fear and Hope: The Making of the North Atlantic Treaty, 1947–1949*. Toronto: McClelland and Stewart.

——. 1980. "The Miraculous Birth of the North Atlantic Alliance." *NATO Review* 28 (December): 12–18.

Rendel, Alexander. 1979. "The Alliance's Anxious Birth." *NATO Review* 27 (June): 15–20.

——. 1980. "Uncertainty Continues as Atlantic Treaty Nears Completion." *NATO Review* 28 (April): 15–19.

Reuter, Heinz. 1954. "Der Sinn der Europäischen Verteidigungsgemeinschaft." *Europa: Idee und Aufgabe*. Cologne: Verlag Wort und Werk.

The Right Divine of Kings to Govern Wrong! 1821. Printed for William Hone. London: Ludgate Hill.

Risse-Kappen Thomas. 1994. "Ideas Do Not Float Freely: Transnational Coalitions, Domestic Structures, and the End of the Cold War." *International Organization* 48.2: 185–214.

Riste, Olav. 1981. "The Genesis of North Atlantic Defence Co-operation: Norway's 'Atlantic Policy' 1940–1945." *NATO Review* 29 (April): 22–29.

——, ed. 1985. *Western Security: The Formative Years. European and Atlantic Defense, 1947–1953*. New York: Columbia University Press.

Ritchey, Russel. 1962. "The NATO Military Education Conference." *NATO's Fifteen Nations* 6.8: 121–24.

Robins, James. 1987. "Organizational Economics: Notes on the Use of Transaction Cost Theory in the Study of Organizations." *Administrative Science Quarterly* 32: 68–86.

Rose, Holland. 1912. *The Personality of Napoleon*. New York: Putnam's Sons.

Rosecrance, Richard. 1968. *Defense of the Realm: British Security in the Nuclear Epoch*. New York: Columbia University Press.

Rosecrance, Richard and Arthur Stein, eds. 1993. *The Domestic Bases of Grand Strategy*. Ithaca: Cornell University Press.

Rosenau, James. 1990. *Turbulence in World Politics: A Theory of Change and Continuity*. Princeton: Princeton University Press.

Rosenberg, David. 1982. "U.S. Nuclear Stockpile: 1945–1950." *Bulletin of Atomic Scientists* 38 (May): 25–30.

——. 1983. "The Origins of Overkill: Nuclear Weapons and American Strategy, 1945–1960." *International Security* 7 (Spring): 3–71.

Ross, Steven. 1969. *European Diplomatic History: 1789–1815*. Garden City, New York: Anchor Books.

——. 1988. *American War Plans, 1945–1950*. New York: Garland.

Rothenberg, Gunther. 1982. *Napoleon's Great Adversaries: The Archduke Charles and the Austrian Army, 1792–1814*. Bloomington: Indiana University Press.

Rothwell, Victor. 1982. *Britain and the Cold War, 1941–47*. London: Cape.

Rubinstein, Alvin. 1964. "Stalin's Postwar Foreign Policy in Perspective: A Review." *Journal of Conflict Resolution* 8.2: 186–93.

Ruge, Friedrich. 1971. *Bündnisse*. Frankfurt: Bernard & Graefe Verlag für Wehrwesen.

Ruggie, John. 1983. "Continuity and Transformation in the World Polity: Toward a Neorealist Synthesis." *World Politics* 35 (January): 261–85.

——, ed. 1993. *Multilateralism Matters: The Theory and Praxis of an Institutional Form*. New York: Columbia University Press.

Russett, Bruce. 1968. "Components of an Operational Theory of International Alliance Formation." *Journal of Conflict Resolution* 12: 285–301.

——. 1971. "An Empirical Typology of International Military Alliances." *Midwest Journal of Political Science* 15.2: 262–89.

Salter, Noel. 1964. "Western European Union: The Role of the Assembly 1954–1963." *International Affairs* 40.1: 34–46.

Sandholtz, Wayne and Alec Sweet Stone, eds. 1998. *European Integration and Supranational Governance*. Oxford: Oxford University Press.

Sandler, Todd and Jon Cauley. 1977. "The Design of Supranational Structures." *International Studies Quarterly* 21.2: 251–76.

Sandler, Todd, Jon Cauley, and John Forbes. 1980. "Burden Sharing, Strategy, and the Design of NATO." *Economic Inquiry* 18 (July): 425–44.

Schäder, Hildegard. 1963. *Autokratie und Heilige Allianz*. Darmstadt, Germany: Wissenschaftliche Buchgesellschaft.

Schelling, Thomas. 1960. *Strategy and Conflict*. Cambridge: Harvard University Press.

Schenk, H. G. 1947. *The Aftermath of the Napoleonic Wars*. New York: Oxford University Press.

Schilling, Warner, Paul Hammond, and Glenn Snyder. 1962. *Strategy, Politics, and Defense Budgets*. New York: Columbia University Press.

Schlesinger, Arthur, Jr. 1979. "The Cold War Revisited." *New York Review of Books* 26 (October 25): 46–52.

Schmalz, Hans. 1940. "Versuche einer gesamteuropäischen Organisation 1815–1820." In Werner Näf, ed. *Berner Untersuchungen zur Allgemeinen Geschichte*. Vol. 10. Aarau, Switzerland: Verlag Sauerländer & Co.

Schmid, Carlo. 1951. "Germany and Europe." *International Affairs* 27.3: 306–11.

Schnabel, James. 1979. *The History of the Joint Chiefs of Staff: The Joint Chiefs of Staff and National Policy: 1945–1947*. Vol. 1. Wilmington, Del.: Michael Glazier.

Schneider, Gerald, Patricia Weitsman, and Thomas Bernauer, eds. 1995. *Towards a New Europe: Stops and Starts in Regional Integration*. Westport, Conn.: Praeger.

Schroeder, Paul. 1962. *Metternich's Diplomacy at Its Zenith: 1820–1823*. Austin: University of Texas Press.

Schuman, Robert. 1953. "France and Europe." *Foreign Affairs* 31.3: 349–60.

Schwabe, Klaus. 1992. "The Origins of the United States' Engagement in Europe, 1946–1952." In Francis Heller and John Gillingham, eds. *NATO: The Founding of the Atlantic Alliance and the Integration of Europe*. New York: St. Martin's Press.

Seaman, L. C. B. 1963. *From Vienna to Versailles*. New York: Harper & Row.

Shlaim, Avi. 1983/84. "Britain, the Berlin Blockade and the Cold War." *International Affairs* 60.1: 1–14.

Shulman, D. 1963. *Stalin's Foreign Policy Reappraised*. Cambridge, Mass.: Harvard University Press.

Siegfried, Andre. 1950. *Switzerland: A Democratic Way of Life*. New York: Duell, Sloan, and Pearce.

Simon, Herbert. 1961. *Administrative Behavior*. 2nd ed. New York: Macmillan. (Original publication: 1947).

Singer, David and Melvin Small. 1966. "Formal Alliances, 1815–1939." *Journal of Peace Research* 3: 1–32.

Skalnes, Lars. 1992. "Allies and Rivals: Politics, Markets, and Grand Strategy." Ph.D. diss. University of California, Los Angeles.

———. 1998. "Grand Strategy and Foreign Economic Policy: British Grand Strategy in the 1930s." *World Politics* 50.4.

Sloan, Stanley. 1990. "NATO's Future in a New Europe: An American Perspective." *International Affairs* 63.3: 495–511.

———. 1995. "US Perspectives on NATO's Future." *International Affairs* 71.2: 217–31.

Snyder, Glenn. 1984. "The Security Dilemma in Alliance Politics." *World Politics* 36.4: 461–96.

———. 1991. "Alliances, Balance, and Stability." *International Organization* 45.1: 121–42.

Snyder, Glenn and Paul Diesing. 1977. *Conflict among Nations*. Princeton: Princeton University Press.

Spaak, Paul-Henri. 1971. *The Continuing Battle: Memoirs of a European, 1936–1966*. Boston: Little, Brown.

Sperling, James and Emil Kirchner. 1997. *Recasting the European Order*. Manchester, U.K.: Manchester University Press.

Spofford, Charles. 1951. "Toward Atlantic Security." *International Affairs* 27.4: 434–39.

———. 1952. "NATO's Growing Pains." *Foreign Affairs* 31.1: 95–105.

Spruyt, Hendrik. 1994. "Institutional Selection in International Relations: State Anarchy as Order." *International Organization* 48.4: 527–57.

Stein, Arthur. 1990. *Why Nations Cooperate: Circumstance and Choice in International Relations*. Ithaca: Cornell University Press.

———. 1993. "Disequilibrium and Equilibrium Theory: Explaining War in a Theory of Peace, Explaining Alliances in a Theory of Autonomy." Paper presented at the Annual Meeting of the American Political Science Association, Washington, D.C., September 5.

Steininger, Rolf. 1985. "Das Scheitern der EVG und der Beitritt der Bundesrepublik zur NATO." *Aus Politik und Zeitgeschichte* 17 (April): 3–18.

Stikker, Dirk. 1951. "The Functional Approach to European Integration." *Foreign Affairs* 29.3: 436–44.

Stimson, Henry. 1947. "The Challenge to Americans." *Foreign Affairs* 26.1: 5–14.

Stinchcombe, Arthur. 1968. *Constructing Social Theories*. New York: Harcourt, Brace & World.

Stockholm International Peace Research Institute. 1970. *SIPRI Yearbook of World Armaments and Disarmament, 1968/69*. New York: Humanities Press.

Stoetzel, Jean. 1957. "The Evolution of French Opinion." In Daniel Lerner and Raymond Aron, eds. *France Defeats EDC*. New York: Praeger.

Stromberg, Roland. 1963. *Collective Security and American Foreign Policy*. New York: Praeger.

Taylor, Howard. 1970. *Balance in Small Groups*. New York: Van Nostrand Reinhol.

Teece, David. 1986. "Transactions Cost Economics and the Multinational Enterprise." *Journal of Economic Behavior and Organization* 7: 21–45.

Temperley, Harold, and Lillian Penson. 1938. *Foundations of British Foreign Policy*. Cambridge: Cambridge University Press.

Teune, Henry and Sig Synnestvedt. 1965. "Measuring International Alignment." *Orbis* 9: 171–89.

Thuerer, Georg. 1971. *Free and Swiss: The Story of Switzerland*. Coral Gables, Fla.: University of Miami Press.

Thursfield, H. G., ed. 1950. *Brassey's Annual: The Armed Forces Year-Book, 1950*. New York: Macmillan.

Tilly, Charles, ed. 1975. *The Formation of National States in Western Europe*. Princeton: Princeton University Press.

Trachtenberg, Marc. 1988/89. "A 'Wasting Asset': American Strategy and the Shifting Nuclear Balance, 1949–1954." *International Security* 13.3: 5–49.

Trachtman, Joel. 1994. "Reflections on the Nature of the State: Sovereignty, Power and Responsibility." *United States Law Journal* 20: 399–416.

——. 1996–97. "The Theory of the Firm and the Theory of the International Economic Organization: Toward Comparative Institutional Analysis." *Northwestern Journal of International Law and Business* 17: 470–555.

Trebilcock, Clive. 1981. *The Industrialization of the Continental Powers: 1780–1914*. New York: Longman.

Truman, Harry. 1955. *Memoirs: Year of Decision*. Vol. 1. Garden City, N.Y.: Doubleday.

——. 1956. *Memoirs: Years of Trial and Hope*. Vol. 2. Garden City, N.Y.: Doubleday.

Tucker, Gardiner. 1975. "Standardization and the Joint Defense." *NATO Review* 23 (January): 10–14.

United Nations Treaty Series. 1948. "Treaty for Collaboration in Economic, Social and Cultural Matters and for Collective Self Defense [The Brussels Treaty]." In *Treaties and International Agreements Registered or Filed and Reported with the Secretariat of the United Nations*. Vol. 19, no. 304 (March 17).

United States Arms Control and Disarmament Agency. 1966. *World Military Expenditures and Arms Transfers.*

U.S. Department of State. 1945. *Foreign Relations of the United States.* Vol. 2, Conference on Berlin.

———. 1946. *Foreign Relations of the United States.* Vol. 2, Council of Foreign Ministers.

———. 1947. *Foreign Relations of the United States.* Vol. 2, Council of Foreign Ministers; Germany.

———. 1948. *Foreign Relations of the United States.* Vol. 1, General: The United Nations.

———. 1948. *Foreign Relations of the United States.* Vol. 2, Germany and Austria.

———. 1948. *Foreign Relations of the United States.* Vol. 3, Western Europe.

———. 1949. *Foreign Relations of the United States.* Vol. 3, Council of Foreign Ministers; Germany and Austria.

———. 1949. *Foreign Relations of the United States.* Vol. 4, Western Europe.

———. 1950. *Foreign Relations of the United States.* Vol. 3, Western Europe.

———. 1950. *Foreign Relations of the United States.* Vol. 4, Central and Eastern Europe; the Soviet Union.

———. 1951. *Foreign Relations of the United States.* Vol. 3, European Security and the German Question.

———. 1952–1954. *Foreign Relations of the United States.* Vol. 5, Western European Security.

Valasek, Tomas. 1999. "European Defense: Slumbering No More?" *Weekly Defense Monitor* 3.19. Center for Defense Information (May 13).

van Creveld, Martin. 1991. *Technology and War: From 2000 B.C. to the Present.* New York: The Free Press.

Vigers, T. W. 1951. "The German People and Rearmament." *International Affairs* 27.2: 151–55.

Walker, Mack, ed. 1968. *Metternich's Europe.* New York: Walker & Co.

Wallander, Celeste. 1999. *Mortal Friends, Best Enemies: German-Russian Cooperation after the Cold War.* Ithaca: Cornell University Press.

Walt, Stephen. 1987. *The Origins of Alliances.* Ithaca: Cornell University Press.

———. 1988. "U.S. Grand Strategy in the 1990s: The Case for Finite Containment." Mimeo., UCLA Strategy Workshop.

Walton, Clarence. 1953. "Background of the European Defense Community." *Political Science Quarterly* 68 (March): 42–70.

Waltz, Kenneth. 1964. "The Stability of a Bipolar World." *Daedalus* 93.3: 881–909.

———. 1967. *Foreign Policy and Democratic Politics: The American and British Experience.* Boston: Little, Brown and Co.

———. 1979. *Theory of International Politics.* Reading, Mass.: Addison-Wesley.

———. 1993. "The Emerging Structure of International Politics." *International Security* 18.2: 44–79.

Ward, A. W. and G. P. Gooch, eds. 1922. *Cambridge History of British Foreign Policy.* Vol. 1. New York: Macmillan.

———. 1934. *Cambridge Modern History*. Vols. 9 & 10. Cambridge: Cambridge University Press.

Ward, A. W. and D. Litt. 1919. *The Period of Congresses*. New York: Macmillan.

Warner, Geoffrey. 1970. "The United States and the Origins of the Cold War." *International Affairs* 46.3: 529–45.

———. 1971. "The Reconstruction and Defence of Western Europe after 1945." In Nelville Waites, ed. *Troubled Neighbours: Franco-British Relations in the Twentieth Century*. London: Weidenfeld and Nicolson.

———. 1985. "The United States and the Rearmament of West Germany, 1950–54." *International Affairs* 61.2: 279–86.

Weber, Katja. 1990. "Alliances and Confederations: A Transaction Costs Theory of Security Arrangements." Paper presented at the Annual Meeting of the American Political Science Association, San Francisco.

———. 1992: "Hierarchy amidst Anarchy: Transaction Costs and International Cooperation." Ph.D. diss. University of California, Los Angeles.

———. 1997. "Hierarchy amidst Anarchy: A Transaction Costs Approach to International Security Cooperation." *International Studies Quarterly* 41: 321–40.

———. 1998. "Varying Degrees of Institutionalization in the European Union: Going Beyond the Neofunctionalist/Intergovernmentalist Debate." Georgia Tech Center for International Business Education and Research Working Papers. No. 97–007 (March).

Weber, Steve. 1993. "Shaping the Postwar Balance of Power: Multilateralism in NATO." In John Ruggie, ed. *Multilateralism Matters: The Theory and Praxis of an Institutional Form*. New York: Columbia University Press.

Webster, C. K. 1922. "The Pacification of Europe, 1813–1815." In A. W. Ward and G. P. Gooch, eds. *Cambridge History of British Foreign Policy*. Vol. 1. New York: Macmillan.

———. 1931. *The Foreign Policy of Castlereagh: 1812–1815*. London: Bell & Sons.

———. 1963. *The Congress of Vienna: 1814–1815*. London: Thames and Hudson.

Weinstein, Franklin. 1969. "The Concept of a Commitment in International Relations." *Journal of Conflict Resolution* 13.1: 39–56.

Wells, Samuel, Jr. 1979. "Sounding the Tocsin: NSC 68 and the Soviet Threat." *International Security* 4.2: 116–58.

Wendt, Alexander. 1992. "Anarchy Is What States Make of It: The Social Construction of Power Politics." *International Organization* 46.2: 391–425.

———. 1994. "Collective Identity Formation and the International State." *American Political Science Review* 88.2: 384–96.

———. 1995. "Constructing International Politics." *International Security* 20.1: 384–96.

Wiebes, Cees and Bert Zeeman. 1983. "The Pentagon Negotiations March 1948: The Launching of the North Atlantic Treaty." *International Affairs* 59.3: 351–63.

———. 1984. "Baylis on Post-war Planning." *Review of International Studies* 10: 247–50.

Wiener, Friedrich, ed. 1974. *Taschenbuch der Landstreitkräfte Bd.1: Die Armeen der NATO-Staaten.* Munich: Lehmanns Verlag.

Wiener, Joel, ed. 1972. *Great Britain: Foreign Policy and the Span of Empire 1689–1971: A Documentary History.* Vol. 1. New York: Chelsea House.

Wiggershaus, Norbert. 1986. "Außenpolitische Voraussetzungen für den Westdeutschen Verteidigungsbeitrag." In Alexander Fischer, ed. *Wiederbewaffnung in Deutschland nach 1945.* Berlin: Duncker and Humblot.

Williams, Emlyn. 1952. "The German Federal Republic Today." *International Affairs* 28.4: 422–31.

Williams, Phil. 1994. *North Atlantic Treaty Organization.* Vol. 8. New Brunswick, N.J.: Transaction Publishers.

Williamson, Oliver. 1971. "The Vertical Integration of Production: Market Failure Considerations." *American Economic Review* 61: 112–27.

———. 1975. *Markets and Hierarchies: Analysis and Anti-Trust Implications: A Study in the Economics of Internal Organization.* New York: The Free Press.

———. 1979. "Transaction-Cost Economics: The Governance of Contractual Relations." *Journal of Law and Economics* 22: 233–61.

———. 1981. "The Modern Corporation: Origins, Evolution, Attributes." *Journal of Economic Literature* 19: 1537–68.

———. 1985. *The Economic Institutions of Capitalism: Firms, Markets, and Relational Contracting.* New York: The Free Press.

Wilmot, Chester. 1953. "Britain's Strategic Relationship to Europe." *International Affairs* 29.4: 409–17.

Wohlstetter, Albert. 1968. "Illusions of Distance." *Foreign Affairs* 46.2: 242–55.

Wolfe, Thomas. 1970. *Soviet Power and Europe, 1945–1970.* Baltimore: Johns Hopkins University Press.

Wolfers, Arnold. 1959. "Stresses and Strains of 'Going It with Others.'" In Arnold Wolfers, ed. *Alliance Policy in the Cold War.* Baltimore: Johns Hopkins University Press.

Woyke, Wichard. 1993. "Foundation and History of NATO, 1948–1950." In Norbert Wiggershaus and Roland Förster, eds. *The Western Security Community, 1948–1950.* Oxford: Berg Publishers.

Yarbrough, Beth and Robert Yarbrough. 1985. "Free Trade, Hegemony, and the Theory of Agency." *Kyklos* 38.3: 348–64.

———. 1987. "Cooperation in the Liberalization of International Trade: After Hegemony, What? *International Organization* 41.1: 1–26.

———. 1990. "International Institutions and the New Economics of Organization." *International Organization* 44.2: 235–59.

———. 1992. *Cooperation and Governance in International Trade: The Strategic Organizational Approach.* Princeton: Princeton University Press.

———. 1997. "Dispute Settlement in International Trade: Regionalism and Procedural Coordination." In Edward Mansfield and Helen Milner, eds. *The Political Economy of Regionalism.* New York: Columbia University Press.

Yavlinsky, Grigory. 1998. "Russia's Phony Capitalism." *Foreign Affairs* 77.3: 67–79.

Yergin, Daniel. 1977. *Shattered Peace: The Origins of the Cold War and the National Security State*. Boston: Houghton Mifflin.

Young, Oran. 1983. "Regime Dynamics: The Rise and Fall of International Regimes." In Stephen Krasner, ed. *International Regimes*. Ithaca: Cornell University Press.

Ziebura, Gilbert, ed. 1966. *Nationale Souveränität oder Übernationale Integration?* Berlin: Colloquium Verlag.

Zielonka, Jan. 1991. "Europe's Security: A Great Confusion." *International Affairs* 67.1: 127–37.

Zucker, Lynne. 1984. "Production of Trust: Institutional Sources of Economic Structure, 1840 to 1920." Mimeo., UCLA.

INDEX

191

SUNY series in Global Politics
James N. Rosenau, editor

List of Titles